GEORGE ANDERSON'S

LESSONS FROM THE LIGHT

LESSONS FROM THE LIGHT

*Extraordinary Messages of
Comfort and Hope from
the Other Side*

GEORGE ANDERSON

&

ANDREW BARONE

G. P. PUTNAM'S SONS
NEW YORK

In some instances the names of the persons George Anderson makes reference to have been changed to protect the privacy of their families.

G. P. PUTNAM'S SONS
Publishers Since 1838
a member of
Penguin Putnam Inc.
375 Hudson Street
New York, NY 10014

Library of Congress Cataloging-in-Publication Data

Anderson, George (George P.)
[Lessons from the light]
George Anderson's lessons from the light :
extraordinary messages of comfort and hope from the other side /
George Anderson and Andrew Barone.
p.   cm.
ISBN 0-399-14510-9 (alk. paper)
1. Spiritualism.   I. Barone, Andrew.   II. Title.
BF1286.A52   1999   98-56039 CIP
133.9—dc21

Printed in the United States of America

3   5   7   9   10   8   6   4   2

This book is printed on acid-free paper. ∞

BOOK DESIGN BY JENNIFER ANN DADDIO

CONTENTS

THE MESSAGES

*I would like to dedicate this book in loving memory to my father,
George "Andy" Anderson, and my dear friend Vincenza A. Barone,
for her kindness and insight both on the earth and now in the hereafter.
This book is also dedicated to my beloved pets and pets everywhere,
who show us the grace of the Infinite Light every day of their lives.*

GEORGE ANDERSON

*This book is also dedicated with love to my angels—
Andrew Petrone, Victoria Petrone, and Colton Barone—
three beautiful, shining examples of the presence of Heaven on the earth.*

ANDREW BARONE

Acknowledgments

For their patience, for their tears, for their hope, and for their joy in helping others, it is with profound gratitude and respect that we acknowledge the following people, both here and hereafter, for their contributions in word or deed:

Tracy Martin Bravin and Michael Bravin, Mr. Neal Sims, Ms. Dianne Vitucci and the Vitucci Family, Ms. Anna Max, Doreen and Roger Hemp and the soul of Mr. Stephen Hemp, Ms. Susan Marek and the souls of Master Ryan Marek I and Master Ryan Marek II, Connie and Phil Carey and the soul of Ms. Michele Carey, Ms. Colleen Carey, Monsignor Thomas Hartman, Sister Julianne Speiss, S.S.N.D., Dr. Elisabeth Kübler-Ross, Ms. Dianne Arcangel, Elaine and Joseph Stillwell and the souls of Ms. Peggy and Mr. Denis O'Connor, Dr. Raymond Moody, Dr. Bruce Greyson, Dr. Ian Stevenson, Ms. Sharon Friedman, The Edgar Cayce Foundation, Dr. Risa Levenson Gold and Dr. Ken Gold, Ms. Carol Bowman, Mary, James and Kelly O'Reilly and the soul of Master Colin James O'Reilly, Ms. Cherie Andes and the soul of Master Nicholas Andes, Mr. Jerome Stricker and the soul of Ms. Kimberly Stricker, the Barone Family, Mr. Bernard Weinstock, Mr. Bill Doyle, Erin and Daniel Tomcheff and the soul of Mr. Theon Daniel Tomcheff, Peggy and Joseph Edwards and the soul of Mr. Corey Alan

Edwards, Ms. Beverly Jones and the soul of Ms. Kerry Lynn Cochran, Ms. Deborah Scholes and the soul of Mr. John Scholes, Ms. Roxie Strish and the soul of Mr. Larry Strish, Ms. Deborah Bloomstrom and the soul of Ms. Nicole Bloomstrom, Shelley Grod Tatelbaum, M.S., C.G.T., Ms. Geri Hashimoto and the soul of "Annie," Connie Costa Trivelli and Art Trivelli and the soul of Geoffrey Costa, Pauline and Dennis Patterson and the soul of Jeff Patterson

GEORGE ANDERSON'S

LESSONS FROM THE LIGHT

Prologue

THE JOURNEY
OF OUR LIFE

AFTER CLOSE TO FORTY YEARS of maintaining an ongoing relationship with the souls in the hereafter, I have come to understand this one statement to be true above all: We are, each of us, born into our exact situation in life in order to fulfill our spiritual journey on the earth. It makes no difference who you are or what you will be—if you are here, lessons will be learned. We have all embarked on a mission we have chosen for ourselves in a previous existence and accepted the challenge of walking on the earth with faith and hope as our only roadmap. We have also been furnished with the circumstances we will need in order to learn and grow from our experiences here, so that we can accomplish the goals we are expected and predestined to meet. We were already told that the lessons would be many and difficult, and the time we have to complete them is so short. Whatever the lessons we needed to learn—courage, patience, forgiveness of others or for-giveness of ourselves—our soul is sent from the hereafter into a human form, into a human family, into the career of our life's work, and we begin the process of struggling to overcome and learn from whatever has been pre-planned as our les-son on the earth. The lessons come in many differing circumstances, and our op-tions in those circumstances number more than the stars in a night sky. It is a process of choices—some good, some bad, but each of them important to the fulfillment of the reason why we are here—to complete our spiritual schooling, our life's journey. And it all is for one purpose—to learn from the knowledge, the pain, the hope and the struggle of this lifetime so that we can benefit from it in the joy of the hereafter. The souls in the hereafter know this already, but it will take us a lifetime—and our passing—to understand.

We all have a reason to be here, and we all have a specific purpose and meaning in our own life as well as in the lives around us. Each of us has a different road, but each of our roads leads to the same destination. For some, the road is paved by the tragedy of loss. And for some others, even the loss of hope. No matter what the circumstance, we all must continue struggling to learn while we are here. We all have one thing in common on our individual walk to the Infinite Light—at key points in the journey, we will be either teacher or student in different circumstances and for different reasons. We will teach by example or we will learn by example. We all have a responsibility to our own soul growth and to the soul growth of others. In my own journey, I have been given the responsibility to be an instrument by which the souls in the hereafter can deliver to us the gift of hope. I do not know whether I chose *them* or they chose *me*. But I do know, just as each of you will come to understand, that there is a reason and a purpose for everything here. It is not a luxury for the souls in the hereafter to communicate—sometimes it is a necessity. The encouragement they provide is badly needed when hope is lost or tragedy finds us. By their lessons, the souls there provide us with the gift of hope. As I walk through my own journey on the earth, I have relied on the unshakable conviction of the souls in the hereafter that the tragedy and hopelessness we experience lead us also to peace and understanding—perhaps here, but certainly in the hereafter. We are all—mother, father, lover, friend, foe—given a role in this lifetime, and we are all outfitted with the life that will best allow our learning to take place. As I came to understand why the souls in the hereafter would choose someone as unlikely as me to interpret and communicate their messages of hope to grieving families here, I need only look back through my life to see how specific was my upbringing to the purpose I would eventually serve. I also have been born to the exact circumstances that I will need to benefit from my job as a "messenger" when my lessons are over and I return to the grace of the hereafter, as all of us will. To learn hope, I was shown a vision of the hereafter and its beauty. To learn compassion, I have found people who care, no matter what. To learn humility, I have dealt with being thought of by people as either unique or worthless. And to maintain an emotional perspective through other people's pain, I was placed in a family that had trouble dealing with my ability and who to this day still understand so little of my work. Each of these facets of my life makes up who I am and how I will learn from my own life experiences, as well as affect the experiences of others.

When I was born, in August 1952, it was a time when Long Island, New York, was still mostly farmland, and doctors made house calls. I missed, by forty-eight hours, the opportunity to be born on the fifteenth, the feast of the Assumption of our Blessed Mother. That is a major coup de grâce if you are the product of an Irish-Catholic background, as I am. There was nothing remarkable about my birth, except for the fact that it had pretty much been decided that I would be the last Anderson born to my parents, Eleanor and George. My parents, having met each other after their respective first marriages each produced one daughter before ending in divorce, decided to create at least two more children—my brother, two years my senior, and myself. This completed the perfect family in their eyes—two girls and two boys. In the early forties my father worked on the Pennsylvania Railroad as a baggage clerk until an accident nearly cost him his life. As a result of the accident, he had a near-death experience, the effects of which stayed with him for the rest of his life. Somehow, the memory of his experience put him in a better position to understand what I do and why. After surviving his accident, my father found work at KLM airlines while my mother contented herself being housewife and family custodian. My parents were simple working-class people, and our lives revolved around Catholic school, work and Thursday night outings to the local hamburger restaurant—but only if we kids behaved ourselves.

Although my recollection of being six years old is not very good, I do remember contracting chicken pox. The thing that I remember most, though, is that it progressively got much worse. I could tell by the alarm in my parents' voices and by the constant doctor visits that I was not getting better, and I felt sick all the time. I came to understand later that I had contracted encephalomyelitis from the chicken pox, and that in most cases children who contracted this illness did not survive. Encephalomyelitis is a virus that attacks the brainstem and produces a swelling in the brain and spinal cord that usually leads to paralysis or death. It was a tense time for my family because the illness seemed to linger for a few weeks and I lost the ability to move my limbs. When the virus had run its course and seemed to lift slightly, I began to feel better and was eventually able to sit up. We were all hugely relieved. Unfortunately, even after the illness had subsided, I still had no use of my legs.

A child's brain is an amazing organ. To me, it is very much like the hereafter in that it can heal, repair, change and work around anything that throws it a curve. Until the age of ten, a young brain is so flexible that it can not only repair damage, but it can also open up other parts of itself to compensate for the injured or non-functioning areas. I remember reading about an operation done to save the life of an eight-year-old girl where half of her brain had to be removed because epilepsy had progressed to the point that her condition was potentially fatal. Her doctors hypothesized that in removing half of her brain, the other half would compensate for the loss by taking over the processes, like speech and movement, that were controlled by the part of her brain affected by the epilepsy. The operation was successful—the young girl survived, is able to walk and communicate and is now in her teens. It is really a miracle of physiology. As I think back to the time the encephalitis had injured the part of my brain that controlled the movement of my legs, it seems to me as if my young brain had accomplished the same thing by compensating in a different way to control my legs. After three months of having to be carried around and then crawling on all fours, I awakened one morning to find that I could walk again. Knowing what I know now, I feel certain that a part of my brain went into "double duty" to repair itself and perhaps also opened up another area of the brain that was able to see and hear things that no one else could—something, even at that age, I could already sense would change the course of my life.

It was shortly after I regained the use of my legs that I was, quite literally, introduced to the rest of my life. One night after being put to bed, I saw the figure of a woman in my room. She appeared, still and radiant, in a flowing gown surrounded head to toe in the soft hazy glow of lavender. She smiled and did not speak, but I could understand the thoughts that she was "sending" me, which were peaceful and soothing. She also seemed able to reach into my soul to understand my thoughts and feelings in a way that no one else could even come close to doing. Although it only lasted a few minutes, her visitation was a warm and lovely experience that left me exhilarated. When it was over, I fell asleep peacefully. I didn't really think much of it until she appeared again a few weeks later. Again she appeared in the same lavender glow and spoke in such a familiar and loving way that I knew she was *not* of this earth. I gave her the name "Lilac Lady" and did not mention these apparitions to any one else until she began appearing with some regularity. When I told my mother about her, she showed me the same feigned enthusiasm parents show when they hear the stories their children tell about imaginary friends. Lilac Lady was not imaginary, though, and as the occasions of her appearing to me grew in frequency, my stories about her communication began to wear my parents' patience and I was told to stop the nonsense. After that, Lilac Lady would be an experience that I would not share with anyone else.

My young life provided me the most opportunities to learn from desperation and hopelessness and probably had the greatest impact on my work as a medium. I cannot remember many instances when school was not a humiliating and frightening experience. I did not fit in, and I was not at all concerned with the same things that filled the heads of other children my age. My experiences with Lilac Lady only seemed to amplify the differences between myself and the other kids, and for some reason my perspective on life always seemed to raise the ire of the nuns who taught at Our Lady of Perpetual Help School in Lindenhurst, Long Island. My different outlook seemed to frustrate my teachers, most of whom mistook it for insolence. Although now it is unthinkable for teachers to hit their students, at that time the nuns felt free to use whatever means they felt necessary to "adjust attitudes," and it was not uncommon for them to vent their frustrations by slapping me hard in the face or banging my head into the blackboard. The worst though, by far, was the verbal humiliation by some of the teachers who became frustrated by their own inability to understand me. I became shy and fearful, and I felt there was no one I could turn to for help. Admitting to your parents that you were so unruly that the teacher had to hit you would incur much worse at home. At the beginning of just about every school year, my parents would meet the nun who was to be my teacher and promptly tell her, "If he gives you any trouble, you have our permission to let him have it." My parents were intimidated by authority and felt if someone had a title, they were more important and somehow they knew better than they. That sentiment would come to overwhelm them with misplaced trust and bad decisions about my welfare until I was a teenager. As the instances of seeing visions and hearing voices became more frequent, I came to assume that perhaps *everyone* received visitations and that there might be nothing out of the ordinary about them. I even told a neighborhood kid about the communication I received from his grandmother who had recently passed on. In this vision, she described to me the happy place where she now lived and how at peace she was. This revelation angered and frightened his parents, and I learned a hard lesson then about telling anyone about these occurrences. I decided that, for my own safety, it was probably best to keep them to myself for now.

Youth has no discipline, and neither did my ability to hear and see those people whom I had now come to understand as being the souls in the hereafter, who regularly came through with soothing and hopeful messages. They started to become my only true friends. The visitations continued to come, sometimes randomly, like the vision of the smuggling of the Dauphin, Louis XVII of France, to safety in England after the French Revolution had broken out. During a class discussion in St. John the Baptist High School about the last ruling family of France, I smugly told the teacher that although she taught that the children of Louis XVI and Marie Antoinette were murdered with the rest of the family, my vision of them told me that they had actually been secreted away and their lives spared. The fallout from that one statement and spontaneous admission of my ability was disastrous. I was ridiculed by the other students at a time when most young teenagers are desperate to fit in, and it was suggested by my guidance counselor that my parents be called in to discuss psychiatric help. My parents, taking to heart the counselor's recommendation, took me to the only authority that they felt could be of real help—the Catholic Church.

Catholic Charities is an organization that serves families in the community who find themselves in crisis by providing programs for, among other things, chemical addiction, domestic violence, alcoholism and psychological counseling. For working-class people, with neither the means nor the resources to seek out private counseling, they are the only game in town. My parents, in heeding without question the advice of the school—since they "knew better"—felt the Catholic Charities Mental Health Center would know best what to do to help me. After a few months of inconclusive tests and experimenting with medication that kept me in a perpetual daydream, they seemed no better able to explain why the visions were increasing in frequency and were, in fact, becoming clearer.

In my sophomore year in high school, there was an incident where I had to defend myself with aggression against a bully. My counselors concurred that their course of treatment was not helping me to "straighten out," and the psychiatrist decided I had reached the point of complete mental collapse. I was diagnosed with paranoid schizophrenia, and it was suggested that I be admitted to the Central Islip State Hospital "for a rest," because the visions I saw and my inability to fit in indicated to them proof of "episodic psychotic behavior." So on we went, my mother, father and myself to the office of the admitting doctor in a state mental hospital for his professional diagnosis. Once inside the facility, which was a daunting and cheerless place filled with people who, for the most part, suffered from severe and violent mental illness, we met the doctor who was to admit me into the hospital. After speaking separately to my parents and then to me, he decided to call in another psychiatrist for his input and diagnosis. I don't think there was another point in my life where I was so gripped with fear that I felt numb and help-less, knowing that my life could be taken from me at any moment by the decision of someone in a position of authority who "knows better." It is a fear that has re-mained with me through my adult life and has also had an impact on the serious-ness in which I take my own work and the thoroughness I demand of my ability. After talking to me for about ten minutes, though, this second doctor went back to the first and told him that he was reluctant to admit someone as young as me since the chance of being beaten and raped by the other inmates was not only pos-sible, it was probable. He also felt that essentially there was nothing wrong, except that I was perhaps overly stressed by the same things that stress many high school students who also don't fit into their surroundings. He told my parents that I needed some time away from school and expressed his anger at the previous coun-selors who had suggested that I needed to be sent to a state hospital at the age of sixteen. My parents gathered my things and we went home, all of us having learned something different—they, having learned that no one has all the an-swers, and I, having learned how to listen and trust the voices that told me, *"This is an experience you will learn great things from."* How right they were.

It has been said that those who do not learn from the events in history are doomed to repeat them. This is a stunningly accurate statement, both here and hereafter. We are given the tools and materials for what will be our soul growth on the earth, and it is up to us to make of them what we will. Some take these life ex-periences and build out of them something constructive and lasting. Others col-lapse under the weight of that burden and walk away, bitter and miserable, having learned or accomplished nothing. It is our choice. In looking back over the events that shaped my young experience with regard to my ability, I now understand that the stage had to have been set this way so that I could learn some very valuable things that would resound in my life. I learned many things in my early experi-ences that I needed to learn in order to understand fully what was to come later. Like the people who come to me who have suffered from the loss of a loved one and continue to suffer from the loss of joy and hope, I was humbled by circum-stance and taught how truly frightening the loss of our control of our existence is. Yet these are the very lessons that will shape our existence here and from which we will benefit when our journey on the earth is done—when our suffering re-wards us with the return of our lost joy in the hereafter. It is up to us either to build from the wreckage of loss or walk away broken and hopeless. Along the way, we are uplifted by signs of hope and consolation, even if they are momentary. Hope was given to me by the people who understood that my differences were what made me special. For the bereaved, some hope comes when they learn they are never alone in their grief. These very small signs of hope have enough buoyancy to keep us alive and on the road to peace.

When any of us experiences a loss, there comes a time in the grief process when we shake our fists skyward and yell, *Why?* It is the wrong question. The question we need to ask is *"What is the journey and what is the growth that I must accomplish by suffering the loss of someone or something so meaningful to me?"* It is the first step in the long and winding road that is to be our life's spiritual journey. There is a reason why the lessons are hard. It is a reason that is closely guarded by even the most helpful of souls in the hereafter. But they promise that there *is* a reason. If we rely on our strength, faith and hope, the reason will become as clear to us as it is to them once we join them again in that happy place. Knowing that there *is* a reason is sometimes the only consolation we may have for now. As much as I know about the hereafter, there are things that the souls there cannot even tell me. It is because I am also on my own road of faith and hope on the earth. I do know this, however—if you are at least *trying* to cope and maintain even the smallest shred of faith and hope, then you have survived the lesson. If you are at least *trying* to make sense of the senseless, then you are moving toward the Light. What we live through and continue *in spite of* is our spiritual lesson.

I have come to understand that the very things that I used to consider random, unfortunate circumstances in my own path actually made me the right instrument by which the souls in the hereafter can pass their messages of hope to grieving loved ones here. We have a curious bond, they and I—they need me to fulfill their growth in the hereafter, and I need them to fulfill my growth here. Just as the souls in the hereafter will send signs of encouragement to loved ones here, the souls in the hereafter have directed the people and circumstances, some good and some bad, to me to help me understand my place in the universe. I have learned a lot from the circumstances and people who have played a part in my journey, both here and hereafter. Like Sister Sophia, a teacher who taught me at a young age the importance of charity and kindness in the face of fear, and my enduring relationship with the extraordinary souls like Mother Cabrini, St. Philomena, St. Theresa, St. Edith Stein (St. Theresa Benedicta of the Cross), St. Joseph and St. Thomas More. They have taught me that not only do they help keep us to our purpose on the earth by their incredible examples of faith and humility, they are also the custodians of our spirituality and our soul.

In many ways I consider myself the bridge between the souls in the hereafter and their loved ones on the earth—it is part of my lesson on the earth. Our loved ones, from their unique place in eternity, continue in tandem with us until the road leads back to the peace and joy of reunion in the Infinite Light. But we have to continue—the souls there are adamant about that. We cannot stop, because if we stop, we cannot heal, and our lessons here were wasted. We have to move on, holding the smallest shred of hope that there is a purpose to everything we will experience on this bumpy road. This is the most profound lesson of the Light. While we cannot control the lessons, we can control the outcome after the lessons are learned. In the words of St. Edith Stein, "Whatever does not lay in God's plan lay in mine." Truer words have never been spoken.

One

COMMUNICATION WITH THE SOULS IN THE HEREAFTER

THE WORDS *PSYCHIC AND MEDIUM* are not interchangeable. A psychic will feel, intuitively, circumstances or information about the sitter or the sitter's loved ones, depending on the psychic's own field of intuition. That intuition very often can include circumstances of loss or elements of the future around the person that is being read. True mediumship is very different. With mediumship there must be two factors in place—direct communication from a soul in the hereafter and someone here to receive the messages. Unlike psychic ability, mediumistic ability relies solely on the information supplied by the souls in the hereafter. Where the psychic relies on intuition, the medium relies on communication. I consider myself a medium. A medium becomes a link between the souls in the hereafter and their loved ones here, and mediumship is the method by which their thoughts, feelings and messages can be communicated to those who otherwise could not hear or feel them. Just as an artist needs the medium of paint to express his feelings and ideas on a canvas, the hereafter will use me as their "medium" to play the role of their "voice" on the earth. Unless the information comes from the souls in the hereafter, I will not know it, and I do not have any messages from the souls unless they transmit them to me. Mediumship is not a per-

11

fect science and sometimes a few messages may fall victim to my misinterpretation. But it does help provide those who are bereaved with real understanding of their loss by hearing the messages of hope from their loved ones in the hereafter. I suppose I could tell families from my own perspective and experience that their loved ones are happy and at peace in the hereafter, but it is only until they hear it "directly" from their loved ones that the same information takes on dramatic and valuable meaning. Used as a resource in the quest for healing, mediumship can bring real comfort and closure to those who just need to know that their loved ones are happy and at peace where they are. It is something that the souls there are very willing to help with. Too much dependence on mediumship is not constructive, however. The souls do not want us to rely on it as a way to sidestep the healing process. Those who want to depend on mediumship to maintain a constant dialogue with their loved ones in the hereafter are quickly disappointed to find the souls reminding them that in order to learn from and understand loss we have to move on with our lives and continue our spiritual journey on our own faith. The souls also try to help us understand that they cannot sort out or run our lives from the hereafter. Some of the lessons of the earth we must accomplish on our own. As helpful and comforting as mediumship can be, it also cannot fill the hole that a loved one's passing has left in the heart of the bereaved. It can only help them to understand that loss is a part of our journey on the earth, and that perhaps the hardest lesson of that journey will be having a loved one pass in our lifetime. The souls want to give us the hope and courage to continue until we see them again and to make the unshakable promise that we *will* meet again.

Many people who have heard about me understand that I communicate with the souls in the hereafter. What I do is actually the reverse—the souls in the hereafter communicate with me, and I listen to them and report the information to their families here. Their purpose in communicating through me to their loved ones on the earth is to help their families to understand that the loss they suffer is only of the physical, and that, in their reality, nothing has really been lost. While we may not be able to see them or be together, we can come to know and understand that they are happy and well in another place. Since the souls can be close to the earth as they are needed, they do not feel the physical separation quite as much as we do, and they can draw near to us in our times of turmoil or trouble. The souls there have told me that *we* can communicate with them anytime we want by just thinking about, praying to, or just speaking to them aloud. They have also told me that they hear *everything* that we tell them and try to help when they can in their own way. With mediumship, however, they have an opportunity to "answer" their loved ones here and address some of our concerns about them or offer some hope and consolation. The souls tell me that they communicate for only one reason—because they *want* to. While they no longer feel the pain of loss that we struggle with here, they still see us and understand our pain in missing their physical presence. Through mediumship, the souls in the hereafter are afforded the unique opportunity to tell their families here that they have not disappeared. They are no more gone than if they lived in another country, where, although we cannot see them or be together, we still know they are safe and happy. For them it is as simple as this, since they can be with us whenever and as often as we need them. They have explained that they do this willingly, it is never a bother for them, nor are we keeping them from their spiritual growth by depending on their help. In their own words, they understand that love is a bond that cannot be broken, even by death, and that nothing separates us but a little time. They know that eventually we will all graduate to the other side when we have completed our spiritual journey on the earth and are reunited.

I call what I do a "discernment" because I don't like the word "reading." Reading implies that I am looking for information, which is an inaccurate description of what I do. I discern, or "pick up" the souls that draw near to the family who has come to me, and I listen to the information the soul wants related to their loved ones. During a discernment, although I can seek information from the souls there, my job is to listen and convey the information that they have come to tell their loved ones. The discernment is the soul's forum—they seem to know how best to accommodate their loved ones with the information they want to communicate because they are with us, often at our darkest hours. Whatever information they communicate is from their own perspective, and as much as I know the family has its own agenda for how they want the discernment to work, I cannot *make* the souls say what the family wants to hear. It seems that the souls have come prepared with what *they* want to communicate, and for me it is only a matter of understanding and interpreting what messages they give me. Although people credit me with the ability to understand and interpret this information, I am only the instrument through which these souls can communicate with their loved ones here. Part of the soul's continuing spiritual vocation in the hereafter is to help their families to understand that we are all on our own spiritual journey, and when we are finished, no matter how long or short the time, we leave the earth, and experience the benefit of having learned what we needed to learn here. After leaving this existence and understanding the reason and purpose of *every* experience, good and bad, on the earth, their concern for us is not to get sidetracked by our loss and to accept it as one of the experiences we have to go through on the earth to benefit from it in the hereafter. During the discernment the souls have a lot to say to their loved ones here to try to get them to continue their spiritual journey and also to understand the importance of going on with their lives and lessons until they are reunited on the other side.

Contrary to what most people think, I don't spend my days being bombarded by the souls who drop by, ad-hoc, to say hello. There has to be a reason for them to communicate to me, and that reason is the presence of their loved ones who need to hear from them. Otherwise, they have no reason to appeal to me to have their presence felt. There are occasions where the souls there will impress upon me to communicate to people that I know or that I am around. On one occasion, some friends had come to New York from South Africa where we met at a bereaved parents group and made plans to have dinner together. During dinner, I could feel the presence of their son, Stephen, who kept at me until I made mention of the fact that he was around. Needless to say, his parents were overjoyed to hear this spontaneous communication, and being too polite to *ask* me about him, were grateful for his insistence. There are other times when the souls will impress upon me to contact their loved ones (whom I know) and send a message or even a gift around a certain time or holiday. Right around Mother's Day, my friend Tracy's mother, killed in a car accident in 1979, asked me to find a teddy bear and send it to her. She was specific about what type to buy and even impressed upon me what to write in the card. The message and gift had its intended effect on Tracy, and I was glad to be a part of this cherished gift from her mom.

Normally, when it is time for me to work, the souls will begin making their presence known and I will feel a whirring in my head, very much like a generator starting up. I can feel the increase in energy, and while I am discerning I am part of the exhilarating electromagnetic force that the souls use to transmit their messages. That energy will stay with me until the discernments or the series of discernments is over, and then it will gradually fade down as the souls leave. I won't feel that drained feeling until a few hours or even a few days later, but it does come. The souls seem to understand that they cannot use my brain for longer than a few hours, and even if I think I can go a little longer, especially in a group setting, the souls decide that I have had enough and they shut me down. They know that the amount of energy I use during a discernment has a cumulative effect on my system, and it is up to them not to overwork my flawed human body and brain. This is why I cannot work every day, and I do my best to limit the amount of work

I do. The nice thing about the souls is that they know when to leave me alone when I need a rest.

What I have found fascinating about the souls in the hereafter is that they are able to appeal to me in many ways to transmit information so that I can understand them. In some instances, they will appear so clearly that I can read the number on a football jersey; in other instances, they will speak to me directly on a wavelength that only I can seem to hear. In many instances, though, they have the capacity to use my brain as a big toolbox, pulling out any information that I have read or seen and using it to illustrate what they want to say. I think the most unique way they have used my brain for this purpose was for a family from Wichita, Kansas, who lost a daughter named Stephanie. During the discernment, Stephanie showed me a character from an old movie whom I remembered as the 1930s black comedian Step'n Fetchit. When I asked the family if that meant anything to them, her very surprised mother told me, "It was her nickname!" Although it was the most bizarre nickname I have ever heard for a young girl, it showed me once again that the souls in the hereafter are resourceful when it comes to communicating information from the hereafter. There are also instances in my daily life when I am reading or seeing something and I will hear a voice telling me, "Remember this—you're going to need it later," and it comes up in a discernment the following week. But I am not a player in the discernment of the soul for a grieving family, nor am I expected by the souls there to have any involvement. They have told me that it is not necessary that I understand the information that is sent, nor do they expect or want any of my input or suggestions. But I am human, and it is impossible not to feel for a family who is suffering greatly or be moved by the tragedy that surrounds the circumstance of passing. It is also difficult not to add my musings about the situations that the souls are communicating. When it seems that I am becoming too involved on an emotional level, I am at first politely reminded and then sternly warned by someone there who acts as an emissary for the souls to pull my feelings out of the discernment. They will hold things there until I regain my objectivity, and then they proceed as usual. They understand that I must stay as detached as I can, probably in order to preserve my sanity or to keep me from feelings of hopelessness after hearing about so much tragedy. During one recent reading, I discerned the son of a woman who had come to a small group session. He had taken his own life because he was so overwhelmed by this existence and was afraid all the time. In giving me the emotional feeling of how it felt to be "in his shoes" when he was on the earth (as they sometimes will do to get their point across), I also was overwhelmed at how closely his pain resembled my own during my teenage years, and I felt myself begin to weep in front of a group of people. I instantly felt the connection go dim momentarily, which shook me out of my emotional state. I was then reminded by one of the souls not to let myself get caught up in the discernment. It is a difficult thing to do sometimes, but for the sake of the people listening to the discernment, my own emotions are something I must keep in check.

Many people ask me why, if the souls are able to communicate so well from the hereafter, their messages are unclear or able to be misinterpreted by me. In a perfect world, the souls would be able to say through me, "Hi, this is John, your brother who passed after falling down an elevator shaft. Give my regards to mother, father, Billy, Grandma and Rose." The only sticking point to the communication of messages from the hereafter is that they have to go through *my* brain, and that is often an obstacle course of its own. I am human, and therefore prone to the same misunderstanding of thoughts and ideas as someone who is repeating a secret that eventually gets convoluted into something entirely different. Although I have been more careful during the past years to keep my own ideas, idiosyncrasies and skepticism about the messages relayed out of the discernment, I occasionally fall victim to interpreting what *I* think the souls mean, rather than let the information mean whatever it will to the loved ones here.

This type of misunderstanding of the soul's messages also tends to show me again and again that I am not as smart as I think I am. But in spite of the missteps that occur during the discernments, the soul will keep at me (or their loved ones) until they are completely understood. Sometimes, I have to admit, the goof is not entirely mine. During one discernment, I told a woman, "Your father is telling me from the hereafter that your husband is also deceased." She shook her head no. "You mean he is still on the earth?" I asked, surprised. "No," she answered. "Then where is he?" "He's dead," she answered. I can still hear the souls joking, "We *are* talking to the *living*, aren't we?" Understandably, those who come to me are sometimes overwhelmed when their loved ones come through and their thinking becomes less than straight. Sometimes they need a lot of patience with us. We hear but we don't listen.

Each of the discernments I have done is unique in its own way—circumstance, relation or information to the families. Some things are constant, though, and those are the fundamental things that our loved ones in the hereafter must tell us over and over—they are not gone. In fact, they are often closer to us than they ever could have been on the earth, and they often help us in our daily life of working and grieving. During the discernments, the one idea the souls try to convey to their loved ones is that they have not lost anything by leaving the earth—they have gained everything. The only tragedy in their passing is that they have "graduated" before us, and we are left scrambling for ways to deal with that tragedy. After crossing to the other side and everything becoming clear to them, they now understand that *we* are the ones that are left behind. What is also interesting about the discernments is that the souls speak so matter of factly about the circumstances of their passing. Though we may see their passing as tragic or accidental, they now understand that there are no accidents in the universe, and that the manner in which they passed was only the process that got them from here to there.

The souls in the hereafter have also come through during the discernment to let their families know that they do communicate with them in small ways to let them know that they are still around. Sometimes it is a familiar smell or lights that go on and off. It can be as simple as a song on the radio or as profound as a visitation in broad daylight or in dreams. Unfortunately, people have a tendency to dismiss these signs as fluke, coincidence or a figment of the imagination. Yet these same people come to me, understanding that their loved ones will communicate. No amount of wishful thinking could produce a visitation, so accept them for what they are—a special message from one who loves you. Many have told me that since the passing of their loved one they have prayed for some sign or visitation. A woman named Susan told me that she prayed every night to her son for him to appear in her dreams—but to no avail. It made her even more despondent, but her son was way ahead of her in helping her to handle her grief. I know that when the souls in the hereafter feel we are far enough along in our grief so that we won't depend on them for our very existence, they will accommodate us. But not until then. I asked Susan if she would even bother getting out of bed in the morning if her son appeared to her in dreams. She admitted that she would probably live from sign to sign, and then she began to understand how her son, by his silence, spoke volumes about his wanting her to pull her life together. Our loved ones in the hereafter, who truly know what is best for us, will not commiserate with us. They look for ways to get us back on the road to completing our spiritual journey here. Incidentally, a year later I got a chance to speak to Susan, who told me that her son has been showing her small signs to let her know he is with her. No burning bush, of course, but enough to let her know she is still loved.

Why the souls feel the need to communicate from the hereafter is both simple and complex. The simple reason is that they see our pain and truly want to help us understand that they are only separated from us by the physical, yet are still connected by the emotional. Now that they have had an opportunity to understand their existence and, in a large part, ours, they want very much to be able to keep us on the "straight and narrow," namely, our spiritual journey on the earth, so that when we graduate to the hereafter we will have benefited from all that we have learned here.

SPONTANEOUS COMMUNICATION

You do not need to be a medium to have an experience of communication from the hereafter. Many bereaved persons have told me incredible stories of having seen their loved ones, both in dreams and in waking moments. Others speak of receiving communication in symbols, such as a smell of flowers or in a "coincidence" of nature that has their loved one's name written all over it. The souls in the hereafter have told me many times that they communicate somehow with their loved ones, sometimes just to let them know they are near. It could be as simple as a song that comes on the radio at the precise time you are thinking of your loved one or as profound as an apparition where they can be seen in full figure. Many souls have told me that they have allowed their loved ones to "peek behind the veil" that separates our dimension from theirs, if only for a second. It is very easy to dismiss these experiences as waking dreams or wishful thinking. Scientists, in their infinite wisdom, have even coined a term for it—"grief psychosis." I hate that term. It implies that because you are grieving the loss of someone you love, you are somehow mentally ill and subject to delusions. How little science really understands the bereaved. While there are some people who cannot distinguish fantasy from reality, the overwhelming majority of bereaved people are thinking, rational people who can understand this very profound gift from their loved ones in the hereafter. That they care enough to make their presence known to us even briefly helps restore our hope.

There are so many ways that the souls in the hereafter will manifest themselves to their loved ones on the earth that describing them could fill a book. I have found that the most common manifestation, besides visitations in dreams, is the use of smells or the manipulation of anything electrical. Every once in a while I can still smell the pipe that my grandfather smoked even though no one smokes in my home. Other times, the smell of lilacs is almost overwhelming, even though there are no flowers in the house. Our loved ones try in many ways to let us know they are near. My friend Connie Carey, who acts as a sponsor when I come to her hometown of Syracuse, New York, had related to me hearing the sounds of her daughter, Michele, as she would get ready in the morning. Connie simply surmised that her daughter, killed in a car accident in 1993, produced this "sign" for her in an effort to show her mom that she was still around in a very normal and familiar way. It is very apparent to see the good this sign has done for Connie, who still has trouble accepting her daughter's passing. Connie's other daughter, Colleen, related to her mom that Michelle visits her in dreams—they are so vivid that Colleen frequently wakes up physically exhausted from them. No matter what the circumstance, these visitations help to emphasize to the families that their loved ones are "back to normal" in terms they can understand. They also help to strengthen the conviction that those who have passed before us are still "around"—a point that the souls in the hereafter make repeatedly in the discernments.

Unfortunately, nightmares are also given false credit for being visitations. Some people have told me that they have had forboding dreams where their loved ones are in turmoil, which upsets them greatly. But I know for a fact that souls in the hereafter transmit a very positive energy, and I have never had an occasion where a soul was unhappy or in turmoil. Because their existence is so superior to ours, they are happy and at peace. They have also come to a greater understanding about themselves and the universe, and they approach their existence (and ours) with that greater understanding. Forboding dreams don't feel as real as the visitation where sight, sound, smell and feel are involved. A dream that puts souls in a negative situation is usually a manifestation or projection of our own fear. These should be considered nightmares and not visitations. After a true visitation from a loved one in the hereafter, the difference will become quite clear.

Some bereaved people, upon hearing all the glowing stories about visitations from their peers, begin to get concerned if they have not had one. They begin thinking that their loved ones don't want to be around them, which is *never* the case. I recall a woman who came to me after the loss of her daughter in an automobile accident. She told me that every day she prayed to her daughter, that she would show her a sign, but to no avail. She obsessed about it so much that her work, life and relationship to her other children were beginning to unravel. During her discernment, her daughter made it clear to her that only when she is truly ready to accept a sign from her would she begin to receive one. The mother needed to be at a point in her grief where she is not living in the past when her daughter was on the earth, but at a point where she is coping with the loss and able to understand that one of the lessons in her spiritual journey here is to experience the loss of a loved one in her lifetime and to grow from the experience. This is very hard for the grieving to understand, but, believe me, the souls in the hereafter are only concerned for our welfare. They tell us that for our soul growth here, we must do some things alone and unaided by them. I have noticed in discernments that the souls in the hereafter will not pull us back into our grief by constantly reminding us that they have passed, but they will work with us from their unique vantage point to help us understand that we must continue our lives although we are in a grief situation. This is particularly true of bereaved parents. When the bereaved are coping and able to regain their perspective about having lost a child, only then will they be able to understand signs from the hereafter for what they truly are—evidence that while our loved ones can't take our pain away, we will see them again.

THE HOLY HELPERS

I cannot take all the credit for the ability to discern loved ones from the hereafter. I am helped in large part by the appearance of many spiritual "helpers," who were spiritual people when they were on the earth. Some religions call them "saints," as do I, but no matter what they are called, they were ordinary people who accomplished extraordinary things and lived lives of great spiritual development while they were on the earth. I am fortunate to have a constant dialogue with them, and they often appear in discernments as a positive example or to symbolize that it is possible for each one of us to accomplish great things on the earth. They are people who can be counted on to help when we need them, and their lives are examples of what unbelievable things can come out of faith and hope.

My first experience of seeing the Blessed Mother (the Virgin Mary, Mother of Jesus) was when I had suddenly become ill in Ireland when I was around nineteen years old. Growing up Catholic, I was hard-pressed to believe that the woman we think of as the Mother of the Universe would appear to the likes of me in a vision. But when she appeared to me, she was so serene and peaceful, and she emitted the feeling that she, too, was a simple person but for her amazing faith. When I told my Irish relatives about it, they listened and accepted my account without question. That is what faith does. On the other hand, my brother wrote to my mother back in the States, telling her I'd gone off the deep end again. Since that vision, the spiritual helpers like St. Philomena, who represents to me the patroness of a happy birth, St. Joseph, patron of a happy passing, Christ, patron and counselor of all who passed in turmoil, St. Jude, who helps hopeless causes, among many others have made their presence known, not as religious symbols but as symbols of faith, hope and spiritual fulfillment. They, like the rest of the souls in the hereafter, teach by their example and show that we are not alone in our struggle. It is as Mother Cabrini had once told me in a moment of my own turmoil—"I am in your corner."

Mediumship cannot cure grief, and the souls there *will not* take the valuable lesson of grief away from us. I have been told by the souls there that the only cure for grief is our own passing into the hereafter when we are finished on the earth. Sometimes the communication with the souls there opens up more questions than it answers, because we as human beings are desperate to understand those things that we cannot know. Much of what we experience on the earth is an exercise in a faith that has its reward only when we pass. There is no magic potion that will take away the pain of loss. The physical loss of someone we love is an enduring pain that will follow us until we are no longer separated. In a very real way, I consider mediumship the "best of second best." *Best* would be never to have a loved one pass on, but that is not possible. The second best that we can hope for is to understand from our loved ones that they live on.

Two

THE PASSAGE
FROM THIS WORLD
TO THE NEXT

WE ARE A PEOPLE truly living in the information age. Everything in the universe is available to us through means that were inconceivable even as recently as twenty years ago. Through computers, the internet, television, fax, radio and phone, there is no source of information that cannot be retrieved the instant we need it. Resources abound to teach us everything we need to know about our life and the world around us. Everything except the hereafter. While there is information that can be found on the subject of death from an earthbound perspective, not much information exists about death as a *gateway* to the rest of our spiritual life. We do know that, for whatever reason, when the physical body we occupy will no longer sustain itself on this plane, it ceases to exist. Physical death, as we know it, is only a static factor in passing, much the same way that pregnancy, while part of the birth cycle, is only a factor of birth. Not much is written (or even discussed, for that matter) about where we find ourselves *after* the actual process of death has happened. What happens after life is over is the subject of unending controversy, because like those who scoffed at Marco Polo and his descriptions of a fantasy place called "China," many people tend to scoff at or fear what they can't physically see or understand. As a result, the subject of passing and what little is recorded about the subject gets fractionalized and subdivided into the New Age, religious or quackery categories. While many argue that life begins at conception—or sooner—the physical, active and conscious life begins as a result of birth. But what many people don't understand is that like birth, our physical, active and conscious after-life begins as a result of death. During pregnancy, the soul about to enter this world becomes equipped with the thing it will need here—a warm-blooded body to adapt itself to living productively on the earth. It is very much like an astronaut who needs a special suit to adapt to a different atmosphere. At the time of death, however, those things we needed on the earth can now be discarded since they will not be needed to exist in the hereafter. From the point of death and onward, we will continue with only what we will need—our spirit body and consciousness. After our death on the earth, we begin our new spiritual journey in the hereafter just as a baby will begin a new journey here.

ONE ROOM TO ANOTHER

I have been told by the souls in the hereafter that passing from this world to the next is as easy as walking from one room to another. Although many incredible descriptions of blinding light and tunnels with good and evil and magnificent beings have been told by some who feel they have had contact with the hereafter, those who have *actually* passed on assure me that the transition is much more pleasing and subtle. Some of the souls who have come through during a discernment or "reading" have told me that, in some instances, the actual "change" was so subtle that they had not really noticed. Edna and Stu Graham came to me after the passing of their son, Kyle, in an automobile accident in Florida. Kyle recounted to me (and them) that immediately following the accident, his first thought after looking at the wreckage of the family van was "My folks are going to *kill* me!" In an effort to ease the tension and make them laugh, Kyle told his parents that the good thing about passing that night was that he did not have to deal with their wrath when they found out what happened to the car. There have been many instances where the souls have talked about a passing so subtle that it took a while to realize that they were actually in the hereafter. One soul from the hereafter whose boat had capsized during a storm recounted to me during a discernment that after realizing he was drowning, he began to feel more and more at peace and then suddenly found the energy to swim to the surface. When he got to the surface, the weather had cleared to a beautiful day, and he began to swim to the shore. As he neared the shore, he began to realize that this was no longer the earth. He continued toward the shore, where relatives who had passed on before him waited, smiling and waving, to welcome him.

Other souls have also recounted complete surprise at having found themselves passed on to the hereafter, remarking that they thought there would be a more obvious transition. During an afternoon break on a tour stop in Hawaii in 1996, I had the time to visit the battleship *Arizona* Memorial to the seamen who had lost their lives in Pearl Harbor on December 7, 1941. In wandering around, one soul had come to me, telling me that his name was Benjamin Steimetz, which we found on the memorial roster. After showing me the circumstance under which he passed (he was on the *Arizona* when it was hit) he told me how shocked he and his shipmates had been upon learning that they had passed. At first, he told me, he was "madder than hell" at having passed on when, he figured, he had his whole life to look forward to, but after realizing the fulfillment of his soul growth on the earth and the opportunities for growth in the hereafter, he quickly came to understand that his passing was a pretty good thing after all. He was also proud to be part of American history and to be memorialized as a hero.

There are other souls who were not surprised at all by their passing and, in some cases, welcomed it gladly. Many of those who have passed on due to terminal illness have reported to me having been able to see the portal to the hereafter and their deceased loved ones before actually leaving the earth. Called "deathbed apparitions" by people such as Dr. Elisabeth Kübler-Ross and Dianne Arcangel, who have researched them, these visitations from relatives, friends and even pets happen in order to help prepare the terminally ill patient for that walk through the portal to the other side. Shortly before my father, George "Andy" Anderson, passed on in April 1997, he told me that he had seen his mother-in-law, Annie (of whom he had been quite fond), who told him that they were all waiting for him. In the time immediately before he passed, the incidences of these "deathbed apparitions" increased in frequency, and he also reported seeing his old Army buddy (killed in World War II) and even the family cat, Boo-boo, who had passed on some time before that. A few weeks before his passing, he told us that our family doctor, Dr. Wellman (who passed on thirty years before), came for a visit and asked him how he was feeling. The closer my father came to his passing, the more he saw relatives and friends, all passed on, with whom he also spoke. Even though I am a bit cynical when I hear these types of stories, I must say that I am hard-pressed to find a reason to discredit his apparitions as dreams or delusion, since he was not in any pain or on any heavy medication. Also, his apparitions were very lucid and detailed. On April 28 of that year, I was on my way to a friend's birthday party, being driven by my assistant, but we got a bit lost and drove aimlessly for a while. While sitting in the car, I had a visitation from a neighbor who lived next door to the house I grew up in, who had passed on years ago as a young woman. She told me that they were waiting for my father and that she would be one of the people who greeted him as he came to the hereafter. She disappeared at the same time we found our way and continued to the party. My father passed on six hours later. Yet with all these experiences he had, he never once felt frightened or anxious; quite the contrary—they were pleasing and comforting to him. I believe the visitations helped him greatly to prepare for his own passing. Whatever the circumstance, those who pass on to the hereafter have described their passing in very simple and natural terms, which leads me to the conclusion that our physical death only creates the circumstance that carries us to our new life in the hereafter. All in all, at the moment of our physical death on the earth, we can look forward to our journey to the hereafter as an experience of great peacefulness, without struggle or fear at the moment of passing.

When the soul has passed into the hereafter, he or she is met by someone or something familiar to them to help with the inevitable moment when they reckon with the fact that they are no longer on the earth. Some people, because of what they were taught on the earth about "the other side," might be temporarily frightened. Sometimes the hereafter has to be creative in welcoming someone to the other side who is confused at their circumstance of having found themselves in the hereafter or do not have anyone like a friend or relative whom they would follow into the light. This is especially true with children or those who are distraught prior to their passing, especially those who have taken their own life or victims of violent crime. In that time immediately following passing, the hereafter seems to create circumstances that we will respond to, like the figure of Santa Claus for children, or the grouping of small animals in a pasturelike setting, or even a field of beautiful flowers and happy people. In short, the hereafter does whatever it takes to create an atmosphere of trust and comfort to ease the transition between the two worlds and to display an attractive setting that will draw the soul to it.

THE LIFE REVIEW

Upon our entrance into the hereafter and before our journey to the Light, there comes that time where all things that happened to us on the earth become clear and understood—what those souls in the hereafter call the life review. It has been described to me as a "living movie" of all the circumstances where we have accomplished good and circumstances where we could have done better. We see the impact our life has had on others—from an impartial point of view. It is through the vehicle of the life review that we begin to understand that our life on the earth and the struggles we endured had a definite purpose in fulfilling our spiritual growth, which continues in the hereafter. It is interesting that the souls in the hereafter say that we all can remember in detail the rotten things we have done to others, but we never seem to remember that we all have done many good things worthy of praise. These things have not been forgotten by the Infinite Light. Conversely, there are some who have acted in a way that their conscience dictated and did things that hurt others, without understanding that those things were fundamentally wrong. A person who has been taught prejudices and narrow religious or political beliefs from childhood and could not recognize that they were not acting in the better interest of others will also experience the impact of their deeds from the perspective of the person they tormented or oppressed. There are also others, fully aware of their actions in committing murder or violent crime, who begin to understand the horror and damage their actions created among their victims and among their victims' family. Even though they felt they had no control over their actions on the earth, they come away from the life review with the knowledge that theirs will be a long road to spiritual growth and understanding.

The life review is not a way to assess punishment—it is actually the "answer sheet" to the test that was the person's life on the earth. There is no punishment in the hereafter in the literal sense. Each person judges his or her own actions and decides what must be accomplished in their spiritual education in the hereafter to compensate for lessons missed on the earth. Through the life review and the grace of the Infinite Light, we can see where we have failed in our attempts to act in kindness and love, and we can better understand that our failings on earth are completely fixable in the hereafter. These lessons that were not learned on the earth must be continued in the hereafter so that the soul can move ever closer to the Infinite Light.

THE NEAR-DEATH EXPERIENCE

I have noticed that the one thing people who have had near-death experiences all seem to have in common is the fact that they are treated to a glimpse through the portal to the hereafter and see their lives on the earth and the impact of their lives on others in broad view. In experiencing this short physical "death" (lasting only a few seconds of *our* time), people's lives are changed forever. Why? Because during the time that people have left their physical bodies in "near-death," some have actually experienced the beginning of their life review and see the greater good of life in perfect love and light. They see their life on earth as an opportunity to do good for others and learn the real meaning of the things that we do and are done to us by others. The experience changes some so profoundly that they leave the life they know to follow another, perhaps better, spiritual path on earth. Dianne Arcangel, whom I mentioned previously, was once a day trader on the stock exchange before a routine operation caused her to "die" for a few minutes. She later recounted the incident to me and tried to make me understand how the hereafter made it possible to "feel" such beauty and to understand that because we are so loved by the hereafter, nothing we do is beyond the comprehension and compassion of the Infinite Light, no matter how miserably we think we have failed here. After this experience, Dianne left her high-paying job to work with the terminally ill in a hospice. My father also experienced a similar feeling many years ago when a work-related accident caused him to experience a very profound near-death experience. He related to me that he felt himself running through a meadow filled with flowers, some of them in colors he had never imagined possible. He ran under a magnificent sky, brightly lit but without a sun, until he came upon three men clothed in white. They motioned him to go back, telling him, "This is not your time, George. Go back." As he made the conscious decision to turn around, the next sensation he felt was that of the operating room nurse trying to shake him into consciousness. In a very big way, this experience altered his way of thinking about this world and the next and also played a large role in his acceptance of death as a natural passing into the hereafter. Although many NDEs are dismissed by "experts" as a form of delusion or psychosis, they are beginning to be taken more seriously by the medical community as a form of "altered state." One doctor explained to me that while dreams are powerful, they gradually lose their detail when they are recounted more than once, since they are in essence products of our subconscious. The difference with near-death experiences is that they have unmistakable characteristics. Those who have experienced them can recount the experience over and over again without losing any detail or substance. They do not fade in time as dreams do, but remain as vivid and intense as the time they happened. Whether you believe them or not, the incredible stories of glimpses into our destiny provide many with proof that a hereafter exists, that the passing from this world to the next is an easy and beautiful one and that the experience is profound and enduring.

THE WAY HOME

Some people are at odds to understand that despite the tragic circumstances surrounding their loved ones' death, their passing into the hereafter was a happy one. "All suffering stops once the spirit leaves the body," I have been told, and after that "it's cake," according to an eight-year-old girl from the hereafter whose family had come to me years ago after she had been found beaten and murdered. She explained to me that she never felt a thing—her time here was finished and, with the other side sensing the inevitable, her soul was taken to the hereafter before the "body" was dead. I (and her family) was pretty amazed to hear that. Since that time there have been more than a few other souls in the hereafter who have recounted the same experience of painlessness upon their passing.

After the life review, when we have been given a clear understanding of the life that was and of the spiritual work we will continue with in the hereafter, the life we have lived and known begins to fade into memory, and we gradually become acclimated to our new existence. It becomes clear to us that we are coming *home*. It is the place from which we have come, and the place to which we return when our work is done. Now the reward for having struggled and worked and gone without on the earth is shown to us, and we accept, understand and *release* the troubles that bound us to the earth. We continue into the Light, pure of heart, to unite with friends and family and begin learning, understanding and fulfilling the spiritual purpose in our new life in the hereafter—our *home*.

Three

WHAT IS THE HEREAFTER LIKE?

IN THE THOUSANDS OF DISCERNMENTS I have done for bereaved people, I have noticed that each circumstance of passing is unique in its own way. The only constant is the destination—the hereafter and the Infinite Light. Through the souls in the hereafter who communicate about their new lives on the Other Side, I have been given a real education in how things work in this other dimension. Each soul offers new and different information about their experience on the Other Side, providing me with yet another piece of this seemingly endless puzzle. It is a world of constancy, yet always building to suit the reality of the individual who inhabits it. I suppose it is not so much a place as a state of being.

While the hereafter is a different place for all who are there, some things about the experiences of those who pass from this world to that one remain the same. These have to do with the actual "place" that is the hereafter. Many have called it a "Fourth Dimension" or "Heaven" or "Nirvana," but according to the souls there, it is a fixed place with many levels of consciousness from which the souls, after completing their spiritual education, move forward to the Infinite Light. The difference between spiritual levels is not so much higher and lower or greater and lesser, but rather like that of the school system on the earth, where one person may have a high school diploma, while another, after extensive education and life experience, would possess a Ph.D. With the higher elevation of consciousness, or spiritual "degree," comes freedom to explore and understand the Infinite Light. As we have lessons that we must complete on the earth, so do we learn and grow in the hereafter in order to "graduate" or come ever closer to the Infinite Light. That is our ultimate destination. It is easy to understand how this system works by using examples on the earth. Someone like Mother Teresa, who exemplified spiritual grace, has benefited from her selflessness and caring for others on the earth and has no doubt earned her reward for her incredible work by moving that much closer to the Infinite Light. Others, like murderers who continually fail to understand the fundamental reason why they are here, come to that understanding when they pass into the hereafter and set upon their long road to spiritual understanding and the Infinite Light. No matter what the circumstance, though, the road to salvation always moves forward, and all of the souls in the hereafter are afforded, if they want it, the opportunity to progress.

THE SOURCE OF PEACE

The hereafter, the actual "place," has been described to me like a perfect endless summer day. The temperature is mild, and everything is bathed in a beautiful light. I have been told that there is no nighttime or periods of darkness, since there is no need for the souls to rest. There is also no direct source of light, like the sun. Everything and everyone is energized by the love and peace of the Infinite Light, which is like a generator of endless light and love. Some souls from the hereafter have told me that there are colors, flowers and objects there that we could never even imagine and that everything has a life and soul—even flowers and stones—that radiate energy from the Infinite Light. Things are beautiful in the hereafter because they are created *with* and *by* love. As fantastical as that sounds, the souls there tell me that life for them is amazingly like that of the earth, but in a much better circumstance. Their entire existence is predicated on peace and tranquillity. They live in communities, are productive, and have enduring relationships with others. They see relatives there, have fun, and work together in a wonderful type of harmony. Very often in readings, the souls make a point of this to give their grieving loved ones a point of reference that is tangible and easy to understand. The real difference between the worlds is that they live to love and serve others and the Infinite light, and there are no problems, no pain, no trouble or illness. In many ways, they tell me it is like the perfect, carefree, permanent vacation. I am very fortunate in only one way with regard to my ability—when I am discerning, I am able to experience briefly their total joy and understanding. It is really hard sometimes to experience our existence here after having even a brief taste of theirs.

Since we enter the hereafter with only our earthly reality as our point of reference, we have to be introduced into this new reality one step at a time, but the things we understood from the earth will stay as our reference point until we feel we no longer need them. The hereafter must accommodate our reality the way we recognize it, especially when it comes to the "staple" items of the world we left—clothing, housing and food. As we start to understand more about this new world around us, our reality slowly changes from the material to the conceptual. For as long as we need it, the hereafter will be for us a reflection of life on earth—with the exception that everything is perfect and glowing with the energy of the Infinite Light and its peaceful environment. I have also been told that we are able to choose the life we wanted that somehow eluded us on the earth. Whatever was longed for materially on the earth can be provided in the hereafter—we can choose our dream home, car, etc. These things are ours for as long as they are needed. Eventually, the soul begins to grow and material trappings become unimportant. The soul slowly gives way to living in the conscious, where the tangible is no longer necessary. There are many souls with higher spiritual understanding who help us in every aspect in this new life. They act as "guidance counselors" when they are needed to help in the transition period between our old reality and our new one.

THE UNDERSTANDING

After we are situated in the hereafter, we place ourselves on a level that most reflects how we have lived and learned from our experiences on the earth. Life on earth is considered a "proving ground" of sorts, where we place ourselves in learning situations previously thought out by our past stop in the hereafter. We come to the earth and use whatever situation we are in, whether good or bad, to complete the lesson that is to be our life's work in service to others. Our work in this life on earth may have been to struggle with the loss of a child and to go on doing good in spite of it or to learn understanding and forgiveness living with a spouse who is abusive or alcoholic. All circumstances on the earth, including success, wealth or achievement here, have their own set of problems and struggles that we work with to complete our learning experience. I remember the shock and surprise people had when Christina Crawford wrote her book about her mother, Joan Crawford, and the hidden struggles and heartache that went on behind the facade of their very "glamorous" life. One thing that I have learned from my experiences in working with all types of families, rich and poor, successful or unsuccessful, religious or atheistic—is that there is a personal struggle in *everyone*. We need this struggle—it is the tool that helps us to understand why we have been placed on the earth and what we need to complete our lesson on the earth before we return to the hereafter. From this struggle, no one escapes. We do with our struggles what we can, and in the meantime we learn to benefit others and be a beacon of hope for those around us. That is why we are here. When we have finished our learning experience on the earth to the best of our ability, we go on to the hereafter and continue our progress, that much closer to Eternal Light. This goes a long way toward explaining why some people live to be one hundred years old and others just a few days. Our mission, it seems, is twofold—we complete our own work on the earth, and we also become a player in another's learning experience. The baby who passes at birth may only have had to learn the joy and love of an earthly birth, while at the same time it will be the fulcrum of its mother's life experience to cope with the loss of a newborn. Our roles are predetermined by what lesson we will have to learn before we move on to the Other Side. Also, the way we pass, whether in our sleep or as a result of a painful terminal illness, is as important to the learning process as the life itself. This is something that mystifies those who have lost a child who suffered so greatly from terminal illness. They sit during the discernment, mouth agape, as their child tells them that every second of the pain they endured they would gladly go through again to benefit the same way in the hereafter. It is a hard concept for us to understand—nothing happens to us that is not absolutely crucial to our spiritual journey on the earth. The lessons all center around the same concept, both here and hereafter—Love. In the life review, we are able to assess how often we were able to use love in situations where we could have been of real service to another. When we have understood the circumstances that kept us from feeling love for another, we have our lesson and purpose of being in the hereafter. As we learned on the earth, so do we continue to learn in the hereafter. The only difference in our learning in the hereafter as opposed to here is that, over there, the lessons are a joy to learn, without the hardship or struggle that accompanied the lessons on the earth.

Since life in the hereafter, like life on the earth, is about choices, we are the only "judge" of our performance with regard to how well we managed with the life we had on the earth. As much as this statement will upset some members of organized religions, the Other Side has stated emphatically that there simply is no "hell" or eternal life of punishment as many have come to fear. *Nothing* is unforgivable in the hereafter, and no sin is beyond the understanding of the Infinite Light. This is a hard concept for people to understand, especially if they or a family member were the victim of violence at the hand of someone that they hope at some point would be "rotting in hell." This probably says more about us and how much we need to understand and forgive, even when it is physically impossible to do. Since we are made to comprehend our actions fully during our lifetime and the effects of our actions on others, we come to understand the happiness and peace or pain and anxiety we brought to another's life. Those souls who did not take advantage of the opportunity to do good in their lifetime or caused pain in others on the earth begin to understand their actions from the point of view of the people whose pain they caused. Knowing this, they voluntarily place themselves on a lower level of enlightenment. These lower levels of enlightenment or consciousness are farther from the Light and are therefore not as warm or bright. The souls who place themselves at these levels understand completely that they must go down a long road of understanding and forgiveness in order to progress closer to the Light, and they do so willingly. There are discernments that I have done for families whose loved ones lived a painful existence here and resorted to murder or destruction so that the world around them could also feel their pain. No one escapes the full understanding of their actions in the hereafter, which should be of some consolation, but the circumstance of judgment is different for each soul. St. Bernadette had a hard time hoping to convince the local religious of Lourdes, France, that she had received a vision from the Virgin Mary who spoke to her in a grotto near what was essentially the town dump. Doubtful of her story, the priests tested her own reasoning ability by posing this question—"What is a sinner?" She confounded her detractors by explaining that "a sinner is a person who *loves* evil." That was in direct opposition to the generally held notion that a sinner is someone who *does* evil, and it speaks volumes about the differences between the two. For those who want to learn from their mistakes and move closer to the Infinite Light, the opportunity is always within reach through the grace of the Infinite Light and with the help of friends, relatives and guides on a higher conscious level. Some souls, even though they are not as spiritually advanced, have told me that it was only through the grace and intercession of the Infinite Light that they were able to communicate with loved ones on the earth, if only to apologize for the pain they caused. They need our forgiveness to help them progress, and it is part of our *own* spiritual journey to forgive and help them, no matter how it hurts.

THE WORDS WE NEED TO HEAR

I remember a discernment I had done for Rita and Joseph Stuart, who came to me after the loss of Joseph's daughter from a previous marriage. During the discernment, his daughter, Jessica, told me that she had come through once before at a discernment for her father, but this time she had Rita's mother and grandmother with her, who needed to communicate with Rita. This came as a bit of a surprise to Rita, a successful surgeon, who never had a close relationship to her relatives and saw no reason why they would want to communicate anything to her. Rita's mother explained to me from the hereafter that through the grace of the Infinite Light, she was allowed to come through during the discernment as part of her own spiritual therapy on the Other Side. She explained that Rita was the only daughter in a family of boys, and the emotional and verbal abuse from her mother and grandmother was unrelenting during her childhood. Now that they had come to the hereafter and seen how the abuse had affected Rita, both in her childhood and adult life, they were truly sorry for the constant torment and worked every day as "guardian angels" to help Rita through her feelings of failure and nightmares as an adult. They asked for forgiveness and promised Rita that their journey in the hereafter included making amends to her, which is why they were grateful for the opportunity, through the grace of the Infinite Light, to communicate this information to her. After the discernment, it was obvious that Rita was badly shaken but quite moved by this communication. She confessed to me that the years of abuse that she suffered had tarnished many parts of her life, and feelings of worthlessness had crept into her adult relationships and work, but hearing this information was a breakthrough for her and an opportunity to let old wounds heal. It was a life-altering experience for her to hear two simple words from the hereafter—"I'm sorry."

The hereafter also has the capability to handle every circumstance of passing to help people on the road to the Infinite Light. When people pass due to terminal illness, they have gone through perhaps one of the hardest struggles on the earth—to maintain their hope and courage through their pain and suffering. In this respect, the hereafter is quite resourceful—those souls, weary from battling physical and emotional pain after passing from terminal illness, are brought to a "house of reflection" where they can rest and recuperate before beginning their new journey on the Other Side. The souls who have been there have told me that it is a marvelous place, filled with fields and meadows, flowers, birds and small animals, all exuding peace and security, to help bring rest and peace to the troubled soul. They are also comforted and cared for by souls of higher spiritual understanding and energy, who help them come to terms with their passing and gain full understanding. Once souls, completely rested and at peace, are ready to move on, they are introduced to the hereafter and their higher purpose of being.

PARADISE FOUND

The souls in the hereafter have also told me that, contrary to the popular idea of clouds and harps, they lead productive lives on the Other Side, often gainfully employed in their choice of service to another soul. During a discernment with Vincenza Barone, the mother of my co-author and director of our grief support programs, it was interesting to note that her mother, Adriana, told me she worked as a "grandma" on the other side, welcoming children into the hereafter. This information dismayed Vincenza, since she could remember even as a young girl her immigrant parents working day and night to provide for six children. She had hoped that at least in the hereafter her mother would finally be able to rest. But for Adriana, the work of welcoming little ones to a beautiful new world was a joy that she chose willingly as part of her own soul growth in the hereafter. The fact that the souls there can choose their own reality is almost mind-boggling when you think that we are taught all our lives how the "dead" are "resting." They waste no time in telling me from the hereafter that their lives are too good to rest. Many have described it as "the perfect existence" or "the opportunity to really live." They explain that while their new lives superficially mirror their lives on earth, the sense of joy and feelings of happiness and peace make their existence "heaven." A sense of well-being and true pleasure in service to others prevails over there, and they welcome the opportunity to contact us in whatever way they can to help guide our life and our spiritual journey here. Many souls have communicated during the discernments that their spiritual work in the hereafter is to act as "guardian angels" for their loved ones still on the earth. They also tease good-naturedly that they do not want us to make it a "full-time job" for them. It is also interesting that in my more than twenty-five years of discerning souls in the hereafter for the bereaved, not one of those souls has ever expressed anything except true happiness about their new life.

THE INFINITE LIGHT

So much has been written about the Infinite Light, from Moses to the present, that another opinion would only be just that. It is rather like the parable of the blind men and the elephant—depending on your vantage point or religion or education, everyone experiences something different. With respect to the definition of the hereafter and the Infinite Light, the souls in the hereafter have told me that every religion has a facet of the diamond, but no one has the complete diamond. The Infinite Light is every name it has been called from God to Allah, and that while every religious persuasion believes theirs is the one true religion, the only spiritualism the other side has espoused is in the concept of faith in the Infinite Light and in love in its purest form. All the rest are different words to the same song. So how does the Infinite Light settle the issue? It doesn't. I am amazed sometimes at the inventiveness in the hereafter when it comes to making people understand spirituality during a discernment. In a discernment where the family is Christian, symbols like the Blessed Mother and Jesus will appear to me, as well as different saints. When I discerned a family recently in Japan, the symbols became Kanon Sama, the Goddess of Mercy, and Buddha. What is most extraordinary is that they are the same beings, just with different earthly names. Many of the names and likenessess that I remember from my Roman Catholic education come to me during discernments. Saints like Philomena, Anthony and Theresa can come through during a discernment, each representing a symbol that I would recognize from their vocation. They come mostly as symbols of spirituality in the hereafter that would be recognizable to those here on the earth. These were extraordinary people who live very close to the light and offer peace and consolation to us when we need it. They know what it was like on the earth and want to help in any way they can. For my benefit, they have chosen the titles that I would recognize and understand. I remember a woman who had come to me six months after she lost her son in a car accident. During the discernment, the Blessed Mother came into the room to offer condolences and support, as she put it, "one mother to another." When I told the woman about this, she looked confused. "I am not Catholic," she said, at which the Blessed Mother answered, "Neither am I." If you are now blanching at the thought of Our Lady making a joke to lighten someone's spirits, don't. These extraordinary people were also human and bound by the same emotions we experience. They also retain their sense of humor and their humanness.

Although the hereafter is many things to many people in the hereafter, it provides the living with a profound sense of peace and joy, which emanates from those who communicate to their loved ones here. Very often during a discernment, there is a fragrance in the room that can be smelled by the family. This fragrance, which smells very much like lilacs, is the fragrance of sanctity that follows the souls from the hereafter. Many souls have come across during the discernment to say that they would never leave the hereafter—life here was too hard. They understand that in the hereafter, life is about the very joy they sought on the earth but often never found. But it is important to understand that life is so hard here so that things can be so good there. Tragedies, like having a loved one pass in our lifetime, are some of the hard lessons we endure and benefit from when we ourselves return to the hereafter. These souls who have struggled on the earth come through during the discernment to teach us that not even death can sever the bond between loved ones, and that we must use the time we have here constructively and spiritually. This is the gift that our loved ones give us—a sense of hope that we, too, will have the "perfect existence."

Four

TERMINAL ILLNESS
AND REINCARNATION

I HAVE COMBINED these two aspects of existence with each other because I feel they represent opposite ends of the same spectrum. Terminal illness and reincarnation are linked to the hereafter very much like a prologue and epilogue to a great narrative. Their common goal is the hereafter, which makes the transition to and from the earth as natural as possible. Since the souls are in the hereafter, that seems to be their only concern when they communicate to their loved ones here. But they do want to help us understand that the Infinite Light is a many-spoked wheel, and, at the very least, they can help us come to terms with circumstances that have been muddled by our feeble attempts at explaining what cannot be understood. One of the advantages of life in the hereafter that I am glad to hear about is the fact that all things of the earth become clear to us when we pass. Not only is there so much that we don't know, but there is even more that we have contorted and confused by our own beliefs or what the so-called "experts" tell us. The only true experts of things not of the earth are the souls in the hereafter, and they can be trusted entirely. They also know that, for our own benefit, they cannot solve the big questions about our existence here. They can only point us in the right direction and hope that we understand. They know that there will come a time that we will.

THE TERMINALLY ILL

People seem surprised when I tell them that many people come to me when they or a loved one are faced with terminal illness. To me it seems perfectly reasonable for someone to want to know what awaits them in the next life, very much the same as researching an area before relocating to another city. It helps to know that we will not just disappear. Knowing about their next home helps to give someone who is invariably suffering both mentally and physically hope that the suffering will not be for naught. When we come to the point where we understand that physical death is inevitable, the only choice we have is to look ahead to the promised fresh beginning and the reward for the hardships we will have to endure until we are ready to pass. I really believe that years of understanding the workings of the hereafter have helped me understand how not to fear the end of my physical life, and I hope that those who read this book can also come away with the understanding that there is nothing at all to fear. Knowing about who we will meet in the hereafter and how we will make the transition helps make things a bit easier to bear for those facing imminent passing and for their families.

Most people who have come to me for a discernment when they are terminally ill are amazed to find the number of people who are lining up in the hereafter to help make the transition a peaceful one. It seems to be an organized reunion of family and friends who are ready, willing and able to help in the transition process, because they truly care about the person who is ready to pass on. It is a heartwarming and comforting spectacle of souls, all wanting to assure the person that there is nothing to worry about. They often talk about things like where they will live and how happy and peaceful everything is in the hereafter in an effort to bring some sense of three-dimensional reality to a place we cannot yet see. Their concern for the well-being of the person who is near passing is almost overwhelming, and my clients tend to leave our session with a sense of assurance and much less fear than they originally had. A few years ago I did a discernment for Dr. Elisabeth Kübler-Ross after a stroke had left her largely incapacitated. It was an interesting prospect to discern for a woman who has been called the "mother of all Death and Dying issues," because she had touched so many lives in her lifetime and helped so many people face the prospect of their own death. In a way I was honored to help make her preparation for transition a little easier. During her discernment, there were so many souls in the hereafter who were waiting for her with open arms that I think she was bowled over by the fact that those she helped to pass would be around to return the favor. They spoke about the many great things she had done in her lifetime, and they promised that whenever she felt ready to make the transition, they would be there in force for her. After the discernment, Elisabeth seemed different—lighter somehow, and in much better spirits (no pun intended). It just proved to me that no matter how much you know about the hereafter or dying, the prospect of change is a frightening one, but we can count on the souls in the hereafter for all the help we will need.

The souls in the hereafter do not necessarily need me to be able to communicate these thoughts and ideas to their loved ones who are about to make the transition. My good friend Dianne Arcangel, who has spent many years studying the "death-bed apparitions" of those in her care at the Kübler-Ross center in Houston, Texas, has documented the visions that patients have had about loved ones in the hereafter who call to them and spend time with them in an effort to make the transition easier. Although medical science mostly discounts these visions as the result of powerful medication and semi-consciousness, they are in fact very real and powerful to the patient. It also does them a world of good in understanding that they are not just "dying" but instead are moving on to greater things. The souls there will help point out the "portal" from where the patient will exit this existence, and they want us to understand how little our existence will change from what we know it to be. Ask most people you know who have had a loved one pass from a terminal illness, and they are likely to recount for you incredible stories their loved one told them about the visitations they received from the souls in the hereafter, and how truly comforting the messages were.

The discernments of those who are near passing are not just for that person, but for the whole family. Watching a loved one "die" physically is very difficult, and it is a big strain on our souls. We tend to lose our hope because we are powerless to stop what cannot be stopped. We sit by idly and watch precious loved ones slip through our hands. It is important to understand where the next destination is, as much for the patient as for the family, because it helps to take away the finality that physical death seems to bring with it. Families who have come together for a discernment with someone who has not much more time on the earth have told me after the loss of their loved one that they have a new focus on the hereafter, and they tend to concentrate on that instead of the fact that a loved one has left the earth. It is a very helpful attitude, to say the least, and a much less painful way of dealing with the inevitable.

I have been encouraged in recent years by the fact that the medical community has begun, at least a bit, to reckon with the fact that there is much more to a passing than just a body that is no longer alive. Even some in the medical community concede that they have taken more notice of the process where the soul begins to free itself from the body and patients begin to state as fact having seen or heard loved ones who have already passed on. Some medical professionals have even confided in me that this phenomenon already brings them a personal sense of hope. Most doctors, whether they like it or not, conceive of losing a patient as a "failure" in that they could not sustain life, but as they begin to understand that there are other agendas at work, they must bow to a higher calling. When my dear friend Vincenza was dying of bone cancer, it became evident to her family that she was conducting ongoing dialogues with loved ones who had preceded her to the hereafter. At first, she would seem surprised at an appearance and call, "Mama? Anna?" and then she seemed to reconcile that they were around for a reason. Some hospital social workers who help families of the terminally ill to understand and cope with imminent loss have begun to reconcile that no drug-induced dream could produce lucid dialogues of the kind they were witnessing. They acknowledge that the occurrence of these dialogues directly coincides with the time a patient goes into active passing, days before the body begins to die. I was surprised but glad to hear that one of the social workers was familiar with the books written about mediumship and the hereafter as a way to help families prepare for loss. While it will take some time for this type of work to enter mainstream medical practice, the information is already being put into use by health care workers willing to go the extra mile for families of the terminally ill. Even the wife of one oncologist I know has told me that some doctors in this very difficult field of medicine have to come to grips with the fact that, with regard to the soul's cycle, the end is actually the beginning, and most patients facing death are being prepared *by someone or something* for the time when passing occurs. In a discernment I had done for this oncologist, the family of one of his patients came to *him* to express their concern and let him know that his patient was not alone. I think it made a rather large impact on his ideals as a doctor—at least I hope so.

Terminal illness is an ugly, cruel way to pass—there is no doubt about that. So much of our loved ones are lost even before they pass, and the anguish of watching a love one in so much pain has a lasting effect on those who are left to grieve. But once passed, these souls insist that it was necessary, both for us and for them, that the spiritual lesson of pain and suffering prior to passing be learned. They tell us that not only did they benefit from the suffering in the hereafter but that we also stand to benefit from this difficult time as it is a spiritual milestone we have passed. I can see the faces of astonishment in a discernment when a loved one in the hereafter says that they would gladly endure their pain again to gain the same reward in the hereafter. They also acknowledge that no matter how bad things got, *all* of it was necessary for the completion of their lessons on the earth.

One of the most important things that the souls who pass due to terminal illness try to help us understand is that *no one passes alone*. This issue often comes up during a discernment for someone who is terminally ill. Their loved ones in the hereafter are concerned about removing the fear that most of us have of dying alone. They promise that there will always be someone with them to walk them through the portal of this life. Although they cannot be seen or even felt by anyone other than the one passing, they indeed are there, and they wait patiently for when the time comes to help guide the way to a world free of pain and struggle, out of a body that has finished its usefulness and into magnificent light.

REINCARNATION

Reincarnation is a subject that few want to acknowledge—even in the hereafter. The only reason I discuss this subject is because bereaved people have so many fears about what awaits them in the hereafter, and because some organized religions are reluctant to even discuss the possibility of reincarnation. I generally don't like to discuss reincarnation (and neither does the hereafter) mostly because we live in the advent of the New Age and everyone only seems interested to find out if they were once an Indian chief or Cleopatra. People have a fascination about who they were, as if the knowledge will change things for them now. It won't. When people actually ask about this during a discernment, I can usually count on an impatient answer from their loved ones in the hereafter. "What difference does it make?" is the usual answer from the souls on the other side, and also, "You accomplished your spiritual growth in that lifetime. Concentrate on *this* one." Although what they say is always in good humor, there is a lot of truth in what they say. Usually the souls in the hereafter are reluctant to mention past lives because it tends to sidetrack us from understanding our goals in this life. The object of our experiences in a previous life was to learn a particular lesson in our soul growth. In this life, there is a completely different set of circumstances and a different spiritual lesson.

There are some occasions in discernments when the souls will tell me that the relationships in this lifetime had also been in other lifetimes as well. They will use the information of a past-life relationship to help their loved ones understand that the strong bond they experienced on the earth has in fact transcended time. They hope to help us understand by that information that we are not only connected to each other in this lifetime, but in many lifetimes to come—perhaps here, but mostly in the hereafter. In the discernment of a couple that had lost two sons, the boys had related to me that they were not only brothers, but father and son in another lifetime. It usually comes as no surprise to the family, since the relationship was so special that they know it had to have been generated by something greater than what is evident here. Very often, when people speak of "soul-mates," they generally mean that the relationship on earth feels as if it were only a continuation from another time. That may very well be the case. The souls in the hereafter have told me that we travel in very large "families" of relations, friends and even enemies, and as we make the conscious decision to return to the earth we will assign each other different roles, depending on the lessons that need to be learned here. Mother in a past lifetime could be friend or sister in this one—even a beloved spouse could return as an adversary if the relationship would be productive in providing a spiritual lesson. I think every person could name those friends who are more like family, and family members who are more like foes.

The thing that frightens bereaved people the most is the fear that their child, spouse or parent will reincarnate before they themselves get to the hereafter. This is *not* the case. Imagine arriving in the hereafter only to be told, "Sorry, your wife just reincarnated five minutes ago." While it sounds funny, it is a very real concern of the bereaved. The hereafter has told me with certainty that this does not happen. It takes eons, I have been told, for the souls to come to such a point of spiritual understanding that they decide to return to the earth and live through another set of spiritual lessons. Because we travel in these large "families" to and from the earth, the souls that are in the hereafter will wait until everyone has returned before even considering the decision to return to the earth. It could also take a few lifetimes on earth for the process to happen. Also, the rush to leave the hereafter is not as great as it sounds. Many still remember fully well how difficult it was here and are not in a hurry to leave, unless returning to the earth would be the best way to experience a certain spiritual lesson. In any event, they promise us they will be there to greet us when it is our time to pass.

Reincarnation is of real value and importance in the hereafter. The souls in the hereafter have told me that while their spiritual growth continues, it is at a much slower pace than here. There, unencumbered by hardship and strife, their spiritual growth occurs quietly and peacefully. I have been told by them that so much more spiritual growth can happen on the earth, because the spiritual lessons come in the form of learning through hardship and adversity. There is also great turmoil here that is not found in the hereafter, and out of this earthbound struggle comes further advancement of the soul when it again returns to the hereafter. We can accomplish on the earth in seventy or eighty years what it might take perhaps ten times longer in the hereafter to learn—thus the decision to return.

Before the souls decide to return to the earth, they will acknowledge the spiritual lesson they would like to benefit from, and then they find the perfect circumstance to return into. Perhaps they decide to return in order to benefit from experiencing the pain of surviving the loss of a child in their lifetime or of a life of poverty and struggle. We may also elect to come to the earth for a very short time to be the child that passes in infancy, providing the spiritual lesson for another. Whatever our lesson on the earth, it always seems to be twofold—we are a principal player in our own life lesson and also a supporting player in another's. This helps me to explain to people what benefit could be gained by their son or daughter living for only a few years if we each have a reason to be here. Some lessons are shorter than others, and some life lessons seem to coincide with our purpose for being here. All in all, the main purpose of returning to the earth after being in the hereafter is to benefit from a sort of spiritual "crash course" and rise to a higher spiritual level in the hereafter. Some religious beliefs also hold to the contention that it is possible for the soul to return as an animal or plant. I don't know, because it has never come up in any discernment. I do believe, however, that with the resourcefulness of the hereafter, nothing is impossible. Neither has it happened that an animal was discerned that told me he or she was once human. Although pets are sometimes so humanlike, theirs is a separate soul growth where they also learn and benefit from their experiences on the earth.

I think that one of the reasons why some parents want to know so much about reincarnation is because they hold to the hope that the child they lost can somehow remanufacture itself back into their family if they provide another birth opportunity. Some families have even come to me before making the decision to have another child solely on the basis that they want to know if this can happen. While I have learned to "never say never" with regard to the power and resourcefulness of the hereafter, there has never been a circumstance in my discernments where the soul of a child will want to return that quickly. Carol Bowman, who wrote the book *Children's Past Lives*, researched the circumstances of children's memories of having lived another life, and I suppose it is possible for children to have their recollections of *another* life but not to reincarnate back into the circumstances from which they left. Each person on the earth has their own life lesson and soul growth to accomplish, and the lesson of having lost a child would not be a lesson if the child were to return to us somehow. I know that the Tibetan Buddhists believe that their spiritual leader keeps returning to the earth in the form of a child, and perhaps that actually happens as part of their particular soul growth. Again, nothing is beyond the comprehension of the hereafter, but I have not seen it happen in the discernments I have done.

One thing is certain: We have created the reality we have so that we may learn. In the first painful moments of tragedy, people inevitably ask, "Why did this have to happen?" We need to ask, "What lesson am I fulfilling from learning from my life's spiritual course?" Bad things don't just happen to people. The hereafter states emphatically that there are no accidents in the universe, no matter how random things on the earth might look. There are merely scripts, written by us before we arrive here to be played out and learned from the best we know how. Some souls who have found the experiences of the earth particularly painful have stated to me during a discernment that they will *never* return to the earth. They are happy and contented learning at a slow and peaceful pace in the hereafter. It seems that it is our choice alone to decide how we will grow spiritually and in what manner, and we are free to choose to stay in the hereafter or return to the earth.

THE
MESSAGES

Five

WHO WILL CARE
FOR MY CHILDREN?

I HAVE NOTICED that bereaved parents make up the largest segment of those who come to me for a discernment. While the circumstances that bring them to me vary, their intent is always the same—to make sure their children are safe and happy in the hereafter. Like any good parent sending their children across the street or off to camp or college, those parents with children in the hereafter are only doing their job, making sure their children are in good care wherever they are.

Parents who lose a child become part of a club that no one wants to belong to. The hereafter has told me that although all losses are hard to cope with, the hardest by far is the loss of a child. Not only do parents feel they have lost their "future," but there comes with the loss of a child overwhelming feelings of guilt and shame. No matter what the circumstance, whether through terminal illness, accident, miscarriage or suicide, parents always tend to blame themselves for the passing or they feel there was more they could have done to stop the inevitable. This by-product of their grief can make the loss seem unbearable.

Another facet of the grief parents face after they suffer the loss of a child is the fact that it forces them to come face-to-face with the fact that their lives are not always in their control and that terrible things could happen to anyone at any time. Many bereaved parents are victims of society's belief that parents who have lost a child were probably not good parents or the loss would never have happened or that somehow they are being punished for some sin they committed in the past. Neither one of these statements is true, and you only need to ask a bereaved parent to know.

The biggest issue that I have found with bereaved parents is not so much their grief but their *alienation* from other parents after their loss. We live in a society that is already too frightened of death, and hearing about the loss of a child makes people even more unnerved. These other parents don't *want* to know that it could happen to their children, too. But it *does* happen. In the hereafter, there is no age consideration in passing from this world to the next. There simply comes a time in which our lesson on earth is finished, no matter what age we are, and then we graduate to the Infinite Light. This message has been given to me time and time again by those souls in the hereafter, especially with regard to children.

Children are my favorite of the souls in the hereafter to discern because they have such clarity of thought, have incredible light and energy about them and are willing to go to great lengths to comfort their parents. They are so eager to come through to their parents because they know how much their parents suffer, and they want so much to make them feel better. Susan Marek, a nurse from outside Chicago, after losing her eight-year-old boy to leukemia, found she had become unable to function day to day because of the burden of her grief. She had become despondent and frequently thought of suicide as a way to be with her son. As soon as she entered the room for her discernment, her son Ryan started like a shot from the hereafter. He talked so quickly that I had trouble keeping up with him. He wanted his mom to know that, although he suffered with his illness prior to his passing, he was happy and at peace. He also told his mother frequently during the discernment that she had to move on with her life and that thinking about suicide was not the answer. She had to finish the lessons put before her on earth and then they would reunite, but *only* when it was her time. During discernments like these, I marvel at the fact that it is now the *children* that become the nurturers and caregivers to their parents.

In many of these discernments, children have been able to come through to set the record straight about the circumstance of their violent passing, much to the surprise of parents who, by witnessing the end result of a lifeless body, are eaten up by thoughts of how their children must have suffered prior to their passing. It seems of paramount importance to these children to explain the fact that they simply did not suffer, no matter how bad the circumstances looked. Again they show through the discernment how the Infinite Light is able to fix any situation and provide for a happy passing, no matter what the circumstance. When I met Margo and Bob Ryan, they had come to me about a year after the passing of their twenty-year-old daughter, Christina, who had been raped and murdered as she walked to her car after her shift at a store in a local mall. During their discernment, Christina related to me that, although her body suffered a brutal attack, her soul had begun its journey to the Light seconds before the beating. She explained to me that when she had been pulled from her car, she understood that her passing was imminent and fell into a "dream state" as she passed to the hereafter. She also asked her parents to "pray for her attacker" (who was caught and convicted of rape and murder) and emphatically stated that, although the scene looked bad, she did not suffer prior to her passing. This is yet another example to me and the parents that the hereafter will provide whatever it must for us to continue a happy life in the hereafter.

Another unfortunate by-product of having a child pass on is the need to blame—to hold someone or something accountable for the passing, as if it were some random accident that could have been avoided. The hereafter has told me time and time again that no matter how things seem otherwise, we all have a time to be born into this existence and a time to move on once our lesson here is completed. I know that this is very difficult for parents to understand, but no matter how "accidental" the circumstances seem, the circumstance is just a "vehicle" to move the child from one existence to the next, allowing them to *graduate* to the other side. This blame factor is so strong that it can disintegrate families at a time when they most need to stay together to work through their pain. Instead, it is each to his/her own corner while relationships between husband and wife or parent and surviving child crumble. This is a tragedy rivaled only by the experience of losing a child.

Children in the hereafter also put themselves willingly into the position of "referee" during the discernment to help these suffering families understand that there is no need to have to blame someone for the loss. They often speak very candidly during the discernment and have no problem presenting the unvarnished truth about their passing in an effort to help bring closure. When Nina Ballard's son, Peter, passed on at the age of three, her marriage disintegrated. During the reading, Peter told me that he was playing on the backyard lawn when his father accidentally ran over him with the riding lawn mower. Peter's father, unable to deal with the pain of being instrumental in his son's passing, blamed Nina for carelessly leaving the baby unattended. Nina could not come to terms with why her husband would decide to mow the lawn while the baby was in his care. During the course of the reading, Peter communicated that ultimately no one was to blame, since it was simply his "time," but conceded that divisiveness between Nina and her husband had become irreparable. Peter communicated that his mom had a life to go on with by herself and that she should look back on her situation only as a chapter in her "life's lesson." To illustrate his point, Peter was able to go into my memory and show me a scene from *Gone With the Wind,* where Scarlett finds the strength and determination within herself to go on despite everything having been taken from her. He told her that any time she feels the pressure from this experience to think about that scene to give herself the strength to carry on. I wonder sometimes if these children in the hereafter realize the great relief they bring their parents when they tell them, "It was not your fault" and "No matter what, I still love you." It means the difference between years of unending misery and forgiveness and hope. No matter how much we try to rationalize by saying, "There is nothing more I could have done," the solace is nothing compared to knowing that your children in the hereafter understand and tell you that blaming yourself or anyone else is a waste of energy. You are only a player in the continuation of their life in the hereafter.

No matter what age a child is when they pass on, children in the hereafter continue to age or mature and will grow to the age that is the age of their soul. Hearing this tends to upset bereaved parents, because they worry about missing their child's growing to adulthood the way they would have on the earth. They also worry about the time when they themselves arrive in the hereafter and meet a middle-aged man or woman who greets them with "Hi, Mom!" This is *not* how the hereafter works. Children who come through to their parents from the hereafter must represent themselves the way their parents would know them and will take on the physical characteristics that their parents would recognize. The only difference will be that perhaps their soul will mature with the understanding received by the hereafter. They can represent themselves to us any way we need them to be, so don't worry about entering the hereafter to find a grown adult you won't recognize. They will be your children as you remember them. They tell me that when we see them again it will seem as if not a second has passed since we last saw them. We tend to think of the body and not the soul. The hereafter, true to form, allows the souls to represent themselves in whatever form they wish. When I discern children in the hereafter, it makes no difference if the child passed on last week or thirty years ago. They will still represent themselves to me and their family at the age they passed. They do this to give me (and their parents) a frame of reference from which to recognize the child.

What is apparent, however is that no matter how old or young the physical body, it is the maturity of the soul that comes through during the discernment. This is why I can communicate with a child who passed at birth or from miscarriage. In the hereafter, the soul, no longer bound by the limits of an infant's body, can speak and have clear thought. This is also true with souls whose physical body was limited by physical or mental handicap. I remember a gentleman who had come to me for an appointment who told me afterward about his apprehensions that his daughter would not communicate since she had been profoundly retarded. During the reading, however, she spoke clearly and candidly about how it was her life's lesson for her soul to be in a body that could not communicate or express needs to the outside world. She also thanked her father for treating her as if she were no different from any other child and talking to her about his life and feelings as if he knew she was listening. I think this is a profound lesson for all of us here who treat the retarded or handicapped as if they are nonhuman or incapable of thought. Their body or mind might appear damaged but their soul is still alive.

Parents of children who pass on due to miscarriage or abortion should receive as much, or even more, regard as those whose children spent time on the earth, because they seem to be in a silent minority by virtue of the fact that miscarriage is not even considered a loss by most people, and abortion is a taboo subject altogether. Although most people's thoughts vary greatly on these two aspects of loss depending on their religious or political beliefs, the hereafter, which seeks always to understand and reconcile, has given me a lot of insight into this area. I must admit that sometimes what I have been told by the hereafter rumples my own belief system, but if I listen without prejudice to what they say, it makes the most sense spiritually. We have to trust them—they know more than we will ever understand in this lifetime. According to the hereafter, the soul does not enter the body until the moment of birth. A soul, recognizing that the body to be born will provide the opportunity it needs to return to the earth to fulfill a specific spiritual journey, will wait until the body has begun the birth process and "jump in." Sometimes, however, plans change for that soul in the hereafter, and for reasons only they understand, the soul changes course and does not enter the body. Since the body cannot survive without a soul, the result is a stillbirth—the soul departs as if it were the end of its life here on earth. For the soul, another opportunity will exist to come back to the earth. Miscarriage, I have been told, happens when the growing body inside the mother is physically unable to sustain the soul waiting for it. The soul, undaunted, waits for another opportunity to fulfill its journey on the earth. Much to the surprise of some families that have come for a discernment because of another loss, the souls of miscarriages or stillbirths also appear as family, whether they are recognized or not. In the hereafter, they still consider themselves son or daughter and will come through that way and also comment that, had the cycle of birth continued, they would have been part of that family. It amazes me that when people hear that a woman had a stillbirth or miscarriage, it is not given the same respect as other aspects of loss. To add insult to injury, parents are often told, "Oh, you'll have another" or "Maybe you're not ready to be a mother." To the mother, the soul is the thing she has bonded to well before birth, and that loss is the same as if the soul had a body she would recognize.

Abortion is an issue so hotly debated that open, rational discussion about it is almost impossible. I cannot take a stand on this issue either way because I am not a woman and will never know what it is like to have to face that decision. The hereafter, however, has provided me with a real understanding of the practical side of this issue and of the depth of compassion the Infinite Light has for a woman facing the difficult prospect of terminating a pregnancy. To make a very simple analogy, the souls liken terminated pregnancies to trains—if one is missed, however disheartening, another will surely come along. If the body they intended to inhabit is terminated, they understand there will be another opportunity to return to the earth down the road. I do not use this analogy to trivialize an important issue, but merely to explain the level of understanding that the hereafter has. They neither judge women for their decisions nor do they encourage decisions to terminate pregnancies. They understand why we must do what we do on the earth sometimes and allow us the compassion we need to reconcile our decisions for ourselves. They do try to discourage abortion, however, because each soul is looking for the perfect situation to be born into here to continue its soul growth. The important thing to remember, though, is that they *understand*. I remember a woman who had called the office rather late in the evening for information. I answered the phone (something I almost never do) and was all ready to inform her that it was much too late to call when I heard the familiar sound of desperation in her voice. She simply asked me if I thought God took her son because he was angry that she had an abortion when she was seventeen. It was heart-wrenching, to say the least. I explained to her that if I could understand that she had to make a painful decision in her life, what would make *me* more understanding than the Infinite Light that understands more than I ever could? The Infinite Light is not vindictive. It understands and has the compassion to let us work through the things we feel keep us from our path toward the light—here or hereafter. Instead of political and religious organizations trying to control a very difficult decision in a woman's spiritual journey, they ought to take a cue from the Infinite Light and try compassion rather than criticism. Don't worry about the souls from terminated pregnancies. Many of them come through during discernments, sometimes simply to tell the mothers that they understand why the decision was made to terminate a pregnancy, and that while they would have liked the opportunity to be born into that particular circumstance, they will have an opportunity to return to the earth in another circumstance. Sometimes, when other family members are unaware that there was a terminated pregnancy in the past, the soul will come through in a way that only the mother will understand, since their goal is not to air the personal laundry in public. They are incredible that way.

Parents of children in the hereafter need to remember that their children will always be their children, and time or distance cannot change that. When we pass into the hereafter, the children will be the first to greet us, and no matter how much time has gone by since their passing, we will know them by their soul. Many of the souls in the hereafter have explained to me that when we meet again in the hereafter, we pick up with each other where we left off on the earth. Time being relative there, parents will still have the opportunity to see their children grow and mature while the children bring the parents up to speed in their new environment. The children will guide us through our new life as we guided them through this one.

Anyone who doubts the determination of children in the hereafter to help their families come to terms with loss need only to speak to Mary and James O'Reilly. Our paths crossed, literally, at an intersection in Bardstown, Kentucky, where I was speaking at a seminar. The O'Reillys and their daughter Kelly have become my good friends since then, and I marvel at the determination that they have *not* to be defined only by their loss—quite the contrary. The loss of their son has propelled them in a new spiritual direction in life. Jim, a construction company owner, has begun to set into motion their dream of building a bereaved parents' retreat in Michigan so that families who suffer loss can unite in a caring and understanding atmosphere and be "people" again. Because it so often happens that the loss of a child changes how families are treated by those around them and in their community, Jim's hope is to have a meeting place where families can be more than just "bereaved." He wants them to get a break from the isolation that so many bereaved families feel and to deal with their loss in a supportive environment. It is an ambitious project, but the O'Reillys have the best co-director possible—their son, Colin James. The following is the story of their journey, written by Mary and James:

MARY O'REILLY

"Our nightmare unknowingly started during the Halloween of 1991. Our son, Colin James, came down with an unusually high fever. He felt too sick to go trick-or-treating, and that worried me. The next day we brought him to the doctor's office for a checkup where they performed the routine tests for the usual childhood illnesses. We were told we would be called when the test results returned. Four days later, an urgent call came from the doctor who told us it was imperative that we meet at 8 P.M. that evening. When we arrived at the office, she was waiting at the door for us. She wasted no time in telling us that Colin had leukemia, but the type had not yet been determined. We went home stunned and prayed a lot that night.

"The next day, Colin was admitted into St. John's Hospital so that they could determine what type of leukemia we would be dealing with. We hung to the hope that it was Acute Lymphocytic leukemia, which is about 90 percent curable. Later that afternoon, we were told that Colin had Acute Myelogenous Leukemia, which is difficult to cure and only had a 50 percent survival rate. Our nightmare began to worsen by the hour. We were told that Colin's illness would have to be treated aggressively and quickly.

"Colin's first treatment series included chemotherapy, and the side effects kept him in the hospital for twenty-one days. During that time we never left his side. When he finished the chemotherapy protocol—eight months of treatments—we left the hospital hoping never to have to return, except for checkups. During that summer of 1992, things seemed to return to normal for our family because Colin was in remission and no longer on treatment. We were able to take a wonderful family vacation that summer and prepare for Colin's and Kelly's return to school in September. Colin returned to school and was in the third grade for only a few days when he started running a fever. It was our worst fear realized—Colin had relapsed.

"On September 16, 1992, Colin was admitted back into the hospital to start treatment once again. He confided in us that he did not want to go through it again—it had not worked the first time, and the pain he experienced from the tests and the chemotherapy was terrible. But we had no choice but to continue with the treatments to make him well again, and we were praying that this time the treatment would put him back in remission. The time before his treatments were to begin we spent as a family, talking and watching movies. One night I hugged Colin and told him that I loved him so very much, and he turned to me and said, 'No, Mom—I love you more.' Those were the last words he was to speak to me on this earth. In the early hours of September 21, 1992, our precious son Colin James lost the battle with leukemia and passed to the other side."

JAMES O'REILLY

"Thinking back on this time, I remember that three days before Colin passed, I sat in bed with my son and was flicking through the television channels, not looking at anything in particular. I came upon a program that featured a medium named George Anderson, and somehow I was drawn by what I saw. This is the first time George had come into my life, and I watched with great curiosity the messages he spoke from people supposedly on the 'other side.' I was amazed, because until that day, I did not even know or care what a medium was, nor did I know I would ever need to seek him out so desperately.

"One night, about a week after our son's funeral, I came home from work exhausted and turned on the television set. There again was George Anderson. I found this to be odd—seeing him again—because I don't watch much television and I was not looking for this type of program. But watching the program, my interest level shot way up and I was amazed that this type of communication with the dead was possible. For me and everyone else who has lost a child or a loved one, the grieving process is so very difficult. Each person has to find his own way, and through that program and the books about George, I felt that I had found mine. From that time on, my mission was to try to get a private appointment with George, and I tried for two years until we found out about the seminar in Bardstown, Kentucky.

"When we got to Kentucky, we drove around looking for a drugstore because my daughter Kelly developed a sudden, unusual stomachache. We stopped at a traffic light, and a man crossed the street in front of our car. My wife looked up and said, 'Isn't that George Anderson?' I looked up, and sure enough it was! I lowered the car window and asked him if he was George Anderson, and he answered, 'Yes, I am.' I told him that we were in town for the seminar and asked him if he would autograph the copy of his book we had with us. To be quite honest, I wanted to kidnap this man after trying for two years to reach him! Instead, I settled for the autograph and asked him if he would consider coming to Michigan. 'Yes. Just write to the office,' he told us, and with that, turned and walked away. We thought maybe this was a sign that Colin would come through during the seminar. He didn't at that time, but what we did hear during the seminar was very touching, reassuring and emotional. For my wife, seeing George was just overwhelming, and the seminar left her with an incredibly warm feeling. We eventually organized a seminar in Detroit in June 1995, and George's gift to us for our volunteer work was a discernment with Colin. Going to the discernment, we weren't sure what to expect, but all our tension and skepticism went away as the discernment progressed.

"The two important signs that we received that told us George was indeed communicating with Colin was his mention of the time our daughter Kelly accidentally ran over a bird while mowing the lawn. It was something only our family knew, and Colin told us through George that he had gotten the bird on the other side and thinks of it as a gift. We also couldn't help but notice our daughter's reaction when her brother came to her in a special way. Colin knew how she was feeling about being a bereaved sibling and having everyone's attention focused on only the parents' needs. This brought a smile to her face that was worth all the money in the world.

"There is a saying that goes, 'When you lose a parent, you lose your past, but when you lose a child, you lose your future.' Still, you go on, and it seems to me that this amazing chain of events was designed by Colin to do just that. Hearing from him through George is an experience that will stay in our hearts forever, and it is always a pleasure to see the reactions and relief on people's faces after their discernments. We know what their pain is because we live it also. Someone who has never lost a child can only sympathize, but they have no idea what pain there is and what path the bereaved parents walk. We started Peace Be With You, a nonprofit foundation, to be able to bring a kind of peace and comfort to people who grieve, and we feel people like George make a difference and touch people's lives in a positive way by helping them to work through their pain.

"In a way, George will always be a part of our lives, like a special friend, because he has given us the ability to allow us another chance to communicate with our precious son. The following is our discernment with our son, Colin James."

THE DISCERNMENT

"Now, whatever I say to any of you, just answer yes or no. Let's see—there's a female who draws near—well, two. Wait—now there's a third—now there's three people. Somebody else is with them now. Four people. There are definitely two males from two different generations—one older, one younger, and there's a female, too. Now another female and another male—somebody else just came in now—quite a crowd here. Two females of different generations also. There's definitely a young male close to you passed over, yes?"

"Yes."

"Because he's coming forward and these other people seem to be much older than him. He's coming forward, and he's going to each of you individually, so he obviously is family. He has an older male with him of another generation—he's also family to him. There's another young presence, too. One keeps pushing *son*—your son passed on?"

"Yes."

"He's the young guy, obviously, and *(To Kelly)* that would be your brother?"

"Yes."

"He keeps saying, 'I'm the son, I'm the brother passed on.' He keeps talking about a grandpa being with him, but I don't know if he means his grandfather or his great-grandfather, so don't say anything yet. He keeps telling me to say 'Grandpa is with me,' and that's the other man. *(To Mary)* Did your dad pass?"

"Yes."

"Yeah, it is, because he just said to me, 'Grandpa is with me,' and he pointed to you—so that's obviously your dad. Now he speaks about your mom *(to Jim)*—did she pass?"

"No."

"No—she's still here—*(To Mary)* Yours is still here, too—yes?"

"Yes."

"Okay—it must be a great grandma, then, but on your *(Jim's)* side, because he keeps saying 'Grandma is with me,' and he went to you. It seems to be your mother's mother, so obviously he's referring to your mom's side of the family and that confused me for a second, where I thought maybe your mom had passed. Her husband too—so that set of grandparents is there. You didn't lose another child, did you? Did you miscarry or something like this? *(Mary nods yes.)* Yeah, 'cause he says there is another child here with him—that there's been the loss of two. You knew the sex? Because it feels like a girl—he gives me the impression that there is a sister there with him. Wait—he says there are three, with him you'd have three. (*To Kelly*) You are the only child left?"

"Yes."

(*To Mary*) That's what it is—you'd have three children, that's what I think he's trying to tell me—technically there are three children. (*To Kelly*) He jokes with you that you're the 'last of the Mohicans' in this world. You're the only one here but he said, 'If all of us were in the flesh, there would be three children.' There would be one son and two daughters—he's saying that had the cycle of birth continued you would have had a daughter, and he states that his sister is there with him—that's the young female. (*to Mary*) Were you close to a grandmother also? Because there's one lady around you claiming to be your grandmother as well. Did your grandmothers pass?"

"Yes."

"Because there is one, and it seems you know one better."

"Exactly."

"One you saw more frequently or something, because there is one—I feel like a flock of people behind claiming to be your grandparents and (*to Jim*) yours also, so obviously all his great grandparents are with him. (*to Mary*) But one lady steps forward and claims to be your grandmother, saying, 'I'm the one she knew better.'"

"Uh-huh."

(*To Mary*) "Your father pass on kind of young by today's standards?"

"Uh-huh."

"He goes before the boy?"

"Uh-huh."

"Because he claims he welcomed your son into the Light, that he's there for him—this is something that you had hoped and prayed for. Did they know each other here?"

"Sort of."

"Yes—they've gotten to know each other better over there obviously, 'cause he says they knew each other here, but maybe not for a long period of time. (*To Kelly*) You and your brother very close?"

"Yes."

"Not that he's playing favorites here, but I feel he keeps going behind you, and I feel I see him standing behind you with his hands on your shoulders—that you and he are great pals as well as brother and sister. He says that it is bad enough to be a bereaved parent, but he says that unfortunately, sometimes you don't know how you are supposed to feel. The focus of attention can go to your parents as having the loss, but you have it also and it's almost like people don't see your grief the same way. Your brother just wants to let you know that he is around you like a guardian angel and he 'breaks your chops' saying that you make him work overtime. He has a great sense of humor, and this is how you will know that he's all right and back to his old self again. He says that if he came in too solemn and ethereal, you wouldn't know that it was him. He had to come in with that personality. (To Jim and Mary) He does pass tragically?"

"Yes."

"In the sense of age as well as circumstance, and he tells me that it looks worse than what it is. He keeps reassuring you that he did not suffer prior to his passing. It seems his death is instantaneous—he tells me that he's gone from one moment to the next."

"Yes."

"I don't understand, so just say yes or no—his passing is accidental?"

"No."

"Why is he saying his health trouble is accidental? Does it come upon him suddenly?"

"Yes."

"Maybe that's what he means, because they confuse me when they say 'health problem, but accidental,' and I say, 'What do you mean—it's either one or the other.' Something cut his air off?"

"Yes."

"He keeps telling me he's losing oxygen. This is not an illness that he was born with."

"Right."

"This is something that suddenly happens. He tells me it happens from one moment to the next. That's why it comes to me like an accident. Did it affect the head at all?"

"Yes."

"There's pressure in my head, and he says it's up there—it's affecting the head. It definitely pressures the brain?"

"Yes."

"Because he tells me that you had no more idea it was there than he did, and that's why he says it's an accident. As far as he was concerned and you were concerned, he says that any of us could have it right now and not know it. He claims it blacks him out—is that correct?"

"Yes."

"That is why it looks like an accident to me. He said to me that I gave you the right information, but it is hard to conceive that he suddenly blacked out. He says that he doesn't want the two of you in any way to blame yourselves, like you should have known something was wrong. How could you know? He didn't know."

"Right."

"As far as you're concerned, he was fine and healthy. He has something like a tumor?"

"Yes."

"That's the best way I can describe it in layman's terms—'cause there's pressure on the head. Wait—he tells me not to use the word *tumor*—something 'pops' up there, yes?"

"Yes."

"Now he tells me it's like an aneurysm."

"Yes."

"That's what it is—there's pressure up there—a blockage. He might have been getting headaches."

"Yes."

"Take a couple of aspirin—it subsides. Yeah, he has an aneurysm. This is why it's like an accident—all of a sudden this thing 'pops' and he's gone."

"Right."

"It happens suddenly. That's why when I said before, he didn't pass from that kind of health trouble, as far as you know, but it has to do with his health and it's there, but it seems to be okay. I mean that when this thing blows, he goes instantaneously, because he states that he blacks out. Oxygen is obviously cut off from the brain, hemorrhaging in the head. As much as you don't want to hear this, he is one of those people whose work on earth got done sooner. 'It was time to move on,' he states. Just like, someday, when your work here is finished, you'll move on also. Again—not to feel that you failed him in any way—you couldn't save him. It all happened so quickly. I see St. Jude around you as a symbol of hopelessness, and you feel hopeless, like what are you going to do—you tried everything. He knows you tried everything but he says that the most difficult thing for you to accept at this time—the fact that it was his time to move on. (*To Kelly*) Are you graduating or something?"

"Yes!"

"Because he keeps congratulating you on your graduation. He keeps handing you white roses, and says he will be at your graduation. You are graduating this year?"

"Yes."

"He says that he'll be there spiritually with you and extends the white roses to you as a blessing. (*To Jim and Mary*) He was always in a hurry? It's like he knew his time here wasn't going to be as long as we would expect. It seems he was always in a rush, trying to get everything done—everything had to be done yesterday. In this case it doesn't surprise me that he finished his work here sooner than anticipated. Is there a Pat or Patrick passed on?"

(*Mary*) "Yes."

"He keeps talking about Patrick being with him and I feel I'm going back—like it's a great grandparent's generation. Also a Sean or John?"

"Yes."

"He didn't pass on, though."

"Yes."

"There's somebody here who's definitely like an uncle figure and claiming his name is Sean or John—English would be *John* of course. Obviously somebody back there spoke Gaelic because I can hear it being spoken."

(*Jim*) "It's got to be my side."

"Yeah, because there is definitely somebody back there who's speaking a Celtic language and I'm assuming I'm hearing Irish—Gaelic."

"Yes."

"Your son states he was complaining about headaches."

"Yes."

"Again, not to feel that you failed him in any way because he's complaining about headaches, and then when this happens—like you should have investigated further."

"Yes."

"But you had no idea that it was there any more than he did."

"Right."

"You know—a headache comes with the common cold or maybe stress, and unless it is something significant, we really don't take it as any type of signal that something is really wrong. He thanks you for the memorial. You must have memorialized him somehow. But good things are being done in his name?"

"Yes."

"It's like a scholarship or something?"

"Yes."

"There's finance in front of me and he says that good things are being done in his name, so apparently that's what he refers to. Is there a James passed on? Wait— your first name is Jim, but more than likely there's someone passed on, too, with that name, like an uncle."

"There is."

"He's there with your son as well. As your son says, you will always have your grief—it's not going to go away, but as he says, look at it as though he's moved to this other place where these relatives live. Also—you lost a pet?"

"Yes."

"Your son keeps talking about the pet that passed on, that is there with him also. Did he pass after?"

"Yes."

"It is almost like when the pet died, it really represented the end for you. He talks about meeting the pet over there, so apparently it passes on after him and it kind of broke your heart again, because it was a link to him, and now there's a feeling of him really having passed on. He doesn't specify the species, so don't say anything but he says the pet is here with me. He says that he's taking good care of it over there. Your son is very independent, yes? Because he seems—he has the relatives over there and he's close with your dad and such, but he likes his own space and to do his own thing. He says that he's very happy and at peace, and he just wishes he could say to you to be more happy and at peace about his passing. You're always going to miss him—that's not going to go away, but as he states, 'I can't say that I miss you, because I'm closer to you than you can imagine.' You've dreamt about him, and he says that there are times that you just feel him there. (They nod.) And even if I didn't exist, meaning George, you'd know he was there. You get the feeling there are times you've turned your head and could have sworn you saw him standing there. He says that you have had glimpses beyond 'the curtain' into the next world, and he says that you have seen him there. The name Robert or Bob mean anything?"

(Mary) "Yes."

"Passed on?"

"Yeah."

"Because he keeps talking about Bob or Robert being with him."

"Robert."

"Is he family?"

"No."

"But like family? It can be a family member by choice, because there's a feeling of 'familyness,' but I don't really feel that he is blood family. Did he pass young also?"

"Yeah."

"Before your son?"

"No."

"Well then, he must have welcomed him, because he talks about passing young also, and the two of them hooking up over there, that they certainly know each other. Also, is there a George? Let me skip it for now. (*To Mary*) Was there another language spoken in your family?"

"Uh-huh."

"Like your grandparents, or such."

"Uh-huh."

"Don't say what it is, but I know I hear something other than English. I would hear it in Europe, though—yes?"

"Yeah."

"Yes, it's a European language. It could be anything, but it certainly is another language in the background. Who is Joseph passed on? Way back—I feel like I'm going way back."

"Yes."

"I feel like about eighty years or something."

"Oh yeah."

"He would speak that language?"

"Yes."

"He did not speak English?"

"No, he didn't."

"Because he seems to be conversing more in his own language and brings his other language up—somebody tells me that he really doesn't speak English that well. He's a father figure, which would be an uncle or something like that. You still have contact with your son's friends?"

(*Jim*) "Yes."

"Because he does thank a lot of his friends for kind of sticking around—it's like you still have a link with him and his memory."

"Yes."

"If you think your friends could deal with this, he just wants you to let them know that he's all right. Without telling me, your son's first name is short?"

"Yes."

"Less than eight letters."

"Yes."

"He tells me that he has a short first name and it's less than eight letters. (*To Colin*) If you can tell me that, why don't you just come out and tell me what it is? I always have to play this game. It's common enough that I have heard it before?"

(*Mary*) "Yes."

"It's foreign sounding?"

(*Jim*) "Yeah."

"He tells me that I might associate it with more of a foreign name—and it is famous, too."

"Yes."

"He says it is a name of fame not only for his memory, but somebody else has the name. Obviously he's trying to warm my brain up to figure out what it is. He's giving me clues, so when I hear it, I won't say that it doesn't make sense. There's also a Margaret? There is an Elizabeth, too."

(*Jim*) "Elizabeth? Yes, my mother had a sister named Elizabeth."

"Passed on?"

"Yes."

"Your son says that she's present there with him also. He would be your only son? That could be the reason why he singularizes himself. He's also the younger?"

"Yes."

"He keeps telling me that he's the baby, which is another reason it hits home so bad. Yes—it may be a little hard for you to accept that say, in ten years, he accomplished here what he was supposed to do."

"Yes."

"He obviously passes on very young. Wait—he's less than ten when he passes, yes?"

"Yes."

"I just threw that out as an example before, but he tells me that he is less than ten when he passes. Somebody saying the Rosary for him? (*They nod.*) Because I keep seeing rosary beads going in front of me and I keep seeing Our Lady of Lourdes appearing also. He states that it's a spiritual instrument, and he thanks you for it—that the rosary is a powerful form of grace in the hereafter, so he doesn't want you to think that you're wasting your time. He shows me seven—is his name less than seven letters?"

"Yes."

"He holds up the five—so it's five letters. The name is famous in literature?"

(*Jim*) "I think it is."

"Without telling me, do you understand why he says, 'A B C D E,' and then stops? The first letter of his name is beyond the E in the alphabet?"

"No."

"Oh—then it's in that cluster."

"Yes."

"Now he shows me 'A B C'—it's not the A or the B?"

"No."

(*Laughs*) "Then it's the C obviously."

"Yes."

"He keeps showing me *The Colin Boy*."

"Yes."

"That's it?"

"Yes."

"He gave me his name right in front of my face and stupid me blocked it out. He told me before that I have heard the name before in my family, and then said to me, 'C O L I N,' and I thought to myself, 'Oh, that's just an example,' and I started going in another direction. He finds it very funny now, that he said, 'I gave it to you.' And he says I used it as an example before—that's why you heard me talking out loud to myself saying, 'If this is the name, I'll want to kick myself in the pants, because I could have had this out ten minutes ago.' (*to Kelly*) You're starting to grow out of friends?"

"What do you mean?"

"New people are coming into your life and other people are fading out. Your lifestyle is changing and you are approaching young womanhood, growing into adulthood—so he says that you might find yourself very moody, and he says that on those days, he's glad he's over there. Not to be down on yourself or make yourself crazy, try to put yourself into balance because it's like you're going through one of the first monumental changes of life and going from childhood to womanhood, and he says that your whole system, your whole outlook, everything within yourself is changing. And he says that it can be a very frustrating time as well, but a very enriching time. It's funny—he's young but he seems older, because I'm talking to somebody who passes, maybe eight years old, but he's more mature. You have a birthday coming up?"

(*Kelly*) "Yes."

"Because he's wishing you a happy birthday, too. I feel him in front of you wishing you a happy birthday and extending white roses to you. He knows you go through anger over his passing, too, and you just can't understand how this could have happened, but he says not to be angry about it. He's not dead, he's alive—he's just not in the physical body anymore. Yes, you miss his presence but you didn't love his body, you loved *him,* and the essence of that which you knew and loved is still very much alive. Sometimes you feel he didn't get a chance in life, eight years and he's just shot down, but he says that life in the hereafter is just continuation—he says that he's going on with his life as if he went away to school. Because that's what he's doing over there—he's in school, and because he is very bright and quick to learn he's over there at what we would consider high school level. He knows that you feel you're not seeing him grow up, you're not seeing him move on, but always remember that they grow in wisdom over there, not in the physical years as we see it. What's this thing about pets—you all have a lot of pets or something?"

"Yes."

"He talks about having a number of pets over there, even if they are ones that he didn't know—maybe he wanted dogs, he wanted cats, he wanted a horse, and he says that he has pets over there that maybe he wasn't able to have on the earth. Was he having trouble with his eyesight? At times, from the headaches he may have had blurriness."

"Yes."

"Because definitely there's a pressure around my eyes and this might have made him feel blurry or dizziness—he admits feeling a little sluggish in the head. He asks that you put yourselves at peace about the entire incident and not to make yourselves crazy over it. *(To Jim)* Now I know you said that you are self-employed, but you're starting to branch out into other areas? You're maintaining the tree trunk, but other branches are coming out. Sometimes you're married to your job?"

"Yes."

"When you are self-employed it's true—'no tickee, no shirtee'—you have no choice, you have to work like that, but he says to also make sure you have some time to yourself and your family. Because since he's passed on, you've kind of buried yourself in your work, trying to keep ahead of your grief. As long as you are working, you're keeping your mind off it, which is good, but you have to have some time for life and yourself. *(To Mary)* Are you employed also?"

"No."

"He's thinking that it may not be a bad idea for you. In your case it would be therapeutic, not really a question of who couldn't use the extra money, but he says that it would be therapeutic because you dwell on this too much. You have too much time to think, and even if it's a part-time or temporary job, you should try to put your anxiety into a more constructive area, because he says you go over it [his passing] in your mind constantly, and he's not being unsympathetic to what you're going through or how you feel, but he said you also have to give your mind a break. His passing happened, and it's not like you're *not* ever going to see him again—he says that eventually you are going to have to come there like everybody else. He knows that sometimes you wish that it was sooner than later, but you still have a purpose here to fulfill. Does the name Helen or Ellen mean anything at all? It seems to be around your dad. Did your father speak a Mediterranean language? Because I'm seeing the Mediterranean, so it's obviously one of the countries there."

"Right."

"That leaves me Greece, Italy, Spain and Portugal. This may be symbolic, but does the name Nicholas mean anything to you at all?"

"Uh-huh."

"It sounds like your father is talking about Nicholas, but I don't know if he's calling out. But your dad knows him."

"Yes."

"Were they pretty close?"

"Yes."

"I don't know why, but your father is saying, 'Tell Nick you've heard from me.' They are relatives, yes?"

"Yes."

"But they're also good buddies. Is there health trouble around him or something?"

"Not that I know of."

"Maybe not him—it could be around him, but it seems he's going through a time of upset. The health troubles could be in the state of things. He says, 'Tell Nicholas you heard from me.' The language is Romantic?"

"Yes."

"Yes, so it is not Greek."

"No."

"Okay, I just wanted to make sure, because he tells me that the language is Romantic. They are speaking a dialect or regional language, which throws me."

"Right."

"Is it actually Italian?"

"Yes."

"Because when I heard it again, it sounded more like that to me than Spanish or Portuguese."

"Is that my father telling you?"

"Yes. When he started speaking again, he said for me to listen closely and it may not be what I hear at the opera, but it definitely had more of the Italian sound to it. Is your anniversary coming up or something?"

"Not ours."

"Then why is your son handing white roses and saying happy anniversary? He's doing it in front of the two of you, so I'm assuming he means you. Well, I'll just leave it with you. (*To Mary*) You took care of your dad?"

"Uh-huh."

"Your father keeps blessing you for being so good to him prior to his passing— your mom did, too, but you all took care of him. He does seem to be very family-oriented and just says to you not to feel like you don't have a father when Father's Day comes up—that, you know, everybody else can celebrate with their father and yours isn't here anymore. He says, 'I'm closer to you than you can imagine,' and one day when you all come back together, he says that you'll understand what they're trying to say. Your son keeps handing you white roses, wishing you a belated Mother's Day, and extends to you (*Jim*) red roses wishing you a happy Father's Day—that he knows that it is up ahead, but he knows that you only feel like partial parents now. Also, try not to be so overprotective of your daughter, your son says. I mean if she has a sniffle now, you watch everything."

(*They laugh.*) "We do."

"There is an essence of independence with her also—he says both of them are guilty of that. (*To Kelly*) He says to me that you'll have struggling time in your teens, but normal struggling times. It's called growing up and finding your way, so he says someday don't feel as if the world is coming to an end. This, too, will pass. He jokes. He says, 'I've been watching you from over here,' and that he's around you like a guardian angel, but says that there are some days you just don't see the forest for the trees. Even he can't do anything about that. (*to Mary and Jim*) Is there a Henry passed on? I don't think so, but I just heard the name fly in front of me, and I don't want to ignore something and find out it means something, like I did with Colin. Also Peter?"

"Yes."

"Sorry, whoever you are! I almost ignored him, too. Your son kept telling me that Peter is here with me, And I thought to myself, 'Oh it's probably wrong' and he said, 'Yeah, just like Colin was,' so I said I'd try it. Is he a father figure?"

(Jim) "A great-grandfather."

"Yes, because also he's a father figure to your son, and also you. Also, is there a Charlie? *(To Mary)* Again around your dad—it looks like somebody he knew."

"I think it was somebody that he knew."

"Passed on?"

"Yes."

"It's not family—maybe a friend or something."

"Yes."

"He keeps talking about Charlie being with him and he comes to you like 'Uncle Charlie'—a term of endearment. Your dad said that Charlie is there with him also. Your mother live in Michigan?"

"Yes."

"He's saying that when you go home, call mom and tell her you've heard from them. He doesn't want her to think she's alone. Is her birthday coming up? *(She nods.)* Because he keeps wishing her a happy birthday also—he says that it's coming up and he extends white roses to her. She obviously prays for him a great deal and he certainly says that he appreciates it and he's closer to her than she can imagine. *(To Jim)* Are you having a lack of communication with a brother?"

"A little bit."

"Your son brings it up—that there's a lack of communication with you and a brother, and it's sort of like, 'What else is new?'"

"Yeah."

"But is seems it just may not ever get any better than what it is. It's just the way it is and you just may have to recognize that it's the way it will be."

"Yeah."

(To Mary) "Did you lose a bird?"

"No."

"Funny, because I keep seeing a bird around the room—your son keeps talking about having a pet bird."

"Oh—I ran it over with the lawn mower!"

"Yeah, because your son keeps talking about the bird being with him. How the hell did you run a bird over with a lawn mower?"

"It wasn't a pet. Actually it kind of was hanging around the house, but he knows it."

"He must have made it a pet over there, because I see a bird fly in the room and he said, 'Tell them the bird is here with me, that it's my pet,' so I said, 'Oh well, then—I guess he has a pet bird over there and that it must be one of the pets he referred to before,' but obviously if you felt that you killed this bird, he wants you to put yourself at peace. He says that the bird is there with him and it has become his pet. Also Thomas?"

(Jim) "Yes."

"Passed on?"

"Yes."

"Someone keeps talking about Tom, Thomas being with them. Again a fatherly figure. Could it possibly be a granddad?"

"Yes."

"So obviously your son's great-grandfather."

"Yes."

"You knew him, yes?"

"Yes."

"Yeah—it seems he always liked you."

"He was very nice."

"He had a brogue?"

"No."

"Was he American?"

"Yes—well, Canadian."

"Yeah, well that's what I'm getting at—he's speaking English, but it sounds different to me."

"Yes."

"That's why I'm thinking that he might have a brogue, because I heard him speaking and I thought, well he's speaking English, but he sounds like he comes from somewhere else."

"Yes."

"So if he had Canadian roots, that's probably why he sounds different to me. Well as they say, Colin is certainly not lonely for company. There are definitely people there around him. He knows you were distressed because he passed on so young, that he'd be frightened over there, but he said that he wasn't afraid—"

"Good."

"—to alleviate from your mind any sense of worry that there was any fear with him. Your son liked adventure, and he looked upon his passing—going through the tunnel and into the Light—as an adventure. He says that it's not a frightening tunnel—you feel like you've done it before. You feel very comfortable and you know what's happening. He knew he was all right. He observed from the hereafter what had happened, and he was more worried about you all being all right. He says that he's come in dreams to tell you that he is all right, he's happy and not in any type of suffering. He was coming through to put you more at peace. He says, 'I haven't been away that long where I don't know how it feels for you to have the loss, but I'm just not in the physical body.' When Christmas time comes around, it should always be celebrated as if he's there, because he tells me it's almost like you want to put a stop on life now, and he says that life has to go on with the three of you as normally as you can. He says that you talk out loud to him, so you must believe he's still around. You keep their pictures out?"

(Mary) "Yes."

"Yeah, because I know they like that—they bring up about your keeping their pictures out. There's a birth coming up in the family or something? There's news of a happy birth ahead."

"My friend."

"No—unless it's somebody you consider like family."

"She is."

"That could be the case, because he's congratulating on a happy birth. I saw St. Philomena appear—a sign of a happy birth—so you must be hearing that kind of news. I keep seeing Christ appearing around you—this is the third time I saw him appearing but I kept getting distracted. He's saying, 'Peace be with you.' That's all he ever says—he's *such* a conversationalist. Your son says again that he's very happy and at peace—as long as you know he's all right, happy and at peace, it is going to make it a little easier. But he says that you all have to try to be happy and at peace also, and go on, because he knows sometimes you just drive yourself crazy over his passing. (To Mary) That's why he suggested getting a little job or something. I keep seeing St. Jude appearing behind you as a guardian angel saint, but also as a symbol of your feelings of hopelessness. Your son says that you keep going over it and asks why you are going over it again. He asks, 'What makes you think that going over it again and again will make it change?' It makes you crazy because you realize the hopelessness of the situation, but you can't do anything about it now—like your hands are tied. He asks you to try to harmonize yourself better, and that you will see him again someday. He is all right and at peace. Not that he's playing favorites here, but he knows that every now and then you get hit with another wave, you deal with it and then all of a sudden a tidal wave comes and you get hit again. Your son states, and your father states too, that it is all right to be happy and to go on with your life. They don't expect any of you to bury your-selves alive. I think that with this, they are going to withdraw from me, but your dad embraces you, your husband and your daughter with love, and calls out again to your mom and family, asking that you tell them that you've heard from him. Colin does the same to each of you—embracing you with love, along with the other relatives and people. As he says, 'It's very hard for you to grasp it, but we are here—just not in your physical world.' He says that it would be as if you were told to live in this room for the rest of your life but could still look out the window to another world out there. You wouldn't be part of it—you'd be separated by the glass, but you could still see it. He says that is what it is like—'I'm here but I am just separated by this dimensional veil.' He says to you (*Kelly*) especially that in growing up, there were a lot of struggles that you had to surmount, but he says, 'We'll get through this one also.' All right, he tells me to let go now, and all of them are sending their love and asking that you remember to pray for them—especially your son and your dad and all the other relatives that are there. Just know that they are closer to you than you can imagine, and until we meet again they send their love and sign off."

THE GENTLE GIANT

The hereafter is at its most fascinating with regard to children who pass. With children unfamiliar with other family members in the hereafter to gravitate toward, the hereafter must build circumstances that children will understand and gravitate toward. One such circumstance is the figure of St. Nicholas or a Santa Claus figure who greets the child who has come to the Light after passing from the earth. This benevolent figure, who is immediately recognizable regardless of culture or religious beliefs, greets them and introduces them to other children in a field where they can play. They are then introduced to family members who have preceded them into the hereafter, with whom they will live and be cared for. In many discernments, aunts, uncles and grandparents in the hereafter have told me that they are taking care of the children who have passed on. They take great pride in their new charge and often affectionately say to the parents here, "Your loss is our gain."

Another figure who came through during a discernment as being a "caretaker" for children came as much a surprise to me as it did to the parents present for the discernment. It was the first time that anyone from the hereafter had mentioned the figure of St. Christopher in recounting their passing to the Light, yet these children of not particularly religious parents related in surprising detail how they came upon this "gentle giant." Ashley and Nicky, both six years old, lived next to each other in a small town in Michigan. Cherie Andes, mother of Nicky and neighbor of Ashley, related the story of two families' tragic loss but renewal of hope as the two children burst into their discernment with a high-spirited account of passing from this world to the next. Cherie wrote this to me months later to tell me about the children and help explain the extraordinary meaning to her of the presence of St. Christopher in their discernment:

"I'D LIKE TO START by giving you some background, just in case you were interested. From the time Nick was born I knew he was special. I knew he was going to be a boy before the doctor told us, and I knew what he would look like. I was thirty-three years old when he was born and my husband was thirty-eight. He was certainly a miracle to us. He was the center of our attention almost all the time, and I believe that we were only apart from him maybe four times in his six and a half years. I was very protective of him and for the first six years watched him like a hawk. It was only the last month or two of his life that I began to feel him start to let go of the "apron strings" and spend more time with his friends. He loved the outdoors and was very busy from the time he was about two years old. He was all boy and going full tilt all the time. Nicky had a big heart, he was sensitive, very affectionate and loving of all around him. His curiosity and love of nature kept us on our toes and young at heart. I felt as though I had a bigger connection with him than just mother and son—I felt our souls were connected. We would at times say what the other was thinking.

"We were a very close-knit family, and we had a wonderful relationship with Ashley and her mom and dad who lived nearby. Ashley and Nicky, even at their young ages, were sweethearts of sorts and went everywhere together. We used to joke about them growing up and getting married someday, but they would act as if that was a "yucky" idea. They had a real best-friend sort of relationship and affection for one another.

"In February 1996, we had an early thaw here. The accident happened the first week of March. It had snowed that day, and the children all wanted to play in the snow. Later on, Ashy (as her mother called her) and Nicky wanted to go to Ashley's house, where I watched him go as he left the house. Apparently later they had gone to another friend's house, three doors down and on the other side of a pond.

"Nicky was warned on a regular basis about the dangers of the pond and the ice. While they walked around the pond to get to the neighbor's, when it started getting close to dark they must have tried to cut across the edge of it to get home.

They were in a hurry and probably even heard me call for them. The snow was deceptive and I'm sure they didn't realize the danger that was there because of the early thaw. All the while, I thought he was in the opposite direction at Ashley's house, which is where I watched him go.

"On the evening of the accident, we found Ashley in the water but still couldn't recover Nick. While Ashley's parents began CPR on her, I tried to go in the water after Nick. Scott, a good friend of a neighbor and an acquaintance of ours, was one of the first rescue workers to show up while I was screaming for someone to help me find my baby. He took his jacket off, tied a rope around his waist and jumped into the icy water, but my Nicky was already gone. Ashley never regained consciousness and died later.

"I had a medal of St. Christopher for many years that my father had given me as a child. Being as none of us are Catholic, I assumed he picked it up at a flea market or something. I in turn gave it to Nick who kept it in his room. I don't think I ever told him who St. Christopher was, but he kept the medal nonetheless. On the day of Nick's funeral I was looking for something special that I had given him to put in the casket with him, when I came upon this medal. Just before my husband and I closed the casket, I put the St. Christopher medal in Nicky's pocket and said, 'St. Christopher, protect him.'"

THE DISCERNMENT

"Okay, now whatever I tell you just answer yes or no that you understand. There's a male presence around—and a female, too. (*George is confused by what he is hearing.*) But see—are you all family?"

(*Both mothers*) "Pretty much."

"All right, let me just leave it go for a minute. There is a male close to both of you passed on?"

"Yes."

"Because it would make sense that he would come to both of you, yes?"

"Yes."

"He walked in the room. He seems very raring to go, and he knows what he's doing. He suddenly just popped into the room and came to both of you. There's a female presence with him, and it's older, so it must be from another generation. I'll leave it go. Ah ha—(*to Sandra*) were you and he romantically involved? (*She is confused how to answer.*) Wait—he's putting a big heart, a valentine heart in front of you. That could be a symbol of fondness. I'll just tell you what I'm seeing and maybe I better not interpret it. There is a big valentine heart over your heads. I don't know if he's trying to suggest romantic involvement or fondness, or both. But he is family by blood to one of you, yes?"

"Yes."

(To Cherie) "But you and he were very close, yes?"

"Yes."

"Because definitely there's a fondness between you, yes, but you're not romantically involved."

"No."

"Exactly—the heart is the symbol of fondness. There is fondness between you, and you're not family by blood, but you are family by choice."

"Yes."

"As he says, which makes you more special."

"Yes."

"That's the way he links it in. Because even though the two of you [the mothers] are not family, you *are* family."

"Right."

"You are *like* sisters."

"Yes."

"Umm—(to Cherie) there's also a female close to you passed on?"

"Yes."

"Knows him?"

"Yes."

"Because they know each other. She just popped in. This other female is your family but older, and she's hanging around but she seems to be keeping her distance. Oh, wait a minute—okay. (to both mothers) You two are family by grief also?"

"Yes."

(To Cherie) "You lost a daughter?"

"Yes."

(To Sandra) "And you lost a son."

"Yes."

"Were they romantically involved?"

(One nods yes, the other nods no.)

(He chuckles.) "You're shaking your head no, and you're shaking your head yes." (They laugh.)

"They knew each other though, yes?"

"Yes."

"Okay, maybe they're not lovers, but they're fond of each other."

"Right. Yes."

"Let's say there's . . . platonic romance there."

"Yes."

"Let's put it that way, because he started explaining that they're fond of each other, they're romantically linked but they're not married . . . and I ask, 'What do you mean?' and he says, 'Well, it's like platonic romance. You know—we love each other but we're not . . . *getting married."*

(They laugh.)

"And now I know why you are family by link—by romance. He kept showing me the heart and telling me, 'No, you're misunderstanding,' but I'm glad that you all didn't say anything he obviously had the chance to explain. And your daughter said to me that the reason she didn't come in immediately is because she knew I would have been confused. I would have been thrown by who has the daughter and who has the son, so he came in first, and it seems that the woman with him is a grandmother or great grandmother."

"Yes."

"She's vaguely there, but just . . . an emissary, I guess. And then your daughter came in, because your son said, 'Give me a chance to lay the foundation, and *then* pop in. So your daughter is here, your son is here—they came in hand in hand."

(They begin to weep.)

"And the fact that you wondered about the two of them being together over there—well, wonder no more, they are together. Did they pass on together?"

"Yes."

"Yes, because they passed on as they were united here—as friends—they united in the hereafter, and they passed in death together. They are together as they passed on, yes?"

(crying) "Yes."

"Because as much as you hoped one would survive, they are glad they didn't."

"I *knew* it."

"As your son says, and your daughter backs him up—'If one of us had survived, the other would have had to live with the memory of being responsible for the other's death.'"

"Yes."

"And both had agreed—as much as you'd rather have one of them here or both of them here, they say, 'Please spare us that.' You know, that they don't have to live with that kind of grief. They know that you're living with the grief, but as they said, 'I don't want to feel responsible for someone else's passing.' Even though they would *not* have been, they still would have thought that—you just can't help but think that."

"Right."

"Your son says, 'Somebody would have pointed a finger—someone would have blamed, and I don't want to deal with that.' They're in an accident together? Because someone keeps talking about *accident*."

"Yes."

"Why do they talk about home—were they coming home?"

"They were going home."

"Exactly, they were on their way home or to somebody's home. Are they in a vehicle-type accident?" (*They are confused and not sure how to answer.*) Wait a minute—was there a vehicle involved?"

"No."

"Not car, but in a vehicle?"

"No."

"You say no and they are fidgeting—something's wrong. I don't understand. Unless the vehicle is my symbol for accident, which it is—an accidental form of passing. I think something's wrong again, because your son is giving me that same flustering feeling that he did with the heart thing. He's obviously showing me something, and my brain is saying, 'That must be what it is,' but you're saying no. Let me give it a few minutes and I'll figure it out. But they are almost home?"

"Um-hmm."

"Yeah, because that's what drives you crazy—they almost made it safely."

"Right."

"All right, I take it they're outside?"

"Yes."

"Okay. Did something happen where they were trapped?"

"Yes."

"That's why I feel like I'm enclosed. Because your son brought it up again. But they're caught in a situation that they can't get out of."

"Right."

"Both of them assure you that they did not suffer prior to their passing."

(*crying*) "Thank you."

"Because that's what scared the ever living hell out of both of you."

"Yeah."

"They keep saying it—and I see St. Joseph appear, which signifies a happy death, and in spite of the ugly circumstances, they don't suffer prior to their passing. They say that they want to assure you of that. Even if they initially survived, they were not conscious. So they're not conscious of suffering."

"Thank you."

"Do you understand why they say they were trapped?"

"Um-hmm."

"They keep telling me they were trapped—that possibly the only way out of this is to die."

"Um-hmm."

"That's what they're telling me—'We're trapped to the point of being enclosed—we can't get out of this unless we die.'"

"Yes, yes."

"Was it very hot? Why do I feel I'm all heated up?"

"No."

"Well, let me go with it again. It could be what leads to it. Anything affect their heads—internally?"

"No—maybe."

"Why do I feel like I'm having my air cut off?"

(*Unsure how to answer*) "There's—"

"I don't mean to laugh, but you're saying no and they're saying yes."

"Well, keep going."

"Because obviously there's been a loss of oxygen."

"Uh-huh, yes."

"They say that they are passing due to loss of air."

"Yes."

"This could be why I'm getting like a hot flash—they may have been getting hot prior to this—"

"Yes."

"—and I'm losing my air, and I'm . . . slowly letting go. I'm getting the feeling of going to sleep. Would there have been the sense of being cold also?"

"Yes."

"That's it. Your son just said—I'm not trying to sound cute here, like I'm fishing it out, but your son's explaining. He said to me, 'I'm cold, but there's a warm feeling prior to the passing.'"

"I understand that."

"He's insisting that he knows what he's talking about. They were—*struggling*?"

"Yes."

"Because there is the feeling of trying to get out of it. But then a feeling of resignation and peace, like, 'Well, we can't get out of it, so we might as well just let go.' It's funny—it's almost like your son was desperately trying to save your daughter—there's a feeling of him trying to like help her over himself, or whatever."

"We understand that."

"Is there water nearby?"

"Yes."

"Because I keep seeing water. Are they drowning?"

"Yes."

"That's what it is. And yes, believe it or not, I've been told a million times that drowning is a very pleasant form of passing."

"Yes."

"It really is, because I heard it from the souls numerous times. Are they in cold water? It may be freezing?"

"Yes."

"That's why I'm hot and I'm cold. Like people say before you freeze to death they feel suddenly warm."

"That's why I said I understand that."

"That's what your son says—(*listening*)—oh, okay, okay. It's a little far-fetched but I'm going to say it anyway—*that's* the vehicle involved. The water is the instrument or *vehicle* that causes the passing. Now that he tells me, it seems like a strange way of bringing it across. Right away when we hear 'vehicle' we think 'car.' Was there ice also?"

"Yes."

"Did ice break or something?"

"Yes."

"Yes, because the ice is breaking. I don't know if your son went in first, or whatever, but it seems that they've cracked the ice and they've fallen in through the ice—and one's trying to help the other. I feel like I'm holding hands, trying to hold on, your son's trying to help her up, both your children are telling me that they do *not* suffer prior to their passing, but they're not going to lie to you that there wasn't a moment of struggle."

"Yes."

"I think we'd all be 'b.s.'ing ourselves if I told you otherwise."

"Right."

"Because they said that there was a moment of struggle of trying to survive, and panic of trying to get out of the situation of being trapped, and then realizing—I don't mean to sound horrible here—it's like, 'We're doomed' and they have to let go. Then they fall—they drift into a sleep. That's why I'm getting the pressure to the head. My oxygen is being cut off, and I'm just slowly shutting down. That's how I would describe it—like getting 'high' and falling asleep. And both of them—plus the water was probably freezing—freezing to death, believe it or not is a very pleasant form of death also. This is why the saint has appeared twice—once we submit to it, we let go. The ice cold turns to very warm—the body is heating up, obviously because the body is in something like shock. That's why I feel hot like I'm sweating. And all of a sudden they just . . . withdraw. Are they isolated when this occurs?"

"Yes."

"It's like nobody could help them. But they—had they been skating or playing—it's funny, it's like they're walking across it, thinking it's safe, and surprisingly turns out—"

"Yes."

"Did this happen in this state?"

"Yes."

"Okay—but it happened when there was thawing?"

"Yes."

"Because I feel like it's winter, but the winter is starting to thaw."

"Yes."

"Because he tells me that to do it a few weeks earlier, that would have been so solid you would have never in a million years have had anything to worry about and you could cross the lake. But the thing is, they didn't realize—you know, the temperature had gone up, but it takes a while to thaw."

"Right."

"Are they centered in it? It's funny—once it cracks, they really are kind of like—they're not in the middle of it, obviously there's enough of a struggle where they can't get out of it then."

"I understand that."

"They're centered in it, they say, and I don't know what they mean, but they say the cold kind of gets to them also."

"I know what they mean."

"Now, they both are little kids?"

"Yes."

"Yeah—I'm not talking to teenagers here. I'm talking to little guys."

"Right."

"—And *gal*."

(*They laugh.*) "Right."

"But (*listening*)—okay, okay. So the romantic involvement could be puppy love as we call it—it's innocent love."

"Right."

"Their dads are still here? Because they call out to their daddies as well."

(*They laugh.*) "Yes."

"They say, 'Tell them that you've heard from us,' and as both children say, 'Whether they believe in this or not—who cares.' It's the message that's important, not the belief system. 'And besides,' they say, 'why would we lie?' So they say to go home and tell the daddies that."

"Were you also afraid that they wouldn't know anybody there?"

"Yes."

"And that's another hang-up you had. They said that—this is the strangest thing—this is the second time I have seen this in a reading—and what I'm about to say has nothing to do with being Catholic, or religion or anything. But the children report your being worried about them not knowing anyone over there, so you were afraid they were frightened after they 'died,' and yet they tell me that the man who came to carry them to the safe place out of the water is somebody I interpret as being St. Christopher. I keep seeing his image appearing in front of me. This man is about six feet tall, who is very broad-looking and stocky, and is simple-minded. I don't mean that disrespectfully, but he's harmlessly simple-minded. And they said that he carried them out of the water to the safe side on his shoulders after they passed on. They refer to him as the 'Gentle Giant.' Eventually they were met by grandparents or great grandparents over there, but the thing is that St. Christopher welcomed them over first. Hmm—what is interesting is that he comes with animals also. They talk about animals with him—cats, dogs and things like that—so they don't feel frightened. Just like a child, their innocence sees animals around a person, and it would immediately put them at ease. Because if the animals respond to this person with such love and affirmation, there can't be anything wrong. So you don't have to worry about them. They were taken to the 'safe side,' they say, which would be the other side, the hereafter. And put yourselves at peace that this was not your fault that this happened. It's like, 'We should have been watching them, we shouldn't have done this, they shouldn't have been alone'—both your children say, 'Beat yourself up no more, because it is not your fault—it happened. And your husbands as well. You can't beat yourselves up for the rest of your lives feeling that you've failed as parents, because you couldn't have them in a bubble for the rest of their lives. They had to go about their own lives. (To Sandra) Also, does the name Christopher mean anything?"

"Yes."

"Passed on?"

"Yes."

"Because the children keep talking about Christopher being with them also. Passed on before them?"

"Yes."

"Funny—they told me that Christopher came with St. Christopher. So Christopher is another child that passed on."

"No."

"Does he pass very young?"

"Maybe—I think so."

"But is this Christopher a relative?"

"Yes."

"Your daughter would know him, yes?"

"No."

"She says she does, so I guess she means now. Because she says, 'Christopher comes with St. Christopher,' so apparently St. Christopher brings them to the other side, and this Christopher meets them. She seems to instinctively know who he is. He is a father figure to her."

"Yes."

"Is Christopher like a father or father-in-law to you?"

"My grandfather."

"Oh, that's my mistake—he would be your grandfather and her great grandfather. He kept coming to you as a father figure, and I thought that it couldn't be your grandfather, but they just explained to me what I did wrong. So apparently it's your grandfather, Christopher, who comes to welcome them both over after St. Christopher brings them over. This is why I was asked to repeat the name twice. Your children—and again, this has nothing to do with religion—but your children impress you to pray to St. Christopher on their behalf and also in thanksgiving. They have great esteem for him since he was the one who rescued them. They keep thinking that he is the one who rescued them from the water, but he did rescue them spiritually, because they were frightened and did not know that they had passed on. They were wondering what had happened, even though it was peaceful, and he lifted them up on his shoulders and takes them to the safe side—to Christopher the grandfather. Any time you see the traditional image of St. Christopher—he is carrying the Christ child over the water—they say that will always be a reminder to you of your children being 'rescued' by him and taken over to the safe happy place. So it should always give you a feeling of security—that everything is all right—especially in your dark days. Also the name Mary mean anything?"

(*Cherie*) "Yes."

"Passed on, too?"

"No."

"Are you sure? Even if it was years ago."

(*Sandra*) "I'm not sure." (*Cherie*) "Passed on, yes."

(*To Cherie*) "Yes, I'm looking at you because your son keeps insisting that Mary is here with him. And I don't know if it is a great grandma or great aunt, but she's there with your son—even if they didn't know each other here, it doesn't matter, because your son refers to her as a mother figure—great grandma, great aunt, something like that."

"Great aunt."

"Your children also call out to—(*to both women*) Do you have any other children?"

"No."

"These were your only ones?"

(*Sandra*) "No, I have another."

"Yeah, because they're saying that there are other children—other *child*—whatever. (*To Cherie*) Are you planning another child?"

"Well, I have a real big need to hear—"

"Because your son is encouraging you to have another child."

(*Crying*) "That's what I needed to know."

"That's why I don't allow questions—let them answer it if they want to address it. But your son blesses you and encourages you to have another child, because you don't want him to think you're replacing him."

(*Crying*) "Yes!"

"That's why he says, 'I know you're not replacing me—you have to go ahead,' because he knows you desperately want to have another child. I saw St. Philomena appear over your head, which is the symbol of a happy birth, and your son says to go ahead and have another child. Hmm—I see another boy around you. I won't stake my life—usually when I predict the sex of children I am ninety-nine percent *in*accurate, but he wants to put you at peace about this. You may think that especially if you have a boy, you might be replacing him, but he says don't start tormenting yourself with that. He is very unique and special, and he knows that you are always going to love him and he'll always love you and his father. That will never change, and he knows you'll always remember him as one of the family, and he says that he wants you to go on with your life. And be careful that you don't become overprotective of the other child. The name Amy mean anything?"

"Living?"

"Yeah, someone is calling to Amy. Did your son know her?"

"Uh-huh."

"Oh, maybe he is then, because I hear somebody calling 'Amy,' so apparently he's calling to Amy, like, 'Tell her you've heard from me.' Also there's a Scott?"

"Yes."

"Living?"

"Yes."

"Your son knows him, yes? Because he's calling out to Scott or Scotty."

(crying) "Yes."

"He says, 'Tell Scott you've heard from me also.'"

"I will."

"Were you thinking of moving?"

(She is unsure.)

"You may change residence up ahead. Your son just wants you to know it's all right. Because you might feel like you're leaving him behind."

"It's crossed my mind and I don't—"

"You have to go on with your life, he says, and you have to go on with your life the way you feel comfortable."

"Okay."

"So if that means moving, if that means having another child—if it means going on with your life, you have to do it. Both children want you to be happy and to go on with your lives. Your families are always—were you neighbors or something? *(They nod yes.)* Your families were always pretty close, but this is an unpleasant way to have to become closer."

"Yes."

"And there could come a time up ahead where there could be a separation of distance—like if you move and live further away, but you will always be linked.

That's what your son says. Again, you have to go on with your lives no matter what, but there will always be a sense of a link or contact of comfort no matter what. *(To Sandra)* Your daughter's first name is short?"

"Yes."

"Less than six letters, yes? *(She shakes her head, no.)* Or is it six letters?"

"Yes."

"That's why she's showing me six letters. *(to himself)* Duh—I should be used to it by now that these two kids seem to know what they're doing. Children just tell it like it is and adults put in what they think it should be. But her name is common?"

"Yes."

"I certainly have heard it before, yes?"

"Yes."

"And it's spelled differently?"

"No."

"Can it be?"

"It can be."

"Okay, that's why she's telling me to be careful how I spell it. There's an A in it? It begins with A?"

"Yes."

"You spell it with one letter—but it can be spelled with two?"

(She is unsure what George means. Ashley is showing George the alternative spelling "Ashli," versus "Ashley"—thus the one letter instead of two.)

"She tells me again, 'Watch how you spell it.' Is there an L in the name?"

"Yes."

"It can be spelled with two L's?"

"No."

"Well, she's showing me the right letters, so I'm glad I'm not fishing for letters. She's showing me names that have the letters of her name in them. She is showing me 'Alison'—her name is not Alison, but that's my clue for the L."

"Oh—I know what she is doing."

"It's like she's trying her best to spell out the name by showing me names."

(Laughing) "I know what she's trying to do."

"There is an E at the end?"

"Yes."

"Okay—she is showing me names—the L is in the middle?"

"Yes."

"Is there an M in the name?"

"No."

"No M or N?"

"No."

"Okay—she's showing me M and N but I don't know why. Would I spell this differently? Because she keeps telling me to watch my spelling."

"Well, you can."

"She's talking about another vowel. There is another vowel, yes?"

(She is unsure how to respond.)

"She keeps insisting there is another vowel. I saw you not answering, but she says, 'There is, there is.' Oh, there's a Y."

"Yes."

"At the end."

"Yes."

"That's the 'IE' sound at the end. Ah—she just gave me a distinct clue—*Ashley*."

"Yes."

"She just played for me the theme from *Gone With the Wind*, and as soon as I heard that I knew the name. She told me it could be spelled differently, and I was going crazy here. Was she ever known as 'Lee'—or something like 'Ashi'?"

"Yes! Ashi—oh my God."

"And that's what was throwing me. She said, 'I'm called by a nickname of Ashley,' and I thought, well Lee, maybe, and she said, 'No, Ashi.' And I thought, well nobody is called by that, and she said, 'Ask *her*.' That was my mistake. Do you all belong to a support group?"

"No."

"It's your decision, and it may not be a bad idea, but you are a big support to each other."

"Yes."

"As your children say, the families were always close like family, but they say that they are happy that a blessing has come out of the passing that has made your families become even closer. You may not have wanted it that way—I mean you don't mind it, and you'd rather have your children—but they look at it from a happy side over there. You were just worried about them being safe and all right over there, and they keep saying that they are in a safe place and that they are all right. Again, they explain that St. Christopher brought them to the safe place.

Are you all Catholic? Nothing to do with religion, but they keep putting the picture of the saint over your heads."

(Cherie) "I'm not Catholic, but I know where that would be from. That has a special meaning."

"Okay, because the picture of him goes over both of your heads, and it's almost like an impression to bring his picture into the home so that you constantly have a reminder of what they are trying to say. So every time you have a down day, which is going to happen, you can look at this picture and think, 'This is the man who took our children to the safe place. Okay—if your son can get his name across a little clearer. Your son's first name is short also, yes?"

"Yes."

"It's short order, he says—he also shows me six, but less than."

"Right."

"It's funny, though—not so common like John or Bill."

"Right."

"His formal name is eight letters or less—no, it is eight?"

"Yes."

"And it obviously can be cut down to less than six letters and he would be referred to by that shortened form."

"Right."

"I didn't say it already, did I? Because he tells me he said it already. I hope he didn't say it and I didn't pay attention or ignored it. Again, his name can be spelled differently."

"It can be."

"Hmm—he stops at the D—the first letter of his name is after the D?"

"Yes."

"Now he stops at the M. Is it the M?"

"No."

"Is it the N?"

"Yes."

"Oh—I'm sorry—that could be me. He must have said, 'Stop at the N' and I thought he said M. Just like with Ashley, he shot right to the letter. (Cherie explained later that Nicky had trouble with the difference between M and N.) His name is biblical?"

"Um-hmm."

"Why is he showing me authors—it is an author's name? He's telling me to listen carefully. He says I'm trying too hard. There is an A in the name?"

"Yes. In his formal name."

"Let's stick with his formal name, maybe that's what he's struggling at. If I do get the nickname, I will know what the formal name is, yes?"

"Yes."

"His formal first name begins with N?"

"Yes."

"And the second letter is a vowel, yes?"

"Yes."

"There's that 'IE' sound again."

"Keep going."

"Is there a Y? Why is there the 'IE' sound again? Does it make sense?"

"Can be. . . . Oh, you did show it to me before."

"Nicholas. St. Nicholas appeared in the room earlier, that's right. He told me, 'I showed it to you before—the man that normally welcomes the children over that you're used to. Also known as Nick or Nicky. That's why I'm getting the 'IE' sound."

"Um-hmm."

"And that's why they both emphasized the 'IE' sound—Ashi and Nicky."

"Oh, God."

"Well, your son was right—he showed me St. Nicholas. Right as he was talk-ing about it I saw the saint appear, and he said, 'Look,' and I thought, 'Yeah, yeah—I know, he normally welcomes the children over, but you're telling me that St. Christopher did.' But also, another reason is that St. Christopher has special significance to you. The saint has touched your life somehow with regard to your son's passing."

"Right."

"And this is confirmation that even before you got to see me, you were getting some sort of a message from over there that St. Christopher had something to do with welcoming your children over."

"Oh my God, yes!"

"That's why I said it has nothing to do with being Catholic. Because your son is telling me that by him describing the 'gentle giant' that carries them to the safe side, he was trying to get you to think about how St. Christopher came into your life. The reason why he was telling you about him was to stimulate your thinking and recognize that you had a sign through that saint. This is why both children tell you to bring the image of St. Christopher into your homes. You have been given a sign previous to our meeting that St. Christopher played a unique role with their safety into the next life. He keeps bringing it up, so apparently something having to do with St. Christopher came to you before today, and he keeps telling you that was the sign before you met me."

"Well, it's something I did."

"Yes, but to do with St. Christopher. You were intuitively picking up this message prior to today, so that the minute you came to see me and I told you that St. Christopher welcomed them into the hereafter, it would hit you on the head like a hammer."

"It did. We're not Catholic, and we didn't even know about St. Christopher."

(To Cherie) "Are you going to Disneyworld, or Florida or something? You are going to travel to a place where there are palm trees. I see them around you."

"Cool." *(Laughs)*

"So there may be news of a happy trip ahead. Family—going to a place where that vegetation exists, and you are certainly encouraged to go. *(Cherie wrote to us six months later, 'A couple of months after the reading, my husband's parents made reservations in South Carolina and wanted us to stay with them. I never associated palm trees with South Carolina, but when we got there, our villa was surrounded with palm trees.')* Your children do not want you to bury yourselves alive—you have to go on with your lives. Are you planning more children?"

"Yes."

"Because they both encourage you *both* to go on with a family. You know you want to do it, but you're hung up about it."

"Yes."

"And again, St. Philomena appears around both of you as a symbol of a happy birth. Both children confirm that having children is life renewing itself, and you have to go on, and they're not going to get pissed off at you. *(They laugh.)* They want you to go on and have other children—yes, you'll never forget them, and you'll never forget the tragedy. Also you have to get over the fear of having another child because of the fact that this has happened. It's another reason that you wouldn't want to have another child—you are afraid. You have to renew and go ahead. Both of you are strongly, strongly encouraged. And one thing about these children, they are very sweet, but if they have an ax to grind, they'll let you know. *(They laugh.)* Obviously they don't have an ax to grind. The both of them keep giving me the feeling of calling to their fathers, saying, 'Tell daddy you've heard from Ashi and Nicky.' Both children call to their fathers and family as well. Did this happen around a holiday time?"

"Um-hmm."

"It must have happened around a festive time, and that always seems to throw a damper on the festive or holiday time, and both children are asking that it still be remembered as a happy, festive time. You have dreamt about them."

"Yes."

"Because they say they visit in dreams, trying to let you know they are near, and also I feel that you have had an apparitional experience—like you could have turned your head and swore you saw one or both of them there. You glimpsed momentarily into the hereafter and it had a feeling of assurance that you'd seen the children."

"Yes."

"It's almost like I see the two of them—when they walked into the room, they walked in holding hands like two kids skipping along—"

"Yep." (*Ashley's mom experienced the same scene in an apparitional experience she had prior to meeting with George.*)

"I keep seeing them on a beach, and they're in a safe, beautiful day over there. As long as you know that they are both happy and in a safe place and are being looked after, it will make it a little easier. Yes, there are relatives that are looking after them now, but the children over there are in such a one-hundred-percent harmonious and safe place, they don't need adult supervision to keep them safe or protected. That's why both children are kind of independent, especially your daughter. It's like, 'I'd rather do it on my own.'"

"Yes."

"And there they can come and go as they please. But actually both children tell me that since they've passed over they've gone with St. Christopher to welcome other children over who don't know anybody—it's like their job. They say that they go with him to the tunnel where people cross over, and they help welcome over other children who may be afraid or not know anyone there. This way, when the child crosses over and they see this man with other children and the animals, they think, 'Oh—this is a nice, safe type of place to come to.' So that's what their job is, they say. Which shouldn't surprise you, because once they felt safe, they would like the fact that they could come and go without any fear. There is harmony there, and it is a one-hundred-percent safe place. That alone should give you a good night's sleep, they both say."

"Yes."

"They are going on with their lives. Not that their lives were cut out, where they didn't get a chance—they just moved to someplace else where they continue, and both of them seem to like the little job they have. They say that it's fun to welcome over the other children—to be playmates and play with them—because they help them to feel safe as they were made to feel safe by St. Christopher. Both children extend white roses to both of you as a symbol of a belated Mother's Day greetings, and to their fathers as belated Father's Day greetings. Definitely on those days you may have felt not too much like mothers because you don't have your children here anymore, but they say, 'You still have us, and that still makes you a mother.' And it still makes your husbands fathers. I guess with this they are telling me that they are going to let go. Yes, there are relatives there, but they seem to like to be on their own—there's a feeling of that, most definitely. Did somebody lose a brother? Did one of your parents lose a brother?"

(Cherie) "Oh, yeah."

"One of your uncles must be there with them, too, because they keep talking about one of your parents losing a brother that is there with them. Let me leave it go, because they're getting ready to wind it down. But in any case, both children embrace you with love, and to their daddies also. They say always to remember to pray for them in your own way, pray for them through St. Christopher, because it is so significant. It's funny—it's almost like up ahead, every now and then when you least expect it, you will get some sort of sign having to do with that saint. It could happen once every five years, but something will happen that will clue you to think back on what they told you about being happy and in a safe place until you see them again. In the meantime they encourage you definitely to be happy and go on with your lives. Go on in the way that you want to—not to be afraid. Thinking that you will offend them in any way by going on—they say that simply isn't the case. They want you to go on, be happy and at peace. It's interesting. I see Jesus appear behind both of you saying, 'Peace be with you, and peace be with your children, also.' But most importantly, peace be with you all, because of the tragedy. All right, on that happy note they tell me that they are going to sign off, so with that they sign off, along with—there are relatives along in the background. They know who you obviously came to hear from—but they're there. They all send their love—and they leave."

WITH THE ANIMALS

Another way the hereafter will ease the transition of children into the Light is with the use of animals, as mentioned earlier in this book. If the child had a family pet passed on, that pet will meet them in the hereafter and guide them toward the Light. As on the earth, animals are a great anxiety reliever, and the hereafter very frequently uses them to comfort those children who were taught on the earth not to talk to strangers and need a trusted friend to help them find the Light. Children might also be met by fawns, puppies, kittens, birds and rabbits to give them a feeling of safety and well-being as they cross to the Light. The children I have discerned have always told me how happy the passing was, and although they understand the separation from their parents, they are not at a loss for love and affection. They come to the knowledge that they can be with Mom and Dad any time they desire. Many have mentioned during the discernment about having come to their parents in dreams for a visit or being close to them when the parents needed them. I think the most poignant example of this was when I had gone to Michigan for a seminar about a year after meeting Mary and James O'Reilly. We had gone out to dinner together where we talked about their work with other bereaved parents and also about people's inability to cope with the subject of death. As Mary spoke about her struggle to continue with a normal life, Colin appeared and curled into her side as she sat, comforting his mom as she spoke. Although she could not see him, I told her about this impromptu appearance by her son and his quiet gift of strength to her. Children in the hereafter often become beacons for the family, often taking the role as "guardian angel" to help the family mend and address the issues that need to be addressed. More often than not I have literally been put in the path of a family in need of healing by children who are most eager to help from the hereafter. I have noticed that many of the souls in the hereafter help "guide" their loved ones to the help they need or even just to the understanding that, where we once thought death was final, some capacity to understand that there is *more* begins creeping into our conscious. I think it is one of the simple graces our loved ones give us from the hereafter, and children seem to be the best at helping to change our perspective about death, and also the most willing to help bring us to that understanding.

Children who are the victims of violent crime come through from the hereafter with a grace that can only be defined by a line in an old hymn, "It is well with my soul." They have a remarkable understanding of their circumstance, and they do not harbor any ill will toward that person or persons who caused their passing—quite the contrary. They understand, accept and forgive the aggressor and ask that we do the same. Although I pass this information to the grieving parents during the discernment, I can tell you that it usually goes over like a lead balloon. Parents are so blinded by rage and sorrow that they simply cannot hear those words, literally from the mouths of babes. It is not hard to understand their anger and bitterness toward someone who took their child away, and I don't blame them for having these feelings—for a while that will be a normal and necessary part of their grief period. Yet their children ask nonetheless to pray for the soul of their killer as a way to help bring about the forgiveness and understanding that is to be part of a very hard spiritual lesson for us on the earth—something we need to work out in this existence. This is their way of helping us past the anger and back to the road to healing.

I could not close this chapter if I did not include the one statement that children make in one way or another to their parents during the discernments. In this instance, I will speak for them:

"PARENTS—while you are mourning the loss of our physical bodies on earth, we have never left your side. We will be your 'guardian angels' and take care of you as you took care of us. It is okay to talk to us out loud and continue to count us with the rest of the children you have on the earth. Thank you for the memorials and good things done in our names, but please remember that we are not saints, icons or monuments. Our rooms or personal possessions are not shrines, nor will leaving the home we lived in make us disappear. You will always be our parents, both here and hereafter. As long as you love us, we live on in your heart, and time, location or moving on with your life will not change this. The memory of my life will not be lessened by having more children or remarrying. As I have finished my lesson on the earth and graduated to the hereafter, so, too, will you, and we will be together. Have the best life you can have until we see each other again."

Six

SUICIDE

WHY?

It has been said that suicide is the skeleton in everyone *else's* closet. There is no statement more true. After the tragedy of having someone you love take his or her own life comes the feelings of failure, humiliation and blame from relatives and friends. No matter how much you beat yourself up about not having seen the "warning signs" (if there are such things), the big question is still *why*. I have seen people and their families collapse under the weight of innuendo and supposition when a family member or friend has taken his or her life. I have also seen people waste all their time and energy in an effort to "get at the truth" of the person who, for whatever reason, had no more strength to continue on the earth.

The issue of passing by one's own hand is a difficult one for us to understand, mainly because what the Other Side has told me with regard to suicide flies in the face of just about every religion. I am not sure why it would, though, because the hereafter's way makes perfect sense. As I stated before, nothing is beyond the understanding and wisdom of the Infinite Light, and no one is punished in the hereafter for their actions on the earth—they are simply shown the impact of their actions on those who love them, and the soul must take it from there.

Because of the volume of mail sent to me on this subject with the same question, which comes up again and again, I will state simply and emphatically that according to the souls in the hereafter, *no one who commits suicide goes to Hell*. I can say this without reservation because, according to the hereafter, there is no "Hell" as we have been conditioned to think about it. The wisdom of the Infinite Light understands the reasons behind every action taken against oneself or another. The souls in the hereafter who have passed by their own hand tell me time and time again that they were not in the correct frame of mind to consider the gravity of their actions. This in itself is a form of mental illness, which the hereafter would try to reconcile—not punish.

I am not sure why religion has taken such a hard stance on suicide. At the very time people need their faith when they are in crisis, some organized religions strip people of their dignity by calling this desperate act a "sin against humanity" and "a slap in the Creator's face." I was told by a woman whose son ended his own life because of his feelings of failure that she could not rest until her son told her that he was *not* in a fiery torture as a result of his actions. Not only was she worried about this because of her Christian education about suicide, but also the fact that the church where she belonged refused to give him the Rite of Burial. During the discernment, her son told her that he is learning from his experience in the hereafter in a very safe and supportive environment, free of pressure and self-recrimination. This woman wrote me a few weeks later to tell me that the night after the discernment was the first time she had slept in four months.

Even the souls in the hereafter will admit that ending their existence here probably wasn't the best idea—that if they had allowed themselves more time to think or ask for help, a way around their problems could have been found. But that having been said, they also tell me that at the time they have made the conscious decision to end their existence here, they are not in a mental state where they are capable of making rational decisions. Many of those from the hereafter have also told me that even though they functioned "normally" on a day-to-day basis, there was a element of mental torture that could not be reconciled with. Having been able to look at their problems from the hereafter has given them the insight and clarity of thought that never was possible on the earth to help them work things through.

When Kimberly Stricker, age nineteen, ended her life with a shotgun borrowed from a friend, more than her own life was shattered. Adopted by Jerome Stricker, a prominent businessman and his wife, Nancy, she grew into a popular, assertive and achievement-minded teenager in her hometown of Covington,

Kentucky, and dreamed of sharing her love of animals by becoming a veterinarian. Rickell Kuby, owner of the Precinct Restaurant in nearby Cincinnati, Ohio, told me, "It seemed like everyone knew Kim. Half of Cincinnati went to her funeral." What devastated her family, however, was the fact that they never saw it coming. During the discernment with Kim, she showed me a vision of herself dressed as a clown—in essence showing me that while she put on a happy facade, inside she was hurting. Only now, surrounded by her adored animals in the hereafter, is she able to reconcile with her unhappy life on the earth. In the course of the discernment, Kimberly related to me that her despondency about an unhappy, unfulfilled life (in her estimation), coupled with the recent breakup with her boyfriend, began a breakdown in her that she likened to a kind of "terminal illness of the soul" from which she could not recover.

Suicide victims in the hereafter provide some of the most fascinating information about the Other Side and its compassion toward a soul in crisis. When souls arrive in the hereafter after having taken their lives, they are immediately taken to a "hospital of reflection" to begin the process of unwinding the turmoil that brought them there. What is interesting about this place is that there are no other humans with whom to create confrontation. It is a place with serene beauty filled with fields and grass. The only beings there are small creatures, like rabbits and fawns, kittens and puppies. Animals are greatly known both here and hereafter for their ability to heal and their unconditional love. They are used as a kind of therapy for the souls there. When the suicide victims are strong enough, they begin the slow process of understanding and learning with the help of friends, relatives and guides.

One very fascinating part of discerning souls who have passed by their own hand is the presence of Christ in their discernments. He seems to act as a counselor to help those souls cope with their confusion and come to terms with their turmoil so that they can continue, unencumbered, on the road to the Infinite Light. During the discernment, Christ appears behind the individual, one hand on the soul's shoulder, radiant in white light and offering only these words: "Peace be with you." He stays for the duration of the discernment, and when it is finished, escorts the soul back to the Other Side. Efforts on my part to engage Christ in more conversation have been futile. He simply beams and repeats again, "Peace be with you."

I think the most important insight I have gained in discerning souls who have passed by their own hand is the fact that they classify their passing as an "accident" or an "illness." It is important for us to remember that this is very much an illness from which they pass—an illness of the mind and of the spirit. Just like physical illness, the mental illness that brings on feelings of hopelessness and failure begin the downward spiral of the spirit, for which the only seeming recourse is to pass on to the hereafter, much the same as heart failure brings the physical body to the point where it can no longer sustain itself in this existence. Hindsight being 20/20, these souls who enter the hereafter and have had time to rest and reflect come to the conclusion that their intention was never to hurt those they left on the earth. Although it is only of small consolation to their loved ones still here, they tell me that they will continue as "guardian angels" from their unique vantage point in the hereafter. They also realize that nothing is impossible on the earth, and help is as close as someone who cares. They also do not recommend suicide as a quick ticket to the Other Side. They realize that theirs is a long road to understanding and healing, and that so much more can be accomplished by working out problems on the earth. They insist that any lessons cut short on the earth *must* be continued in the hereafter and that there are no shortcuts. Since time here is finite, it takes much less time to learn and understand here than in the hereafter, where time is infinite.

If there is any lesson to be learned by those who pass by their own hand it is that our experience on this earth, no matter how privileged, will be fraught with experiences where we will have to make decisions critical to our existence on the earth. These souls encourage us to continue understanding that everything we must go through in this existence is of benefit to us in the hereafter, and that there is no easy way out of the lessons we must learn. What is interesting about their messages during discernments is that they understand that there are circumstances on the earth that are more difficult to deal with than others. The two that are most difficult to deal with are feelings of worthlessness and achievement. It is also interesting that the two are diametrically opposed—one is a failure fearing success, and the other, a success fearing failure. Feelings are the gateway to the soul, and therefore our sense of self-worth can be profoundly affected by the world and people around us. When we don't feel good about ourselves, the soul withers. The same way newborn babies will die without the experience of being held, the soul cannot sustain itself without the nourishment of feeling like we have purpose and value. People are always surprised when I tell them that the Other Side talks about success being one of the most difficult things to deal with on the earth. The fact is that success takes a lot of work to achieve, but even more work to sustain. Those who have become successful by the world's standards have the Herculean job of trying to stay successful and deal with the added responsibilities and problems.

When you are successful, the only way to move is down, and many who have fallen from their lofty position, even just slightly, consider themselves, and are considered by others, failures.

This type of failure is very difficult to endure, since it cuts to the very fiber of who we are. Coupled with feelings of worthlessness, there begins a falling backward from which few survive. Even though these are easy fears to understand, it is also very difficult to see them in ourselves and change without help.

Connie Trivelli is an energetic, fun-loving woman who one would never guess endured the type of tragedy that so few could understand unless they found themselves in the same circumstance—to have a loved one pass from the effects of "success." After having all the trappings of a well-to-do, ambitious and successful existence with her husband, Geoff, she found her world unraveling, and the price of success proved too high to pay when it cost her husband's life. It is a true reversal of fortune that is important to understand when we think of the real meaning of success in one's lifetime. It has also helped Connie to understand that sometimes emotional illness is very much a form of terminal illness of the soul and, in some cases, genetic. This is Connie's story, in her own words:

"I MET MY HUSBAND, Geoff, when I was twenty-one years old. He was tall, and oh—so handsome! We met at a nightclub and danced together all night. At the end of the evening, he kissed me goodnight, and somehow I knew that it was not good-bye. It was that kiss which caused me to rush home and wake up my mom to tell her I met the man of my dreams. I just knew we were going to fall in love. The next morning Geoff called and we started a romance that I knew would last forever. We got along so perfectly well—we had the same goals in life and the same dreams. We were very much in love with each other, and we were never apart. One year later we were married. We bought our first home and began planning to have children. Three years later our first son was born—our beautiful love made a beautiful child. We couldn't be happier, and I really felt we had it all. Geoff had a great job and was getting promotion after promotion, and we were so proud of our beautiful house. Two years later, our second son was born. God blessed us again, and through it all our love was growing stronger and deeper with each passing day. We often took the time to pray and to thank God. We realized how lucky we were to have it all.

"Promotions for Geoff became a way of life. He was a very intelligent young man who was very successful. He truly started at the bottom of his company, and had now just been offered a job at the top. The job, though, was out of state and the decision had to be made soon. Although we didn't want to leave our families, we knew that we had each other and the children, and that was enough to carry our love. Geoff took the promotion, so we sold our home and off we went. I was so proud of him. We knew that because our children were two and four, the move would not be hard on them, and when we reached our new town in North Carolina, we were put up in a complimentary home. It was such a beautiful home that overlooked a golf course. Our boys thought that they had the biggest back yard in the world. Money was coming in faster than we could spend it, and our love life was as passionate as ever. I knew that he truly loved me, and he treated me like delicate china. He was a sensitive man with a heart of gold that never let a day pass without playing with his sons and making them feel so very special. He was a great dad.

"One afternoon, Geoff came home and told me that the company had to fire someone that day, and they offered the job to Geoff. He explained that it was a tough job and not within his area of experience, but it was a great opportunity. Since Geoff had always done everything right, I told him that I would support his decision. After two days he decided it was too good an offer to refuse; he would accept this huge responsibility knowing that it would be tough.

"It wasn't very long after that I saw changes in him. He wasn't himself. One weekend I even went to his office to see if I could help, and could see all the memos on his desk marked, 'immediately,' 'ASAP,' 'top priority,' etc. He was so busy. As time went on, he started getting depressed. One night I got up from bed and found him sitting in the boys' room just staring at them as they slept. He looked up at me and said, 'I'm so afraid I'm going to fail them.' I told him not to think that and that everything would be all right.

"Lovemaking wasn't as often now as it was, but I understood. He had a lot on his mind. Finally he called from the office the next morning and told me about his meeting with the head boss where he told him that he was going to give up his position since he felt that the promotion was just too much. His boss explained that they were very happy with the job he was doing and they wanted him to stay there. That night Geoff drank himself to sleep—something he never did before. From that point on, things got worse. At work, he and his boss went back and forth with the decision to continue on in that same job until Geoff told his boss either he got his old job back or he would resign. He didn't look the same and the gleam in his eyes was gone.

"The once-happy Geoff was now a constant nervous wreck, and his sleepless nights wreaked havoc on his appearance. He was falling apart. Finally, he quit his job. Having such a good reputation, he already had another job interview set up. When we were put up in the beautiful complimentary home that we now occupied, we had put all of our belongings into storage since it had already been furnished. We decided to return to New York and stay with my parents and sister while we looked for a new home and Geoff decided which new job to take. It wasn't that easy, however. Geoff couldn't get over the fact that he walked away from such a prestigious position and was very disappointed in himself. It seemed as if he needed a healing period, but again things got worse.

"Now living with my parents, Geoff was falling apart a little more each day. We finally went to a therapist, who explained to us that Geoff was having a nervous breakdown. Meanwhile, Geoff's boss called from North Carolina to offer him his old job back, but just the thought of it placed Geoff under such extreme pressure that he felt worse. He started telling me that he felt he couldn't get out of the hole he had dug. I told him, over and over, that I didn't care about the position or the money—that I just wanted the old Geoff back—but he slowly became worse.

"He wasn't eating, and he didn't care if he got dressed. The doctors thought he needed hospitalization, and off we went. Geoff started telling me that I'd be better off without him. He had no soul in his eyes—he was empty. I was terribly frightened. He finally admitted he wanted to die. He couldn't pull himself out of this major depression and talked about taking his own life. He explained that he loved us and didn't want his boys to know their father was in an institution, and, since he couldn't get better, we would be better off if he were dead.

"Depression is something that this world has very little true knowledge about and also very little sympathy for. It can cripple a person. It can tear them apart and break them down. It can also take over and destroy—that is what depression was doing to Geoff. After being in and out of hospitals, Geoff got no better. My heart was heavy and my soul was broken. Thank God my parents and sister were supportive during this whole ordeal. Their strength helped me to deal with the trouble, even when our insurance ran out and Geoff was released permanently. Though I was scared for him I couldn't wait to lie by his side, and the children were so happy he was coming home. I thought that with his being out of the hospital, life would get back to normal. I loved him so much that I wanted to shake him, hold him, yell at him—anything that would get into his head and change him back. I would have done anything. I went to our priest and asked him to pray for us.

"We had a normal dinner his first night home, and I never slept so well with him holding me in his arms. But the next morning when I woke, Geoff was gone. My mom had gone out to pick up milk for the children and asked my sister to watch them until I awoke. At first I assumed Geoff was just with the children, but I soon saw that one of the cars was missing. I was frightened to death. Where could he be? I had no car to look for him. When my mother pulled up, I was crying. I told her that Geoff was gone and he took the car. He was gone all day and into the night. I finally called the police and explained that he was not himself and that we were so concerned. Finally, after dark he pulled up. In private he told me that he thought of how to take his life. He felt that he was only going to take this family down and we didn't deserve it. I had such a hard time understanding why my love for him wasn't enough and why my prayers were not being answered.

"We had a system now where we took turns watching him. It was especially hard on my sister, who had, herself, battled cerebral palsy all her life, and now was getting ready to be married soon. Helping out so much at home was difficult for her at such a busy time in her young life, but we were a family united in helping Geoff. He was getting worse each day, and at this point there was not much we could do for him except pray and hope that in time, with love and support, he would grow strong again.

"One morning when we awoke, Geoff was gone again. He took nothing with him except the car. I had no idea when he left or if it was during the night or in the morning. My heart felt as if it had stopped, and breathing was an effort. There was only one car now, so in my nightgown I took off to look for him, rolling down the windows to call his name over and over as if he might hear me. I mostly drove to the beaches hoping he was watching the waves and thinking, but he was nowhere to be found. I remembered that he once spoke of jumping from a bridge, so in a panic I speeded to the nearest bridge. I wasn't stopping at the traffic lights but would slow down to make sure that no other car was coming. I didn't want to hurt anyone, but I had to get to the bridge. I was crying, screaming, shaking and praying all at once.

"Behind me I saw flashing lights and then heard the siren. A police car was forcing me over to the side of the road. I had no time to stop, but I did. He asked for my license, but of course I never took the time to grab my pocketbook. I had no license, no identification, and I was still in my pajamas with no shoes or socks, and I was rambling and not making much sense. I thought the police officer was going to take me in, because I had no registration or proof that the car was mine. Finally, I broke down, unable to pull myself together. He placed me in the patrol car, and I asked him, 'Do you believe in God?' He looked at me and said, '*What?*'

'Do you believe in God?' I asked him again. He softly said, 'Yes.' 'Then please believe me, my husband has been sick and I have reason to believe that he is on the bridge, and if I don't hurry, his death will be on our hands. Please believe me. I think he is going to take his own life, jump perhaps, and I'm scared.'

"He took the C.B. in his hand and called the Highway Patrol, and I gave him the make and model of the car. He asked them to look for it at the bridge while we waited. The response seemed to take forever. Finally they radioed back, and the policeman asked me to stand off to the side of the patrol car while he took the call. After the call, he quietly told me to get in and we took off. Finally he told me that they found the car at the top of the bridge, but they couldn't find him. He put the siren on and we took off, leaving my car behind.

"The ten-minute ride seemed like an endless road to the end of my hope. I thought of our boys, our lives and how much love there was, and that somehow it had all gone so wrong. Words could never describe how truly scared I was when we pulled up onto the bridge. I saw his car among the patrol cars, and then saw a bunch of patrolmen huddling in a circle. I panicked, and then I saw Geoff, the six-foot-two-inch outstandingly handsome love of my life. I ran as fast as I could into his arms. There were no words—there was no reason for them—we all knew why he was there. At this point, this poor soulless man had no reason for words, no reason for life. Because we had no insurance, the police took him to the state hospital.

"A mental institution is no place for a seriously depressed person. People there were talking to the air. Some were rocking back and forth, exposing themselves, dancing or crying. Geoff was not like any of them—he was simply down and out, empty but harmless. Perhaps he was too good for this deteriorated world, but where could he go to get help and not feel as if he was a lost and hopeless case? I visited him the next morning and every visiting hour allowed. He was not like the others, most of whom were seriously mentally ill and others dangerous. Being in this environment only confirmed to him proof of his failure. I discussed Geoff's case with the doctors and they agreed that he could probably be helped and that his stay was not permanent, but I never felt that they were actually helping him. After twenty days of visiting him in this terrible run-down ward, sitting in ripped chairs near barred windows, we got a visit from the state lawyer. She explained to us his legal rights and said that she could take him to the court to plea for his release. For the first time in this whole ordeal, I saw a spark in his eyes.

"When he entered the court ten days later, he looked better than the lawyers in his best suit. He had confidence, class and most of all a smile. All at once I remembered why I fell in love with this handsome man. After he spoke to the judge, he was allowed to go home. The doctors wanted him to continue taking his antidepressant medication for a while. We bought it and brought it home, putting it in the kitchen. My mom had a great dinner waiting, and I really felt that the rest of our lives were going to be just fine. We all went to bed early, and falling asleep in each other's arms was the most peaceful feeling in the world.

"The next morning, we took the children for their checkups at the doctor's and then back to the house. Michael, my oldest son, and Geoff took a bike ride together. My little guy, Geoffrey, was too young yet to ride a bicycle, so he stayed with me. It looked and felt like old times. They came home in just enough time to make a haircut appointment for Geoff. He got the keys to the car and handed them to me. I thought for a moment and said, "No, you drive. You always used to drive." I kidded him by adding, "Well, captain, things are back to normal and you're driving!" and handed him the keys. He got behind the wheel and we left. Things were going so well.

"After about a mile of driving, Geoff said he didn't feel well. He said he had a terrible headache. As I was thinking that, sure, this poor guy has been under so much stress, just then he passed out. I grabbed the wheel as fast as I could. He was out cold. I couldn't reach the brake pedal from the passenger side and tried to move him, but he was too heavy. I finally climbed over him while trying to steer. I pulled the car off the road and kept screaming his name, over and over, but there was no response. Somehow I came to the conclusion that he probably was overwhelmed with everything that happened the past few days, and he had just passed out. I quickly got out and tried to flag someone down for help, but no one stopped. I got back in the car and tried to find a hospital. I had a good idea where it was but still I couldn't find it. Finally I pulled alongside another car and asked for help. They gave me directions, and I drove as fast as I could. As I pulled up to the hospital, I saw a police officer, so I flashed my lights, honked the horn and yelled for help. He knew right away that I was in need of help and ran over. He radioed inside the hospital, and several men came outside. They asked a lot of questions: 'How is his heart?' 'Do you think he had a heart attack?' I told them I didn't think so. They took him in right away and started working on him. All the time I just kept asking, 'What's wrong, what's wrong?' There couldn't be anything wrong. We were just beginning to start a new life. They wouldn't let me into the room, but I could see them somewhat. Very soon after, a nurse came rushing out and asked me if he was on any medication. I couldn't think, and then it came to me—'Oh, yes, how foolish of me. I'm sorry, he's on an anti-depressant. Is he all right?' She told me that they didn't know yet and that she would be back as soon as possible.

"Several minutes later, the same nurse came out again. She asked about the dosage of his medication. I told her, 'I'm not sure—why? Did he have a reaction?' She asked me if there were a way that I could call home and get some more information on his medication, and do it in a hurry. I ran to the phone and called my mom. I could hear my boys playing in the background. I told her, 'Mom, listen carefully. Geoff passed out, and I think it has something to do with his medication. Get it and read the dosage and the correct name of the medicine.' She rushed back to the phone, crying and yelling, 'Oh God, Connie, I can't find it.' I told her, 'Mom, look again. This is important.' My father got on the phone and said, 'Connie, the bottle is missing, we can't find it anywhere. It's not where it belongs and it's not around anywhere.' I hung up and ran to the nurse, telling her what my parents told me. She said softly, 'That's what we suspected. The pupils of his eyes are dilated. He must have taken all the pills. He took an overdose.' She told me that this overdose was a very serious one and that the doctor would be out to speak to me soon. But I just didn't see this as an overdose. I didn't understand it. I thought, well maybe he just wanted to get better faster or there was some mistake. Maybe he forgot to take his first pill and then took another, but I was sure that he would be all right.

"When I was in the emergency room waiting for news of my husband, I felt as if the blood were slowly leaving my body. I finally had to run to the bathroom to throw up. When I came out, I saw the doctor. He told me that Geoff's condition was very serious and that the pills he took could cause his heart to stop. But I knew he was a healthy, well-built, twenty-nine-year-old man. His heart was so strong, so I knew he would make it. I went in to be with him and hold his hand. He was in a coma now, but I talked to him to get well. I told him how much I loved him, and all I wanted to do was to crawl under those covers and lay in his arms. Time passed and my parents and close friends came. I was tired, felt sick and was scared to death, but I would not leave. He was a warm and special man—loved by many—and he had to pull through.

"It was getting late, and from time to time they asked me to leave the room. I sat very close by and prayed. Earlier they had asked for our family doctor, and just then he had walked into the waiting room. He looked so tired. Then, as he began to speak, I saw his face darken. 'Connie, Geoff is gone.' I just looked at him and said, 'You're crazy, I just saw him. He's inside that door, he's asleep.' 'No,' he said,

'Connie, I'm sorry, he's passed away.' I fell to my knees screaming and then started to pound the doctor's chest, telling him to get back inside and work on him. The nurses kneeled on the floor with me and held me. They started to cry. I looked up and saw my dad. He fell into his seat, and a nurse helped him. They were so close, Geoff and my father—more like father and son than father-in-law and son-in-law.

"I ran inside to see Geoff. He had no color. None at all. 'Oh my God,' I thought, 'I think the doctor is right. He's gone—my husband is gone. Oh, God— what am I going to do without him? The children have no father.' None of this made sense. I couldn't believe he was gone. To see other people in the hospital fighting for their lives only to find that my husband had taken his own. I thought, 'Dear God, what will I tell my boys and how could I ever tell them about this? How could I ever go on?' Now I wanted to die.

"In the days and weeks that followed, I felt as if I had to learn to walk and breathe again. Eventually I found a job. The best I could tell the boys about their father was that he had a blood clot and died. They were so young and so upset. My new friend, Artie, would become my best friend in those months after Geoff's passing, and it turned out that my mother knew his family from way back around the time of World War II. I was going through therapy at this time and was still trying to pull my life together when tragedy hit my family again with the passing of my sister at twenty-seven years old, just a short time before her wedding. I tried to make things go as smoothly as I could, but I truly felt like a living dead person.

"I finally told the truth to my children of their father's death when I felt they were old enough to understand. There was no soft, tender way to explain it, and I worried that if I still didn't understand his death, how would they? Michael took it the worst—he was full of anger—while Geoffrey was saddened deeply. Ever since the boys were told the truth, Michael went downhill. I found out he was sneaking out at night, drinking, smoking pot, failing in school and falling apart. Though he's been in therapy for a long time, it doesn't seem to help greatly. I also decided to share another secret with the boys. After their father passed on, a friend told me about a great medium named George Anderson. I never heard of him, but she suggested it would help my feelings if I saw him. It took me three years to get an appointment, and I wondered if it could be true—a man who claims to hear from the other side, from people who have passed on. Is Geoff's soul really alive?

"Well, I went, and the discernment was unbelievable.

"I always wanted to tell the boys that their father was sorry for what he did and that he still loved them and was with them always, so I played for them a recording of the discernment after I sat them down and told them the truth about their father's death. I knew that Michael would have the hardest time, since he was such an intelligent child and was close to his father. He probably sensed more than I was aware of even though he was only four and a half when it happened. The tape was so helpful. They actually had a chance to 'hear' their father. I was one of the lucky people blessed with meeting George. After going to him, I knew for sure that he was telling the truth. I did hear from Geoff, and though it broke my heart, it also mended some of my open wounds. I believe it did the same for my sons. Now that they finally knew everything, I hoped that we could put the past behind us and move on.

"Now, nearly ten years have passed, and I'm in the hospital with Michael and dealing with his depression. I wondered if it would ever stop. As I sat, I thought that if only I could go back to George, but this time with the boys, maybe their father could come through and talk to them! More than determined, I called every day, until I finally got through. This time, George had a private discernment open and without hesitation I booked the appointment. At this time not only was Artie in my life, but we were married. We got married about two years after Geoff's death. He was my strength, and he loved Michael and Geoffrey, which made me love him. Artie built us a new home. It was beautiful, and we feel as if we have a fresh start. God had blessed us with our third son. Joseph was born with a smile and a living, happy heart.

"Knowing how compassionate Artie is, I was sure he would agree for all of us to have a discernment with George as a family. The thought of seeing George again and what peace it might bring to my sons caused sleepless nights of anticipation. I held my breath as we walked into our appointment. It was unbelievable—better than I imagined. Geoff still loved us all, and that brought great comfort. It was amazing to hear how Geoff knew of Michael's hard times. I got much peace from the discernment, and I felt happy knowing that we will still be a part of his life. Even after all this time we knew we had a place in each other's heart, and that is sacred. I thought now that Michael would let go of the past, enjoy his life and move on. Sadly enough this was not true, even after meeting George. Even though Michael said he truly believed everything, even though Geoff himself told Michael not to go down the same road. Here I sit in a waiting room of a hospital. Since I was now experienced with the illness of depression, I was able to see the warning signs one evening and got to Michael before he took anything or did anything to himself. But he still needs help. I lost my husband, Geoff, my sister eight months later, my home and my hope, but never my faith. There is no way that I am going to lose my son.

"Together as a family we will always remain strong and united and understanding that the loss of a loved one is only temporary. It makes it so much easier to go on knowing Geoff is glad I went on with my life, and it helps make the guilt go away. George has taught me that we are here for a purpose. We have jobs to do on the earth and we all have gifts from God. My gift is strength and my job is to save my son whom I love with all my heart, as I do all my sons. I will never give up. George has taught me never to fear death. This will all pass, and then we will go on in the most ultimate beauty.

"This is the discernment that my family attended with George. Thank you to God, George and Artie for your strength being passed on to me and my family."

THE DISCERNMENT

"Well, there's a male presence here in the room so far. Now is he family to you all?"

"Yes."

"'Cause he claims he is family. Have you been married before? Did your husband pass? This (*indicating Artie*) is your husband—this man is coming in claiming to be dad, husband and I'm thinking, 'No, he's sitting right there as far as I know.' (*To the boys*) So actually it is your biological father? (*They nod.*) He leaves in turmoil? He admits not being the happiest person here—true?"

"Not in the end."

"And that's nobody's fault, he says. He especially wants you and your boys to understand that he is not singularizing you but you know where he has to focus at this moment. He just states that he wants his sons to know that it's not their fault, that he was so unhappy when he was here toward the end of his life. He admits being in turmoil, so was he very emotionally up . . . tight or something? Yeah, because he admits being in turmoil. Were you guys afraid that he was mad at you or something? Because he keeps saying that he's not mad at you. Things just started to go downhill for him, so he felt. But he admits being his own worst enemy, that he was making things worse than what they were. You and he were very close at one time? Did he kind of distance himself from you then? He apologizes to you— that you were very close and all of a sudden he doesn't seem to want to be around you anymore, he seems to be cutting you off, he just doesn't want to be bothered anymore. You, especially since he passed on, might think, 'What did I do? All of a sudden this man is close to me and then it seems like he doesn't love me anymore. He doesn't care about me anymore,' but the problem is he was starting to lose caring for himself. Was he also being kind of demanding to you? (*They nod.*) He feels he might have been a little hard on you at different points as any father can be but actually it just seems he's cutting you off, he just backed away from it. He was a very accomplished individual, yes?"

"Uh huh."

"This is somebody who for the period of time that he was here he was extremely accomplished. I take it you all pray for him, yes?"

"Yes."

"He certainly thanks you for your prayer and asks that it please continue. It's true he could be his own worst enemy? Because this is where the trouble starts. He jokes to me that he makes his life an opera; he makes things worse than they really are. He was very successful, yes?"

"Yes."

"Because he had accomplished—he was very successful financially. I'm dealing with somebody who puts his nose to the grindstone and makes it happen. He thinks big, he projects big and he creates big, but with him it's all or nothing, true?"

"Yes."

"That's the key to his downfall, he says. He wants to pass on? Because he admits he wants to die—he wants out. In essence did he take his own life? Because he admits he commits suicide. Now he realizes that is the worst thing he could have done, not that he's in agony or suffering over there, but he realizes that it caused more harm. At the time, he thinks—he might have thought he was doing the right thing and it caused more harm than good, not only for himself but also for his family that he left behind. But he felt he was failing—he felt trapped and cornered, and he admits that when he first got over there he reflected on his life and he was disappointed in himself. Again, we're not speaking to a dumbbell. This guy could have worked it out. He knows he could have surmounted this obstacle and taken on this challenge. He was the type of guy who would willingly take on challenge. Was he hostile before his passing? Because he admits he might have said the wrong thing at the wrong time. (*To the boys*) Were the two of you really getting more of the brunt of it? I mean not that you (*to Connie*) weren't left out either but it just seems that you are maybe experiencing it more or hearing it more. Was he playing favorites at one time?"

"Well, he (*indicating Michael*) was older."

"Yeah, he kind of apologizes that at times it might have felt like favoritism being shown. Like maybe he was favoring your older brother over you, or vice versa, but I think it was more what I said the first time—he certainly wants you to know that he does love you and knows how much you love him. He admits he was showing favoritism but it wasn't being done intentionally, although it certainly looked that way. Did he have trouble with drinking or anything? Was something breaking his system down? Unless it was just his emotions, because I feel like I'm having a nervous breakdown."

"He did have a nervous breakdown."

"Was he on something like Valium?"

"Elavil."

"Maybe that's what it is, 'cause he's talking about taking some sort of drug. I'm thinking, 'Well, what do you mean, do you mean a substance abuse drug or do you mean a legitimate drug?' and then he showed me Valium, so apparently he was on anti-depressants. That's the drug that he was taking. It was helping but it wasn't helping. He goes from one extreme to the other. He's like a normal, hardworking successful guy who suddenly feels his life is going down the toilet, and he's going down with it. For a period of time, though, he had a very happy home."

"He did."

"He had a happy marriage, he seems like a nice father, you have a very com-fortable, contented life. Did he have some failings business-wise?"

"He felt he did."

"He talks about failings business-wise and yet you know I'm not making judg-ment on him, but it's almost like I want to grab him and say, 'What the hell is the matter with you—you're not failing' because he is not failing."

"Exactly."

"He thinks he's failing, and everything just had to be in its place, had to be perfect all along."

(She nods.)

"He is—he's a perfectionist and everything must be perfect. It has to be ex-actly the way he feels secure. He realizes now, not only for his own sake but also that of his family, especially his two sons, the worst thing he could have done was taking his own life, because you might feel he gave you all a royal slap in the face and just said, well, 'F-you, I'm leaving and I'm not dealing with it.' Plus he was constantly yelling all the time."

"Yes, toward the end."

"Yeah—it seems like he's yelling at you all the time or whatever you are doing is not good enough, and you're saying to yourself, 'What did I do wrong?' All of a sudden everything has gone to another extreme. He wasn't eating well, either?"

"Right."

"He wasn't nutritionally backing up his system, so again the medication is helping but it's also hindering—it's breaking the system down also, plus it seems he is sleeping a great deal, but he's not sleeping well enough. He has a nervous breakdown. He might not even know it himself, and you have to admit that turned him from Dr. Jekyll to Mr. Hyde—all of a sudden he was just quite the opposite. He just wants all of you, especially the three of you, to know he is not mad at you, nor did you do anything to add to his anxiety or frustration, nor did you do anything to fail him. He just cut off his nose to spite his face. Unfortunately, he says, I have no one to blame but myself. It's not that he's in some horrible state in the hereafter, but he's looking himself straight in the eye and saying there's no one to blame but me. As he says, it is said many times that you can easily cheat others but you can never fool yourself or the Infinite Light—you have to face up to yourself. Are you all in therapy or something? (*They nod.*) Yeah, 'cause it sounds like he knows you're in therapy because you are trying to piece the puzzle of this back together."

"Right."

"He knows on certain days you just wish you would die, and then you wouldn't have to deal with this anymore, but he says, 'Trust me—don't take the way out that I did because it's not going to solve the problem.' As he says and I can understand that, unfortunately when you get very depressed and feel a state of desolation you don't think rationally. All you think of is 'I'm good for nothing and I want out.' His dad passed on?"

(*She nods.*)

"Before him?"

"I have no idea."

"Oh, 'cause he keeps talking about his father helping him out a great deal over there. Did they have a distant relationship?"

"He didn't know him."

"He says that they had a very distant relationship here, and they have become very close over there, and he states that his father has been doing a tremendous job helping him to help himself over there. (*To Michael*) Have you at times been suicidal? Because he's telling you, 'Don't do the same thing I've done, don't,' he says, and he's right. It will not solve the problem; you will only bring more unhappiness to yourself and as he says, you will survive this, you will get through it, it has to be up to you. In this case you don't want to be 'like father, like son,' he states. Not that he's playing favorites here, but he's been singularizing you more because he knows you suffer in silence a great deal. You kinda keep it in, and he knows you are like a time bomb that could go off at any time. He says again, 'Don't do the same thing that I've done, it's not going to solve your problems, it's only going to make matters worse.' He recognizes it's one thing to lose your father, but it's another thing to lose your father through this process. Was he kind of hurting himself? It's like he was doing things to hurt himself. I'm baffled by this. Anybody who knows him, and knew him well, was probably boggled beyond words to try to figure out what was making him tick now. He admits that he had put up such a severe wall of frustration and despair that you could not even put a dent in it, he just would not let anybody in. He thought that for him to ask for help was a sign of being weak, but he realizes now that it's a sign of being strong. He's recognizing that you do need somebody to talk to and you need help, but he's the type of guy that wanted to figure out every problem on his own. *(To the boys)* Is one of you being picked on or bullied?"

(Geoffrey) "I'm always being bullied by the whole family."

"Because he is talking about somebody being picked on."

"He *(indicating his brother)* picks on me."

"He was saying about stopping it and not doing it, but again it doesn't solve the situation. The three of you have to really try to pull yourselves together as best you can, and he knows it's easier said than done—you are living in the shadow of what happened. Your name is Connie, right?"

"Yes."

"Is there another passed on?"

"Yes."

"Because there is somebody standing behind you—claims her name is Conchetta—is that grandma? Yeah, because I feel her behind you. She has her hands on your shoulders and says you are named in her memory."

"I was."

"And she says she is around you as a guardian angel, and she wants to let you know she's been doing her very best to help your husband to help himself in the hereafter. Is your name Conchetta also?"

"Yes."

"Is there a Joe, Joseph passed on? Two? Just say yes or no—let me tell you."

"I think so."

"Because there are two people around you claiming to be Joe, Joseph. One seems to be a fatherly figure like an uncle or something like it."

"And the other?"

"It's almost like somebody said Giuseppe *[Italian for Joseph]* so he must be a fatherly figure like an uncle, and one is claiming to be Giuseppe who's obviously a grandfather—that would be a fatherly figure also."

"Yes."

"Also the name Peter? (*To Artie*) Remember, people from your family can come in, too, so anything is recognized."

(*Artie*) "I don't know my family."

"Oh, all right, but I did see a female presence hanging around you and she's standing there next to you, but she's saying to me, she knows she's not going to speak up yet because it's obvious that Connie's husband has more of a need to communicate and they sense that. There is definitely a woman around you, she comes to you like a grandmother or such. Also, the name Carl mean anything? (*To Artie*) It seems to be more around you. You didn't know your family at all?"

(*Artie*) "Not really."

"You don't know if there was a Carl or Charlie? Let me leave it with you. Either I'm wrong or it could be somebody that you just don't know who it is. See, that's the thing, these could be people that you can't confirm any more than I could who they are. But the woman around you claims to be your actual grandmother—biologically, she must have been. Whoever was an orphan, were they in a foundation at one time? With nuns?"

(*Artie*) "Probably my mother."

"Because I keep seeing nuns all around you. Did your mom pass?"

"No."

"There's somebody claiming to be grandmother, but I just wanted to make sure [that he did not misinterpret mother for grandmother]. But there are women around you that look like real nuns, the way they dressed when I was younger, and apparently they are a part of this order or foundation that took care of your mom or somebody in your family."

"Is that what the 'Carl' was about?"

"Carl or Charlie seemed to be more family or family-connected, but you just don't know who it is. There are four nuns around you. Was your mother in [an orphanage] in the New York area?"

"Yes."

"Because they claim that it was an order that was near us, so it had to be somewhere like Brooklyn or the New York metropolitan area or one of the boroughs, because they're claiming that the orphanage or the convent took care of them in our area."

(*Connie*) "I believe it's Queens."

"Also is there a Mike or Michael?"

"Yes."

"Passed on?"

"Yeah."

"Knows your husband?"

"He didn't know him, but . . ."

"It's a father figure to him over there, let me just leave it with that. He says that your husband was sent to what we would consider a very exclusive rest home where he was only around animals for a period of time. There were fawns, dogs, cats and things that he wouldn't feel threatened by, until he basically calmed down, and then Uncle Mike came and visited him again and asked him if he wanted him to be there to try to work him 'out of himself.' That's one thing that I have to say about your husband—when he makes his mind up about something, he doesn't change until he's ready to. They knew he'd come around—it would just have to be his idea. *(To Artie)* You didn't lose a brother, did you?"

(Artie) "Not that I know of."

"You didn't lose a step-brother or something like it?"

"Not that I know of. What's his name?"

"I don't know yet, I don't get anything. I just get the feeling of the loss of a brother around you."

(Connie) "Around him?"

"Yes."

"Someone like a brother maybe?"

"Sure, as long as it's somebody that is close."

"Yes."

"That would have been *like* a brother? See, the thing is, they're very cautious not to interfere, not to cut me off yet, because obviously Connie's husband has the most need at this point, but the thing is I can feel people forming around you [Artie] and this person comes to you like a brother, so if you didn't lose a brother, maybe he's somebody who is a brother by choice, or emotionally you look upon him as a brother."

"Yes."

"Did you work with him?"

(Artie) "How do you know?"

(Connie) "I have a tremendous feeling I know who it is."

"Because whoever this male is who comes to you as a brother, he claims there was work contact, so apparently you worked together at one point or . . ."

(Connie, to Artie) "Did you work with him?"

(Artie) "If it's him—sure."

"Just say yes to me so that I know what I'm hearing is correct because he is claiming that you worked together."

"Okay."

"And this will give you a further clue of who it is. Your husband used a weapon with his passing, not in the traditional sense, because he says he uses a weapon. But I don't feel it's like a gun or knife. A weapon could be anything, but not in the traditional sense, but something obviously cut his oxygen off, because I keep feeling like I'm losing my air. Also is there a Sonny?"

"Yes."

"Passed on?"

"Yes."

(To Artie) "Knows you?"

(Connie) "Knows him and me."

"Well, whoever it is, says hello to everybody in the room. He came into the room and said hello to Artie and hello to your boys—he knows everybody, he says. He knows your husband that passed on also."

"Yes."

"He comes like an uncle figure."

"Yes, he is."

"He's present also. Also is there an Anna?"

"Oh please—that's very close to something else."

"Well, don't say it. It's a woman's name, though—yes? And she is passed on? Is she a mother figure? A mother figure could be an aunt, grandmother or anything like that. It sounds like she's saying Anna to me. She would know your husband? She passes young. This is where I am confused—is she family to you, but by blood? *(She nods.)* Okay, but there is a lot of strong friendship as well. She passes before your husband? She claims that she's met up with him over there. Wait a minute— could it be two people with the same name both passed on?"

"Not that I know of."

"Because one claims that she was there first. I don't understand what she means."

"Well, can I tell you?"

"No, I'll let them tell me. *(waits)* I hear Annie. It sounds like Angela, Angelina."

"Yes, Angela."

"Okay, probably what she's saying is Angie, she might have been called Angie at one time—that's why I was saying Annie. She is related to you, yes?"

"Yes."

"She's not only a relative but a friend as well? Because the feeling of friendship is very strong."

"Yes."

"I mean it was bad enough when your husband passed on, but losing her, you felt you got another kick in the pants."

"Yes."

"But she claims that she's a mother figure to your boys."

"Yes."

"She comes to you like a sister."

"Yes, it is my sister."

"It is because she keeps saying that she's their aunt and your sister, but she's also a friend."

"Yes."

"Also, you took care of your sister?"

"Yes."

"Because she does thank you for being so good to her prior to her passing—I see her handing white roses to you. Thanking you for being good to her prior to her passing. Also very fond of your boys?"

"Yes."

"If I didn't know better, I'd think she was the boys' mother. *(To the boys)* She keeps coming to the two of you definitely with a very strong motherly feeling, and she is a mother figure in more ways than one."

"Yes. Are we allowed to respond to them?"

"As long as you are not giving me any information. She does say hello to you, and she knows that you're in the room. Also, a Vincent, but called Jimmy? *(They motion no.)* He's not backing off. Are you sure? Usually if they don't back off, they know they're right. It could be your husband's side too."

"I don't know."

"All right, let me leave it with you. Was there loss of a brother, too?"

"Yes."

(To Connie) "Yours?"

"Yes."

"She's telling me that the brother is here with her also. Did he pass on very young?"

"Yes."

"Because I feel like he's been there since 'Grant took Richmond.'"

"Yeah."

"Actually, I wonder if he was the one claiming to meet your husband."

"You said Michael—that's his name."

"Oh, okay, because there was a sibling claiming that he was there first, that he was present there to help welcome him over, and he claimed he was connected to you. So obviously the two of them are together and Conchetta with your mom? Your mother's mother?"

"My father's mother, but she was almost like her mother—very close."

"Because she keeps saying that they are there with her, and obviously your mom's folks have passed on or something—or at least one of them."

"Yeah."

"Angela and Michael are together—that's what I'm trying to spit out."

"Thank God."

"Because Angela asks that you go home and tell your parents that you've heard from her and the two of them are together."

"Can I say something?"

"No. Also, did you ever miscarry?"

"No."

"Is there the loss of another brother—you don't know if your mom ever miscarried?"

"I think my mother might have had a miscarriage."

"There's another feeling of a boy claiming to be the male who passed on, and, had the cycle of birth continued, there would have been another brother. Without telling me, was your husband called by a nickname?"

"Oh, that could be very important to me, yes, go ahead, yes."

"He's giving me the feeling that he was called by some sort of nickname."

"Yes."

"But it's a code nickname?"

"Yes."

"He keeps writing a code in front of me—that the nickname is a code."

"Yes."

"Without telling me, do you think I've heard this nickname before? That's the only problem—if it's something that my brain has never heard before, it will be like I am hearing a foreign word and it won't make sense to me."

"Okay, yeah, it probably won't make sense to you."

"Okay, for the time being let me say this—he's giving me the feeling that he's calling out that he's called by some sort of nickname, and then he wrote out code in front of me. So even if I don't get it, you know he's trying to push it through, whatever it is."

"Yes."

"Is it connected with his name? He keeps saying that it's connected with his name, like a nickname. It's a short name code."

"Yes."

(To Geoffrey) "Your birthday coming up?"

"Just passed."

"Oh, because your father is wishing you a happy birthday and extending white roses to you. Apparently he's aware of it. *(To Connie)* Without telling me, your husband keeps giving me the feeling of his own name but shortened."

"Yes."

"Was he called by a shortened form of his own name?"

"Yes."

"Now I take it I've heard his name before—it's common enough? It's just not anything I've never heard before."

"Right."

"Does the name Sam mean anything?"

"Yes."

"Passed on?"

"No."

"Your husband knows him?"

"Yes."

"Because your husband is the one saying it. He keeps calling out to Sam."

"Yes."

"I almost blocked it—I didn't know what he was talking about."

"No, that makes a lot of sense."

"Sam is a person?"

"Yes."

"I just wanted to make sure. Your husband calls out and says, 'Tell Sam you've heard from me.' Obviously someone that he was very close with."

"Yes."

"He wants Sam to know that Sam didn't let him down."

"Okay."

"As long as that makes sense to you. Something cuts your husband's air off?

Because I keep feeling like I'm losing my breath and I'm going into a dizzy fading out. He was very good with finance?"

"Yes."

"Because it seems that he definitely knew how to manage money well and make it work and so forth. He's very very brilliant."

"Yes."

"And self-made, most definitely."

"Definitely."

"He's giving me the feeling that he's starting at the bottom of the heap and working his way to the top."

"Absolutely."

"And this is again why he states that when he first got to the Other Side, he realized how silly it was for him not to give himself a chance to surmount his obstacles, because, look at his beginnings and what he had achieved. He was a very positive person and then became very negative."

"Yes."

"You memorialized him? Obviously something good was done in his name."

"Yes."

"He keeps thanking you for the memorial. Did you plant something?"

"Yes."

"But that's only part of the memorial."

"Right."

"You've done a couple of them, at least, because he says you planted something like a tree and did something in his name, but then there was a more substantial memorial or something placed in his name."

"Yes."

"Now he keeps talking about the code again and keeps referring to his surname. Either somebody would call him by his last name or something like that."

"I think I know, but you don't want me to tell you, right?"

"No. He has a short last name, or he shortened it or something?"

"It is short."

"It is no more than five letters, true?"

"It is five letters."

"People call my father 'Andy' for Anderson. It's almost like they called him something with his last name. He keeps telling me that there's a shortening of his last name. The name Peter keeps coming up."

"Peter vaguely comes to me on his family's side, but I don't know."

"It's interesting—it seems to be around your current husband."

"Okay."

"That's the third or fourth time that name has been brought up."

(*Connie, to Artie*) "Maybe that's your grandfather's name."

(*Artie*) "Go with it—can you go with it?"

"I can go with it, but I have to know that there's definitely a confirmation. I have to know that the information they're giving me is correct. I'll just have to leave it go. Your husband's first name, again, can be shortened?"

"Yes."

"Shortened to like three letters."

"Yes."

"His full formal name is no more than eight letters?"

"Exactly."

"It's exactly eight letters?"

"Yes, you may not get it from just counting, in case you're frustrated. I'll just tell you that it—"

"No, no."

"Okay, I just want to know that it's him."

"It's frustrating that he can tell me that it's eight letters, but he can't just come out and say it."

"Why does it happen that way?"

"I have no idea. Imagine how I feel, putting up with it for so many years. He spells it differently?"

"Yes."

"That's where he says I am going to have the trouble. He says if you spell it the way you think it should be spelled, he says you're going to have a problem. (*Pauses*) Oh, that's a good example—he's using the name like Steven—you can spell it S-T-E-V-E-N or S-T-E-P-H-E-N. There's two of the same letters in it? Normally it isn't?"

"No, there is."

"There is. Why is he telling me to double the letters—are they next to each other?"

"Yes."

"He keeps warning me to watch how I spell it. He says I'm going to mess it up by the spelling. Even with the spelling that is the way he spells it, would be no more than eight letters, but he tells me to watch how I spell it, there's an additional letter added in."

"Right."

"He says that's what is confusing my brain. Now he's showing me M and N. Now either that means there is an M and N in his name or he is breaking up the alphabet, but I get the feeling that he's breaking up the alphabet."

"Oh, yes."

"Okay, now we're going for the formal eight-letter name."

"Yes."

"He says A B C D and stops, so I'm going to assume that his name is after the D in the alphabet."

"Uh huh."

"He jumps from the D to the M and says, 'Go further.'"

"Yes."

"Is the name foreign sounding?"

"Some people think—it's not really, but the way it is spelled is foreign."

"That's probably what it is. He tells me to think on the foreign spelling. Now he is hanging around the P, he stops at the P. Is it after the P?"

"No, he's giving you clues."

"His name doesn't begin with the P, does it?"

"No."

"Why is he showing me the P then if it's not P?"

"You want me to tell you?"

"No."

"It's after M, it can't be the O—(pauses) His name begins with O?"

"No."

"Why is he showing me the O then? He's telling me that it's after the M and not further than the P, and I'm saying it can't be, because the name can't begin with O. But is O significant with his name?"

"Yes."

"But not the first letter."

"No."

"But it still signifies the name, he tells me. There's one O in his name, but the first letter of his name is after the M?"

"No."

"Before the M, but it's not the M."

"Right."

"I'm telling you, I'm losing my patience. He's going to have to work harder at this, and faster. There is a G in the name?"

"Yeah."

"It begins with G."

"Yes."

"Now he's at the R. There is an R in the first name?"

"Yes."

"One R."

"Yes."

"Is it G-E?"

"Yes."

"He's telling me that I should know the name. Does it begin like George with G-E-O? That's why he keeps telling me the O like George, G-E-O. He says it has the I-E sound, but I'm going to spell it the wrong—(he pauses, listening) Poet? What poet? Oh—Chaucer—Geoffrey."

"Yes."

That's it—with a G—G-E-O-F-F-R-E-Y."

(Connie) "What poet?"

"Geoffrey Chaucer—as soon as he said Chaucer I said, 'I think his first name is Jeffrey,' and I said in my mind J-E and then I thought, no, the English version would be G-E-O. He said to me, 'If you say it, you are going to spell it wrong and then you are going to block it out.' If he said to me, 'Jeffrey,' I would have spelled it that way."

"Right."

"But he also was called Geoff, right?"

"Yes."

"Did you also lose a pet dog?"

"Yes."

"He says the pet dog is with him. Before him?"

"Yes, before him."

"Because he claims the dog was part of his therapy in the beginning—"

"Oh my God."

"When you are sent to the place where the animals are to learn to kind of get your bearings back—he says the dog was there or brought to him. Also the name Dan or Daniel?"

"Yes."

"Passed on?"

"Yes."

"Your husband knows him or I guess he does now, because there's a very vague feeling—that's why I didn't know if it made sense or not—your husband was just saying, 'Dan is here with me.'"

"Yes."

"Also a Lou?"

(*Artie*) "There is a Lou."

"Passed on?"

"Not to my knowledge."

"Is he family to you—an uncle or such? They're referring to him as Uncle Lou. Maybe his parents have passed on or such. Someone is calling out to Lou here. Is he a widower?"

"Not that I know of."

"Because there is a female voice calling out to him, but it could also be his mom if his mother is passed on. I'll have to leave it with you. That Peter still clings to you, so it has to mean something. I don't know if it's a family friend—whatever—but it keeps coming through, there must be a family connection with it."

"Go with it for a second, because I think I know who it is."

"Peter?"

"Yeah."

"Is he family?"

"Yeah."

(*Connie*) "He just remembered."

"He's more like a fatherly figure."

(*Artie*) "For who?"

"For you, which could be an uncle, grandfather—something like that."

"Okay."

"Would he have spoken Italian?"

"Yes."

"Because he did refer to himself as Pietro (*Italian for Peter*)—It's almost like he could be a grandpa or something."

"Yeah."

"He keeps pushing at me that this is now the fifth time he's come to you, and he says again that he belongs to you. If that's really him, then obviously you had a grandfather Pietro over here. I don't know if it is your natural or your adoptive, or whatever the story is, but there was somebody there by that name who claims that he's around you like a guardian angel."

"Okay."

"In any case, he wants to acknowledge that he's near to you. Normally when they keep pushing at me—the same person—something is being overlooked and they are correct. So I guess with this they are going to fade down. They were starting to before, but I wasn't going to let Geoffrey go until I figured out what he was trying to tell me name-wise—why it was spelled differently—and I finally figured it out. Geoffrey, your father and husband, embraces the three of you with love and he especially reaches out to his two sons, that you remember what he said—that he is all right and at peace, and not to feel, in any way, shape or form, any type of blame for this tragedy that's happened. He says that is one thing about taking one's life—he says you make the choice yourself—nobody makes it for you. Again he asks that you remember to pray for him, and remember what he said about the thoughts about taking your own life. He says, 'Trust me, it's not going to solve the problem. It's not going to solve any of your problems.' He realizes now that there is nothing on the earth that you cannot deal with if you just put your mind to it and take on the challenge and surmount it. He wishes he had realized it before he made his decision in an irrational state of mind. He certainly knows that you love him and you miss him, and the terrible tragedy that you had to go through, but he says that he is coming along—that he is all right and at peace. And continue to pray for him, but certainly he'll feel much better if all of you put yourselves at peace as well. Also, the name Lena mean anything?"

"Yes."

"Passed on?"

"Yes."

"Somebody just walked in over there and that is what made me say it. Somebody just came in and said, 'Hi, this is Lena.' Is she like an aunt or grandmother?"

"Yes, grandmother."

"Is she your mother's mother?"

"Yes."

"She says she's with Angela and Michael also—that they're all together and to tell your parents that you heard from her. Her husband has passed, I take it?"

"Yes."

"Because I can feel him in the room, that he's here, but obviously Lena just appeared over there for a second and then she calls out to everybody, that she's with Geoff as well. In any case, they're telling me that they are going to withdraw, and he withdraws along with the others and all ask that you remember to pray for them, until we meet again."

"Can I ask you a question?"

"Okay."

"I know it's way off the track here, but what do they do on the Other Side? I'm curious."

"Well, everybody has their own specific jobs, but at this point, like in Geoff's case, he's still, it seems, studying himself, like going through a state of reflection and understanding of self, coming to grips with himself and then from then on, he can move on to something else or whatever he wants, helping other people that are in emotional distress over here or over there. It's like in Alcoholics Anonymous, getting help from somebody who's been through it before. In any case, again he steps aside along with the others and with that he signs off and the others step aside, too—and there they go."

FINDING FORGIVENESS

Discernments of suicide victims help me and the bereaved families better understand how important the Other Side's messages of love and service to others are to this existence, how much we need to tune in to those around us, whether we know them or not, with compassion and understanding. Some family members have told me confidentially that it is hard to forgive their loved ones in the hereafter for wasting their existence here and causing so much tragedy within the family. We need to find it within ourselves to understand and forgive, because no matter how senseless we feel their passing is, we can never understand fully the feelings that our loved ones endured prior to their passing. Through their communication, we can only listen and accept that, although they could not continue on this plane, they do continue in a better place, free of turmoil, to learn and move closer to the Infinite Light.

I think the most poignant part of the discernment of suicide victims comes when they communicate to their families that now, having seen the panorama of their life and struggle here, more possibilities existed here to help them than they had been able to see. They often explain that given time and a little clarity of thought, their problems could have been worked out and their existence here spared. Unfortunately, that clarity and vision only come once they are in the hereafter. While they do not regret what they have done, they do understand more clearly the rules of cause and effect with regard to life and family here. This is one of the things they seek to reconcile in the hereafter.

In some rare instances during discernments, souls have come across to me from the hereafter that they are not quite ready to reconcile the circumstances that brought them to end their life on the earth. Although they are now in a place free of pain and torment, they might, at least for a brief time, harbor some resentment about the circumstance of their passing. It is a rare occurrence, happening perhaps three or four times in the thousands of discernments I have done, but they are still there. This is not to say that they are in any further torment in the hereafter. It is rather like having your face slapped, and then after the pain is gone, you still resent having been slapped. They do understand in the hereafter that their pain is gone, but they still must reconcile their feelings. This is only a temporary feeling for them in the hereafter, however, since everything from the moment of their passing becomes easier as time passes. Some wounds take longer to heal than others, but all wounds heal, especially in the hereafter.

THE FIRST TIME I met Erin and Daniel Tomcheff was at a bereaved parents' weekend in Anniston, Alabama, at the home of Dr. Raymond Moody. Meeting them gave me the feeling of having seen J. D. Salinger characters come to life— they are artistic, cultured and intelligent people who seem free of some of the conventions and biases that imprison the minds of most people. To look at them, you would think that fate has been kind to them—it has not. After their reading, I gained a new admiration for anyone who can still see beauty in life despite the tragedy and loss of hope they have suffered. The following is a biography written about their son, Theon, written as only a loving mom and dad could do. It includes the story of their life and the circumstance that brought us together—the passing of Theon:

ERIN TOMCHEFF

"Let me tell you about our son Theon Daniel Tomcheff—born on July 1, 1970, in Westwood, California—beautiful and aware at the very beginning. Daniel had a job that paid well, and I had a featured role in a movie that was scheduled to begin in a few months, but nothing compared to our wonderfully healthy, lively and beautiful child that we loved more than anything or anyone.

"We moved shortly after Theon's birth from California to Bensenville, Illinois, primarily due to the fact that Los Angeles was changing. We wanted to raise Theon in a safe and happy environment. We spent eighteen years in Illinois before moving once again to Colorado.

"Theon had problems in school. During his grade school years, he was bullied and picked on by some of the other children, but, worse than that, he was a victim of the apathy of those school administrators who were in authority. We made the decision to remove him from school and have him home-tutored, where Theon worked toward his GED diploma. Was Theon the perfect child or a paragon of virtue? Absolutely not! On the contrary, he was perfectly normal, had a raucous sense of humor and was a daredevil. As if it had happened overnight, he was maturing into a beautiful young man.

"The three of us had weathered some really hard ideological times, though. One evening as we sat talking about all this, Theon said that he felt that he had gone through a sort of mid-life crisis. 'Mom, I think I had a mini nervous breakdown,' he said, referring to a time shortly after his twenty-first birthday when he began hitting the bars, hanging around with the wrong crowd and collecting guns. Although I was shocked at his choice of words, Theon could always express how he felt to us, and what he was referring to was a sort of breakdown—certainly of what he valued and held most dear.

"Theon made friends with people of all ages, occupations and gender. His tastes were eclectic, his knowledge impressive and his curiosity never-ending. But he had a terrible fear of authority—jail and the police. In 1991, after a minor scuffle with the law, Theon thought he would be put in jail for one night. To Theon, jail was a 'fate worse than death,' and he told his father, 'I'd shoot myself before I'd go to jail—even for one night,' so terrible was his fear of police and jail. Although he was only sentenced to a fine and some community service, Theon became preoccupied with the thought of being sent to jail. He also repeated several times that he would 'die first before I spend one hour in jail.'

"Of all Theon's friends, the ones that would prove most troublesome for him [were] some members of a skinhead group from Denver. But gradually, Theon returned to himself. It was to this period of time that he referred when he said that he felt that he had a 'mini nervous breakdown'—that he had suffered a 'mid-life crisis.' By the winter of 1993, Theon's essence as a human being became more and more visible on a daily basis to all of us. In two more weeks, we were moving into a new house and we were all back together working toward a future that held such great promise.

"On October second at approximately 2:00 A.M., our dog, Tia, woke me with her barking at the front door. I went over to the front door and opened it, turning on the porch light at the same time. I opened the screen door, and there was Theon, standing at the garage, pointing a gun at another man. Theon had watched this man trying to break into three different cars, and had the thought that he would perform a 'citizen's arrest.' The man then came toward me. He was so obviously drunk, and all I could think was 'He's got a gun,' and I called to Theon to come in the house. As the man made his way up the street, Theon explained his intentions to us, but I told him, 'You know, Theon, you're not the honor cop of the neighborhood.' He made some adjustment to the gun and went downstairs to his room. We didn't think to report the incident but, rather, said goodnight and went to bed.

"The next thing I knew, I was being awakened from a sound sleep by a tremendous pounding. I leapt out of bed and to the front door, but looked out and saw no one. Just as I started to pull back inside, a man's voice said, 'Boulder Police! Boulder Police!' They were at the side of the garage, peeking around the edge of it behind a tree. 'Step this way, Mother. Come out, Father,' they shouted. 'My God,' I said. 'Come inside. I'm barefooted.'

"Daniel told me to go inside and put on my slippers, and the police were talking to him. I put on my slippers and returned outside, telling them to come in and asking what the matter was. The policeman kept calling us 'Mother' and 'Father' and was saying something about having received a complaint about a man being threatened with a gun (the one Theon found breaking into cars). I am not clear on that at all, however. I was cold and felt fear in my heart. Finally we all went inside, and they said that they wanted to see Theon. They asked me to wake him up. They needed to ask him questions.

"When I woke him and told him that the police were here, he was confused and asked what it was about. I told him it was about the incident with the man. When we got upstairs, the policeman was talking to one of the two female officers. They asked Theon a lot of questions about his guns and about any tattoos he had. Then Theon mentioned that they were here because of his past association with the skinheads. They denied it. They asked other questions about the man having been threatened by Theon, all of which he denied.

"After one of the female officers made a phone call, she said, 'All right, Theon. You'll have to get dressed and come with us.' When I asked why, she replied in a menacing voice, 'Because this is a felony—very serious—you'll have to come to jail.' 'Wait,' I said. 'I believe we should call our lawyer.' The policewoman ignored us and spoke to Theon. 'We need you to get dressed and come with us. Where is the gun?' The other female officer said to her, 'Don't let him touch the gun—you get it and you go down the stairs first.' 'Why am I going to jail?' Theon asked again. 'Because this is a serious matter,' said the officer. (This, of course was the ultimate fear for Theon, the darkest dread of his life—only we did not realize it at the time. We were not making connections.)

"We opened the door to go downstairs, but our dog Tia started to bolt in. I called for her to come to me, but Theon said, 'No, Mom. I'll get her.' He calmly got her by the collar and handed Tia off to Daniel, saying, 'Take care of her.' Then we once again headed down the stairs.

"Theon was first, the dark-haired policewoman was second, I was third and the blond policewoman, who'd admonished the other female officer about being first and getting the gun, came last. As we got to the bottom of the stairs, Theon ran forward to the bookshelves along the wall, reached quickly for the gun, chambered the bullet, pointed it to his head and pulled the trigger.

"His body rose gently and there was a pop—and then bluish smoke. Theon fell gracefully to the floor, his face turned toward the right and blood flowing rapidly onto the rug. Daniel rushed down the stairs, knocking into the policewoman and me as he rushed to where Theon was. As he reached the basement floor, he was viciously struck to the left eye by the blond policewoman.

"Daniel and I were pushed and shoved and screamed at. God, it was disgusting. 'Get back! Get back! Don't move! This is a crime scene!' shouted the dark-haired policewoman. They seemed at such a far distance. All sound was so far away. My only, only, only son was dead.

"I did not know how we were going to get through the rest of our life. We were brought to jail and were put in a room where the detective questioned us for hours. I hope I told him how intelligent Theon was. I don't know if I did. I also told him that Theon was not suicidal—just frightened of going to jail. At the moment of his death, Theon was reacting to his old and very deep fear of going to jail. So he did the only impetuous thing he could do to escape without any thought of the consequences. It was a tragic, tragic accident. He was not thinking in real terms of death—he just needed to escape.

"Our son Theon was a pilgrim on this earth—he loved all of life, even the less lovable parts of it—but he feared that element in society that has the power to control our lives. Daniel had a dream of Theon about a month after his death. In the dream Theon said, 'Where's Mom?' He paused slightly, and went on, 'I just couldn't take it anymore.' The beauty and the wrenching of the heart for us come in both parts. The first is classic Theon: He *always* wanted to know where Mom was! She was the greatest person in his life. It is the second part that I know should be clearer and that wrenches my heart. The 'it' that Theon refers to is not life—it was his dread of police, jail and the 'justice' system. That is the monster that took his life!

"That first week after Theon's death was full of lucid memories and of no memories. The central issue of that week was singular and easily recalled—'Should we kill ourselves or not?' There was no question in our minds but that the sole meaning for our existence ended in less than a second when Theon died that Saturday morning. Gradually, we began to come to a realization—with our deaths ruled 'suicides' by the police, as they ruled Theon's (though all three of our deaths could be ruled 'murders' by any objective look at the facts in this matter), no one alive could possibly ever know what Theon is like and what might have been the root cause of his action that morning. The police and others in our society who control our lives would never be held accountable for what happened that early morning if we did not, somehow, stay alive and see that justice was done."

DANIEL TOMCHEFF

"In those dark, early months we received insights from friends, which helped our spirits greatly. We also sought out other resources and references to give our own experiences deeper validity. This search began with one of those 'coincidences' that are in fact the 'little miracles' coined by Dr. Melvin Morse, given to us by our loved ones in the hereafter. After waiting for Erin in a bookstore, I saw two titles that caught my eye. One was about a man named George Anderson and the other by Raymond Moody. I related this to the authors some sixteen months later when we met them during a grief therapy weekend in Alabama. During that weekend we learned the last bit of knowledge we needed to understand fully about Theon and the thoughts that led him to take the action he took. By knowing that Theon is well—no, more than well—after what has happened to him here, gives us a sense of peace, a sense that we will be with Theon again. The following is the discernment of our son, Theon, through George Anderson."

THE DISCERNMENT

"Okay, now, of course whatever I say just answer yes or no. And let's see, okay, first of all there's definitely—they'll have to decide who wants to go first—well, there's a male presence around you, there's a female, too, and another male. There's two males close to you passed on? Well, I am going to say yes for you because as soon as I said that, they said, 'Well there is,' so, there are two males close to you passed on. One passes young, yes?"

"Yes."

"It's two different generations?"

"Yes."

"Yeah, 'cause somebody else is with him. Now there's another male and there's another female, too. So that's three males; there are at least two females also that are there. Right. Ah, okay, someone claims to be your son. Did you lose a son?"

"Yes."

"Yeah, he's the young male obviously. He's the first one here. Ah, I can—it's almost as if I can feel him sitting between the two of you, and he has his arms around the two of you, so I'm glad you left a little room. And so he's present. (*To Erin*) Your dad has passed? Yeah, 'cause there's a man standing behind you and has his hands on your shoulders and claims he's dad. Meaning yours. And your son's with his grandfather. (*To Daniel*) Your dad has passed, too?"

"Yes."

"Same thing—behind you, hands on the shoulders. And your son is claiming he's with both of his grandfathers. There's talk of mom. Is your mom gone also? (*To Erin*) Yours has? Okay—that must be the grandmother. (*To Daniel*) Your mom still living?"

"Yes."

"That's probably why she's coming in and she's saying 'mom.' She's not really telling me whose mom she is. So I was a little stuck for a minute there. (*To Daniel*) So she would be your mom through marriage. (*To Erin*) Apparently your mother and father. (*To Daniel*) Your father—and is there also loss of a brother?"

(*Erin*) "Yes."

"Your brother?"

"Yes."

"Okay, because that's what's throwing me. Because your son said, 'Ask about the brother,' and I didn't know if he meant *his* brother or somebody else's brother. So in this case it's . . . your brother passes kind of young also, by today's standards?"

"Ah—fifty-seven."

"Oh yeah, definitely, I consider that young by today's standards—anything under sixty-five. 'Cause your mother, your father, your brother is here. There's also a flock of people in the background among all of you claiming to be grandparents. So it would be like your son's great grandparents. They're there as well. They're all present. Your son very close to you? 'Cause I feel like I'm not only speaking to your son, but I feel as if I'm speaking to somebody who's a good friend to the two of you as well. I mean, as he says, 'You know, sure, as a family, who didn't have their ups and downs, but, you know, we all love each other in any case.' He, ummm—how'll I say this . . . he's kind of a *keeps-things-to-himself-at-times* type of guy? 'Cause he seems very open, and yet I feel there's a small percentage of him I don't know."

"That's true."

"And I think that could be the case with anybody, but he seems to be a very extroverted person, basically, but still this part of him I really don't know, but that's so small and minute it really isn't bad. So on the whole, he's more of an extroverted individual. You obviously pray for him, because he certainly thanks you for prayer and asks that it please continue. He's also inclined to be pretty independent? *(Parents nod yes.)* Yeah, 'cause he's here, and yet there's this feeling of him doing several things at once, you know, that he's very independent. That I do feel that he's family oriented and yet, this sense of him with the independence, doing his own thing and such. Certainly, as he states, you were worried about him being all right over there, and he keeps saying that he's fine, that he's all right, because as you already should have known, he'd be the type that would make friends and have a job like in ten minutes. You know he would definitely find a way to fit in no matter where he had to go to. His passing is tragic? It certainly is beyond his control, yes? Well, that's how he puts it. Don't answer me then. 'Cause he says it's beyond his control, and when you seemed to hesitate, he told me to hold my ground, so I'm going to stay with what I've heard. *(long pause)* Hmm, he *knows* he's going to pass on?"

"Uhh . . ."

"'Cause he says to me he's really not shocked by death. So he says he's going to pass on. He passes very quickly though?"

"Yes."

"'Cause when the time comes, that could be another reason why he says he's not shocked by death, he tells me he passes very quickly. He gives me the feeling like I feel something in the chest, and yet he doesn't pass from a health problem."

"No."

"Because he tells me something in the chest just for the moment, I don't know why. But it seems very remote, but he says to me that he does not pass from a health problem. 'Cause he claims now his passing is 'accidental, but beyond.' So . . ."

"Yes, that's true."

"Yeah, he's telling me it's 'accidental, but beyond.' I think the reason he's telling me that is because my brain will have to classify it in something other than an illness, which would be 'accident,' but there's more to it—it's beyond, he says.

Anything affect his head at all? 'Cause something's funny in the head now. Obviously this feeling I'm getting in the chest was something that kind of cut his air off, or might have, or the circumstances in the head might have caused like the oxygen flow to malfunction and so forth. Yet he keeps telling me to tell you that he's all right. 'Cause this is like something that's obviously driving you crazy. You don't hear him saying anything else, and you just want to hear him say that he's all right because of the circumstances of his passing. Yes, definitely there's a, for lack of a better word—there's injury to the head? 'Cause he says to me he passes on from injury to the head."

"Yes."

"And it's a sudden, swift type of injury and passing. He also wants you to know he did not suffer prior to his passing, because he states that, again, you can see the unpleasantness of it and think the worst. And he states that he's not—you're afraid like he kinda died alone?"

(Crying) "No."

"'Cause he says that he doesn't die alone, but I think he means more in the sense that he didn't die alone because there was somebody here to help welcome him over."

"Okay, that's true."

"Is there a female he was close with? Did somebody pass on? Did he lose a female friend at one time or something?"

"Not that we're aware of. We moved from one place to another."

"Oh—he keeps talking about this female friend of his that passed on that's there, and I feel as if I'm going back many years. So, it could have been somebody that he . . . I don't get a name or anything, I just get the feeling . . . and it could have been somebody that he knew in school, something of this nature. He keeps bringing it up. He's not pushing at it, so it may be something that's going to be vague. So I'm just going to have to leave it alone at the moment. Again, there's that feeling of a hit. Is there a hit to his head? But not like somebody's hitting *on* the head, 'cause there's a hit *to* his head."

"That's correct."

"Umm . . . there is a weapon involved?"

"Yes."

"Yeah, 'cause he's saying to me, 'There's a hit to my head,' but he said *not* like somebody's hitting him with a baseball bat. That's what he means by *not*. 'There's a hit to my head,' he says, but not in the way my brain's thinking what it would mean by 'hit.' A hit in another fashion. And he says it's not like somebody hits him on the head with a baseball bat, he says, but there. In a way, he's more or less in the wrong place at the wrong time."

"Yes."

"That's what he states—'I'm kinda.' I keep seeing Curly from the Three Stooges joking with me that he's a victim of circumstance. And that's what your son says and how I can explain it. He's at the wrong place at the wrong time. He's a victim of circumstance. He's kind of caught in somebody else's squabble?"

"I'm not sure I'd put it that way."

"He's caught in somebody else's squabble or problem. That he's really not a part of it, but happened to be there."

"Yes."

"Why is there talk of work—was there work involved? He wasn't working or anything. Okay—he talks of work, and I'm trying to figure out what he means by that. Okay—well, let me drop it, and he'll hopefully explain it to me. I hear gun shots. There is a shot to the head?"

"Yes."

"Yeah, so someone shoots him?"

"No."

"Well, (*speaking to the son*) what do you mean by *someone* then? He's saying that there is a shot to the head. But accidentally?"

"It's difficult to say."

"He says 'accidentally' . . . he keeps saying to me, 'It's an accident and beyond.'"

"That's right."

"Because he says to me, 'It's an accident and beyond,' because it's not a car accident, which is my symbol of an accident for that type of passing, so he says to me, 'It is an accident, but it's beyond that,' so I'm not going to say car accident. But he says, 'There's more to it, though.' It seems too black and white here. But from his point of view, things are not the way they seemed."

"Right. That's exactly right."

"And he's glad for this opportunity, so he can actually reinforce what you felt. There was tension prior to his passing?"

"Yes."

"'Cause I'm getting, if you'll excuse my expression, the *you-know-what* hits the fan?"

"Yes."

"'Cause he says the *you-know-what* hits the fan prior to his passing, that there is extreme tension."

"Yes."

"'Cause he admits being irrational?"

(Crying) "Well, yes and no."

"That's the thing—I'm not saying that he's going on a rampage, but he's not thinking clearly, 'cause he admits he's not in the right frame of mind. He is irrational prior to his passing."

"Yes, I would say so."

"Had some . . . had he been drinking or something . . . doing a drug or something like this? Okay, 'cause there's something in my system that is making me not myself."

"That's true."

"There's some sort of substance in there—drinking, drug or something of this nature—I don't feel, you know I'm not level-headed. Oh, see, this is what confuses me—well I have to say it—he gives me the feeling he takes his own life."

"Yes."

"But he doesn't commit suicide? *(They acknowledge yes.)* That's what he's telling me, because he keeps saying to me, 'Someone shoots me,' but he's not aware of what's happening. That's why I said before, when he said . . . see, he realized he confused me when he said, 'Someone shoots me.' I thought a stranger, somebody else shot him, and he said to me, when you didn't seem to accept this, he said, 'No, no, back off,' and then he waited a minute and he said, 'Well, I'm taking my own life, but I'm not committing suicide.'"

"That's exactly the way it happened. Yes."

"So 'Someone shoots me,' is 'I'm the someone, but I'm not in the right frame. I'm not the same person.'"

"Yes."

"And again, maybe a police report says, 'Well, this guy killed himself.'"

(Crying) "Yes."

"Well, he says, 'I did, but I didn't commit suicide.'"

(Crying) "Absolutely."

"Well, I'm just repeating back how he explains it, and he says that that's the thing, and he's glad to be able to put you at rest, because the thought is still there—well, we feel he didn't kill himself, you know, commit suicide, but did he? And that's why he's glad to say, 'Well, no, I didn't.' That's why he's telling me, 'It's an accident and beyond.' It's an accidental taking of one's life. He's a victim of circumstance."

(Crying) "Oh, absolutely."

"And the someone who shoots him, yes, it is himself—he's the someone, but he's not himself. That's why he's referring to himself as another person."

"That's right. True."

"Because this seems so out of his character."

(Crying) "Of course."

"This is not him."

"That's right."

"This is someone—someone else. You know, if I were a psychiatrist, like Dr. [Raymond] Moody, I'd say, 'Well, this isn't you—I'm not talking to you.' Yes, I'm talking to your son *now*, but at the time of this tragedy, it was somebody else."

"Yes, it was."

"It might sound hokey to a cynic, but I know what he's trying to say—I can feel what he's trying to say—he's not in the right frame of mind. Was he toying—was he kind of kidding around or something? 'Cause I almost feel like I'm playing a game or I'm toying. Well, without telling me . . . ah . . . let him explain it, because it's interesting—he's telling me this is going to be a little complex for *me* to try to understand, because he's saying there's another side to it. That's why he keeps referring to himself as someone or whichever. Because it's not like somebody just comes up and says to you, 'Blank you—I'm going to kill myself.'"

"Right."

"It's not that simple. You know it's very . . . there's more to it than meets the eye. It's an accident and beyond. He's with people when this occurs? 'Cause he talks about being with people, and yet he's aloof. *(They acknowledge yes.)* Because he's telling me he's with people, but he's alone. That's why before you were worried about him passing alone, you said, 'No, he didn't.' He's like, 'Well, yes and no, now.' Technically, he's not alone."

"Right."

"In his mind he is."

"You bet. That's exactly right."

"Someone else—and I'm glad you didn't say anything, because now I'm starting to feel better about it. He's explaining more what he was trying to say where I thought I was kind of missing. I was going in the wrong direction. 'No, no, no, you're in the right direction, but there's more—it's complicated.' The name Kevin doesn't mean anything at all, does it?"

"Yes."

"Passed on?"

"No, I don't think so."

"A friend of his or something?"

"Yes."

(Kevin, his wife and newborn baby visited Theon the day before his death. It was Kevin and his wife who sent a lovely poem, from all of them, on learning about Theon's death.)

"He kept bringing up the name Kevin before, but I kept blocking it trying to get some more of the details from him about the circumstances, but now he's bringing it up again, and he's just calling out to Kevin. Was Kevin with him at the time or . . . ?"

"No."

"They were just good friends, I guess."

"Yes, they were friends. Whether or not they were good friends, I don't know."

"Well, okay, but he keeps calling out to him as a friend, so there must be a reason he's calling out to him. But he just keeps calling out to Kevin for whatever the reason."

"We understand that."

"You've *dreamt* about your son?"

"Yes."

"'Cause he states he has come to you in dreams. He's trying to reach out . . . umm . . . now, not that he's not in a good frame of mind over there, but he says that he's still trying to understand himself, because it was like . . . umm . . . this is what he's trying to explain to me, 'cause he says it's a very complicated situation, and he understands what happened, but he's all right and at peace, but he still is . . . umm . . . trying to reach out, and this has given him the opportunity to explain it. Again he—okay, okay—he states that it's no one's fault."

"Okay."

"You know. He keeps saying this is no one's fault, this is—'I'm at the wrong place at the wrong time,' and he said he's not saying that to be abrupt, but he's saying that to state the fact as it is. Was there some sort of like argument or whichever? 'Cause again I'm feeling that tension prior to it."

"Yes."

"There might have been an exchange of words, or . . ."

"I would say that's true."

"But it seems a solemn exchange of words. I still feel I'm kind of . . . that 'small percentage of me you're not knowing right at the moment,' or something. *(To the son)* Why don't you just come out and tell me everything exactly so I can—I'm getting more confused trying to figure out what he means, but . . . 'cause he certainly claims, like your parents or people that have gone on before him, were certainly there to help welcome him into the Light. Were you afraid you'd failed him?"

"Oh, sure. Sure."

"'Cause he keeps saying, 'You didn't fail me. You didn't fail me.' And he just wants *that* to be understood. He is kinda hard on himself, though?"

(Crying) "Sure he is."

"Yeah, 'cause he admits—he keeps singing from *Oklahoma!*, 'With Me, It's All or Nothing.' You know that he's inclined to be pretty hard on himself."

"Sure. I know that."

"And I think the tension he's referring to now might have been with himself at one point. He has been going through a difficult time?"

"Yes."

"Yeah, he admits he's been going through a tense, frustrated time prior to this happening, so logically, the stage is set for somebody who could take their own life. It could look that way to us, but that's not the case."

"No."

"That's what he's saying to me. That's why you know the police could write this off as, 'Oh well, it's suicide.' Yeah, because the symptoms and the stage are set for that, but that's just simply not the case, he tells me."

"Correct."

"Was he doing something with his weapon?"

"Yes. You mean a . . ."

"Yeah—it's almost like he's cleaning it, toying with it—he's doing something with it prior. Yeah, 'cause he tells me, not that he's playing 'Russian Roulette,' he tells me he's toying with it. Doing something with it prior to this happening."

"That's right."

"Now he speaks of home. Did this happen at home?"

"Yes."

"Yeah, okay. That's good. That figures. Speaking of home, was he—oh, wait a minute—was he *working* with the weapon?"

"No. Probably there was a problem with it. I know that."

"Maybe that's what he means by working with it."

"Yes, because there was something that didn't work right."

"'Cause he's saying about 'toying' with it. You know like somebody trying to fix a clock or something. He claims he's working with it. He's toying with it. It's funny, too, 'cause he tells me he knows what he's doing with it, but he doesn't know what he's doing (*laughs*). You know, it would be like me. I can't change a flat tire, but if I were stuck, I'd have to make an attempt, and I kinda get the feeling he's making an attempt to do something with it. I feel the gun goes off accidentally. There's a feeling of it going off or something. Again, accidentally because I feel he's not in the right frame of mind."

(*Crying*) "Absolutely true."

"Now, would you say—I get the feeling at the time he'd had too much to drink?"

"He had—he had a considerable amount of beer."

"Yeah, because it seems—he is definitely light-headed."

"He's . . ."

"He's definitely not in the right frame of mind only because of that situation."

"That is true."

"Does someone—why, again—somebody else pass on with him?"

"No."

"Around that time or something? He's—"

"No."

"Okay. At this time is he kind of with the wrong people?"

"That was the end of it. That was before."

"Yeah, because he admits he's with the wrong crowd."

"Right."

"So, umm, maybe at the—just prior to his accident. I don't know what he means. He says—all right, all right, as long as you understand—I'm not going to try to get into it deeper when he says to me, 'Look—I'm with the wrong crowd.'"

"Right."

"And again, this is out of character for him."

"Totally."

"Because I keep feeling I'm a fish out of water, and I didn't want to say to him, 'Well, what the hell are you doing there? You know what you are doing with these people. These people are not like you.' It would be like me walking into one of these red-neck bars down here—I mean, what the hell am I doing there, you know? Yeah, because he—I keep . . . it's funny . . . I keep pointing at the place, I always tease everybody about it when we're down here. 'Oh, let's go there for a drink,' whatever, and they stop me, 'cause it's a real red-neck place. It's like he's saying to me, 'Yeah, it would be like if I walked into there, I don't belong there any more than you would.' (*pause*) So, technically, he has been in a social-type atmosphere prior to this happening? There are people around him, though."

"Yes."

"Okay—that's what they mean by a 'social-type atmosphere,' that they're out with people like in this respect. Had he distanced himself from you?"

"No. Just the reverse."

"Because he—"

"In the past?"

"No, he keeps apologizing—"

"... Well ..."

"—for distancing himself. It's almost as if—because he says to you, 'I forgive and hope you do, because ...'"

(*In tears*) "Instantly."

"He's telling me that he—umm ... what's the word I'm looking for? Oh, yeah, right—he's telling me, 'It takes two to tango.'"

(*In tears*) "He really does forgive us?"

(*Long pause*) "Yeah, he knows—he knows you are in a very delicate frame of mind, so he's trying to be very careful how he expresses himself—but was there a point when he felt banished?"

"It could have happened. (*crying*) Oh, yeah—"

"Yeah—he admits, again he's not blaming, so don't, 'cause he knows the two of you, you're going to read into everything he says, but he says that he felt banished by you at one point."

(*Crying*) "Sure, I can see that."

"And he says he's saying it only to clue *me* into the situation, not to rub salt into a wound. (*pause*) You kinda didn't like his independence?"

"No, I don't think so."

"'Cause he feels like maybe that you didn't like his independence or the direction he was taking, or something like this. But there was some sort of falling out?"

"It's difficult to say—"

"'Cause he's telling me there's tension and there's a falling out, but I'm not saying you're not speaking to each other."

"Yeah, that's true. There were differences—no doubt about it."

"There's tension there definitely. 'Cause he keeps telling me there's tension prior to this. (*The parents believe he is referring to the incident where Theon tried to stop the man who was drunk, trying the doors on the neighborhood cars, prior to his death.)* And it just so happened that this occurred during the highlight of that tension. So it kind of makes things look worse. *(pause)* He keeps telling me that I have to take this slow, because he tells me that it's very complicated, because my brain is going to jump at trying to just find an easy, simple explanation, hand it to you and move on, but he says, 'There's a lot more—again, it's beyond,' there's a lot more here. But the one thing he keeps telling me to tell you is that you have to relieve yourselves and forgive yourselves for thinking, 'Did we play a role in his killing himself, but not taking his own life, but not committing suicide?' and he says you have to let go of that. He just doesn't want you to feel that. He felt at one point—yes, he's being honest—he felt at one point kind of banished, but he doesn't want you to feel that you abandoned him."

"Right."

"And it's very important, because he didn't have a chance before he passed on to iron out the wrinkles, and you certainly have not had the opportunity since this occurred. You have other children?"

"No."

"Did you lose another child or something?"

"No. We talked about that before we came here that there was one time before I became pregnant with him, which was four years before that, but I was late with my period for three weeks—"

"I wonder if you would have had a girl, because he keeps talking about a sister, and when you said no, I was expecting you to say yes, you had another child and obviously you have a daughter. And when you said no, he claims having a sister, so maybe at one point, had the cycle of birth continued, you would have had a girl. Because he keeps talking again about a female being close to him there. There's a vagueness with it and yet a feeling of familiarity, so I'm going to say that you probably would have had a daughter at one point. So I take it he's your only child—only son—which, of course, hits home even worse. *(To Erin)* Your mother been over there for a while?"

"Yes."

"Yeah, because it seems you're almost praying to her that she'll be there for him and help him out or something, and she says that she has been—that the two of them are very close over there—it's like they've become good friends. Your son— he didn't have any health troubles or something, did he?"

"No."

"No? Okay—because I get that little feeling again in the chest. But I think that what I'm feeling is when this occurs—the accident—I'm getting the air cut off. *(pause)* It's obvious that you do pray for him because he thanks you for prayer and asks that it please continue. Ahh—he passes as a young adult, yes? Because I feel like I'm talking to somebody who is a young adult. There is also a pet that passed on?"

"Yes."

"A dog."

"No."

"No, wait. Well, he just says a pet. He didn't say what kind and I jumped at that. All right, let me go with what he said for the moment. He said, 'The pet that passed on is here with me,' so apparently it's there. Did it pass before him?"

"Yes."

"Yes, 'cause he says actually the pet welcomes him over first, because it's something he knows, something he trusts, something he loves, knows loves him—there's a sense of safety and a comfort level with it—so he says the pet welcomes him over first. He admits he was kind of heartbroken when the pet passed on."

"Yes."

"So, this is something he would have trusted and would have followed into the Light thinking, 'Okay, everything's all right.' Because there was this momentary—like when this tragedy occurred—there was like, 'What happened? Where am I? I'm in this, you know, dark vortex—what's going on?' And then he goes toward the Light, and then the animal comes forward, then he realizes, 'Well, I must have passed on if I'm here,' and he followed it, where it crossed him over, so to speak. Yes, he keeps showing me a huge knot in front of you, which means that obviously this has caused quite a knot in your lives. Funny—I guess I shouldn't press the issue, but I can—you know, it's like I'm up at bat, but I haven't hit the home run yet. And I keep saying to him, 'C'mon you know, let me hit the home run now,' because I feel there's something more to be told and yet, you know, it has to work the way he wants it to work, and I'm like, 'C'mon, a little bit more here. I'd like to get into it if I may.' *(To Daniel)* Also, your dad feels he could have been closer to you. Is that true?"

"I think we could have."

"Yeah—it's not that you hate each other by any means—he just feels that you could have been closer to each other, and he just wants to let you know that he always loved you, even if it wasn't shown or expressed in the way that it normally would be. He does call out to your mom, and he also expresses your mother having trouble with her walking. He keeps telling—I mean, I'm not telling you anything you don't already know, but she has to watch where she's walking. It's obviously something she has to live with, and he tells her to be concerned about it. *(pause)* Did someone leave this weapon available?"

"Yes."

"He keeps talking about the weapon being available. And would it be a hand-gun?"

"Yes."

"Because it looks like I can hold it, so I'm going to assume it's not a rifle—it's a handgun. It's funny—it's like he had it—you didn't know about it?"

"Yes and no."

"Yeah, because, again, it's like he has it, but I don't know he has it, but I do know he has it. He keeps telling me that this session is going to kind of like dichotomize me, it's not—'Things are not what they seem,' he tells me. *(pause)* The name Dan or Daniel mean anything at all?"

(Daniel) "That's me."

"Anyone passed on with that name?"

"No."

"I keep hearing your son calling out 'Dan, Daniel' so then he is obviously calling out to you by name. But the thing is, he keeps calling out to you by name because as much as you're both brokenhearted, he knows as a father, you kind of suffer more in silence, so he singularizes you more, so you might be tormenting yourself more inside, because men don't come out with the emotion as easily, or because he knows you are a sensitive man but unfortunately you may not know how to express it. Men, unfortunately, unlike women, really cannot express their emotions as well as they'd like, so he just singularizes you, knowing that you're having a rough time with this. Yes, it's funny, it's like you know he has it *(referring back to the weapon)* but you don't want him to have it. Yet it's still there—there's something peculiar with it."

"Yes."

"Were you concerned that you were not paying enough attention to him?"

"No, I would say just the opposite."

"I don't feel that's the case either. He—that's what I'm feeling from him—he doesn't want you to think that you weren't paying enough attention to him, that's what I'm driving at. The name Stan doesn't mean anything at all, does it?"

"Maybe it's Stan Wollinski."

"Living, though?"

"I don't know. I would assume so."

"It seems like he's calling out. Was he [Theon] also having distance with friends?"

"Distancing himself?"

"Yes."

"Yes."

"He admits having distance with friends—I feel that I'm a—I keep seeing scenes out of the novel *Great Expectations*, like he's becoming a little reclusive."

"Yes, that's true."

"He keeps telling me that he is drawing back—he's kind of going to the opposite of what you normally know him to be."

"Yes."

"He's telling me again, he's a dichotomy, he's very extroverted and yet now he's starting to close in, and he says to me, even now while he's speaking to me, he's not doing this deliberately—but still maintains this, showing that example, so that I can understand that this is somebody who's gone from kind of one extreme to another. It seems like his life is starting to change radically, also."

"Yes, it does."

"And he was coming in touch with himself?"

"Absolutely. That's true."

"And it was kind of freaking him out, *not him*, as much as people around him?"

"Ah—the people that knew him, perhaps."

"He says that it's starting to freak him out, only because maybe the people that know him maybe are not knowing how to handle it or deal with it. He does feel a sense of abandonment from friends, to a degree. He realizes now that it probably was not as important as he might have made it at the time."

"That's probably true."

"But at the time it seemed important, you know. But the key here is, he's coming in touch with *himself*—he keeps bringing that up."

"Uh-huh. No question of that."

"Which you didn't care about? I mean, not that you didn't care, but it's almost like he was his own worst enemy about it. I wish he would just get to the heart of it, so I could make all this other stuff fit because he's giving me pieces here and there and . . ."

"I understand what he's saying."

"See, that's the thing. If they know that you understand what they're saying, they feel comfortable with that to a degree, but I'm kind of *not* comfortable with it. I wish he would just come right out and explain to me what he means to say so that it will all fall into place, like pieces in a puzzle coming together. He jokes in a way like he's going through what I would call a mid-life crisis."

"That's it! You've said it."

"He says to me, 'This is a mid-life crisis I'm going through,' even though he was far from mid-life. But see, that's the thing—he kills himself but doesn't commit suicide."

"That's right. You got it. That's exactly right. Couldn't get it any better than that."

"But I'm saying to myself, 'How the hell could you shoot yourself in the head—' but again he states it's an accident."

"It is! It is, George."

"You understand what he means exactly?"

"Yes."

"All right, okay. Now, he's shot with bullets, yes?"

"Yes."

"Because he says it's a legitimate gunshot. He held it the wrong way?"

"No, I don't think so."

"Was he not holding it?"

"Yes, he was holding it."

"Yes, he says to me that he was holding it, but again he's toying with the— idea, maybe. He keeps saying that he's toying with it. Was there only like one bullet in the chamber, something like that?"

"More than one. Okay."

"But why does he tell me that there's only one? Do you understand what he means?"

"I do."

"All right, as long as you understand. He said to me there's *one*. I said, 'Oh that means there's one bullet in the chamber.' That's how I put it together, but when you said no, he said to me again, 'I said there's *one*.'"

"Right."

"It has to do with his passing?"

"Yes."

"Yes, 'cause he said to me there's one. It has to do with his passing. He should know by now I've ground my heels in, because you've got to tell—I mean you can't sidestep this—you've got to tell me what. I don't mean you, I mean him. Now, okay—now he is holding the weapon, yes? Yes, 'cause he says he's holding the weapon, and there's *one*."

"Maybe there is only one—I thought . . . What we had said earlier in the evening—maybe there is only one."

"Ah, all right."

"It may well be, George, that there is only one."

(To Theon) "You're holding the weapon. He admits he does hold it to his head."

"Yes."

"Yes, he says he does. He says he pulls the trigger."

"Right."

"Okay. *(To Theon)* You said you pulled the trigger—but he says, 'I'm not committing suicide.'"

"Right."

"I don't know. Was there something about the angle?"

"No. It was straight."

"Because I feel it's like right to the head."

"It was."

"And he's the 'someone' pulling the trigger. But he still insists, and once he insists on something, he insists—"

"Right."

"—he does not commit suicide."

"That's right."

"There is also something with, ah—yeah, he admits having a lot of struggle with himself, correct?"

"Correct."

"He keeps admitting that that's correct. He's having to struggle with himself, and I feel you knew about it. He talked about it. He opened up, he talked about it."

"Every day."

"But he said he was going through a lot of inner struggle."

"Yes."

"In a lot of ways, I'm getting the feeling he was kind of his own worst enemy, you know, in some respects. Do you understand why he says he kills himself but doesn't commit suicide?"

"Yes, we both do."

" I wish he'd tell me! . . . so I'd understand. Yes, some friends might have tired—he could have grown out of them, or they faded out of his life or something . . ."

"Oh, definitely."

"He talks about friends, kind of cutting him off or—"

"Maybe the reverse."

"Yeah, because he feels like, well, maybe he felt it both ways, not only them cutting him off, but him cutting them off as well. He admits he was kind of going into his own world, in a lot of ways. I keep seeing a bear hibernating. He's kind of becoming reclusive again."

"Right."

"Obviously he was staying home more."

"Yes."

"He admits staying at home more. Was he in school?"

"No."

"Was he thinking of going? He keeps talking about being in school—maybe he's also telling me that he is [over there] but it was something he was considering doing."

"Absolutely right."

"Okay. Anything to do with a uniform with him?"

"Yes."

"Would he have worn one?"

"No."

"Why do I keep feeling him around you in uniform? Does that make sense?"

"Yes."

"As long as it makes sense, because it feels to me like he's in uniform. But I'm going to have to leave it for the moment."

"Okay."

"Also the name Tad doesn't mean anything at all, does it?"

"Close. (laughing) Oh, yes, very close."

"To his name?"

"To—"

"Well, somebody passed on, though?"

"Yes."

"Sounds like somebody over there is telling me that they're like Lincoln's son, their name was Tad, but that's what it sounds like to me."

"Well, it's a—"

"But does it have to do with his name?"

"Yes—well, no, not really."

"Okay, but someone passed on, though?"

"My brother."

"Because then he knows—'cause he keeps talking about Thad or Tad."

"That's it."

"Your brother's name is Thad?"

"Yes."

"T-H-A-D?"

"Yes."

"Oh, 'cause I said to myself, 'I've never heard that name before.' So, obviously your son is telling me that Thad is with him, and your brother is calling out. That he's present. Yes, your son hands both of you white roses (*symbolically*) and says, 'I forgive, and hope you do, too.'"

"Thank you."

"Did he feel rejected?"

"No. Never."

"Because he was never rejected, but—"

"He may have felt it. I don't know."

"Yeah, because I wondered if he might have felt it nominally or something."

"Without our knowing it—at that moment?"

"Possibly, or something, because I get the feeling again, I know him 95 percent, but there's that 5 percent that's still left that he's keeping to himself. It's making things complex. Did he leave a note or something—was he writing or anything?"

"He was writing all the time."

"Oh, okay, because I keep seeing writing in front of me, and I thought—that's why I asked if he left a note. He jumped at me and said, 'I told you I didn't commit suicide.' I said, 'Oh, all right, all right,' so he said, 'But the writing is correct.'"

"Right."

"And I'm seeing writing in front of me, but it's not like I'm leaving notes. So, obviously he was doing a great deal of writing. I see colors around him. Obviously he was creative."

"Yes."

"And up ahead—ah, he tells me that over there, he still writes."

"Oh, that's good."

"And he's still going on with his life in that type of sense. He says it's easier there, because you're accepted by your value—not like here, where you have to spend time in school for a hundred and fifty years or whatever. So he feels—in his heart he seems to be a pretty spiritual person in his own way, and he says not that he's begrudging this existence on the earth, but he says he feels more at home there. You know, he just—I keep hearing that song on the radio years ago about Vincent van Gogh, that he really wasn't suited for this world, and he says that it's no one's fault about his being unhappy or anything—he just admits that he really didn't like it here too much. (*They agree.*) So, he just wants you to know that he's much happier there and that he's doing all right. He just keeps saying that he's sorry that this happened. It's 'all confusing,' he tells me. It happens at the wrong place, wrong time—that he's a victim of circumstance—it's just, 'It's all messed up,' he says—it's all botched up, and that's why from what he has said to you, even if he hasn't given me the exact details, he wants you to listen to exactly what he has said and try to let most of it go. But, he definitely again states that when this tragedy occurs, he's really not in the right frame of mind."

"I agree. Absolutely."

"He's not in the right . . . it's almost—and I'm not saying this is how it happened—but it's almost like somebody's had a nervous breakdown and doesn't know it. You know, but I'm saying that as an example, he was emotional to a degree but, within, more so."

"Right."

"He's, ah, joking with me that he's like me. He's a little on the eccentric side."

(*Laughing*) "Right."

(*Laughing*) "Thanks! But he's saying that he's eccentric—maybe even a little neurotic—but that's the artistic or creative side of him coming out. And people who are creative are inclined to be very temperamental or—was he writing stories or something? Yes, I keep seeing plays, novels, stories. He was certainly getting—but that was another reason he was becoming a little reclusive. He was getting very much into what he wanted to do."

"Right."

"He had focus, concentration, the whole works. Also there's a John?"

"John? I don't know."

"Anybody passed on though?"

"I don't know, he had a friend that may have."

"'Cause he talks about meeting John over there, and I mean—"

"Oh, John Kalienkov, too."

"'Cause he's an older man. Could be like it's almost like he refers to him being an uncle-type figure."

"That's right."

"Because your son keeps saying, 'John is here with me.' I guess he felt my frustration in saying, 'Well everybody knows a "John" passed on,' and he said, 'Well, it's, like he's not family, but he's an uncle-type figure,' and that he just says that John is there with him also. There's also an Al or Alex?"

"I hope Alex is not passed on."

"Well, your son is calling to Alex or Alexander—something like this—so he may be calling out to somebody by that name that is present [on the earth]. Did anything bother your son's throat?"

"No."

"I forgot—it was the losing of the air. I just felt the sensation again of something wrong there. Maybe this could be the initial feeling of it. Yeah, he was finding life a struggle, yes?"

"That's right."

"Yes, because he admits again the stage is set for somebody, you know, but he admits he was finding life a struggle here, and he seems sensitive enough to speak about it to a degree that's coming out [here]."

"Right."

"Was he also having sexual struggle with himself?"

"Frustration."

"He admits some sort of sexual struggle within himself, could have been sexual frustration—something—he feels very kind of repressed or something."

"I think that's true."

"And he says it's something, I mean not that you have to be a sex maniac, but it's something like when you're not getting enough to eat, there's a sense of, you know, a level that in our bodies, I guess, has to be appeased, or such, so he said he was going through a lot of sexual struggle, or frustration, as well."

"That's absolutely true."

"It's almost as if in a lot of ways he was diagnosing himself. (*They acknowledge.*) You know, starting to, I guess, like 'dissecting myself. I'm trying to pull myself apart.'"

"He's figured it all out. Yes, he told us that."

"He admits that *there* he's doing his writing, and he certainly has no sense of struggle, but he's still learning to understand himself. But things are clearer there, where here, again, we are faced with obstacles that we need to surmount, but *there* he's starting to find things balancing out for him more, because he's seeing things clearer. He also admits that he's kind of giving himself a break."

"Good."

"You know—where, here—he really wasn't, well, giving himself a break. Too much fear is coming into his life, because that's the key—that's actually what is the cause of his death."

"Yes."

"It's more fear, because it's said that, as I was taught as a Catholic, pride was the worst of the seven capitol sins. Fear is the worst of the negative vibrations—from that stems all the other negativity."

"Right."

"And he says he was wrapped up with fear to the point where he was 'afraid of being afraid.' So fear certainly played a great role in hindering—'cause it's funny—just as he said that word, he showed me a key and unlocked the door, and he said, 'That's what I'm trying to say—that fear wraps it all up as to what had occurred.' Was he becoming afraid of people?"

"No—well, he did say . . ."

"I'm not saying that he's . . . you know, not so friendly. I'm wondering, because I see him in a clown costume—it's like he might have smiled on the outside but was a little afraid on the inside. But I think that his friendliness is almost—like in my case, I'm very shy, but my friendliness will be my defense mechanism to cover up the shyness. I'm seeing a lot of how *I* feel in him also. Had he been getting a little paranoid? (*They acknowledge yes.*) He admits that he's afraid that somebody is trying to do harm to him."

"Oh, yes."

"See, now I'm starting to understand a little more, now that he's getting more into the emotional—he's kind of giving himself a *head trip*, and he was starting to, you know—was he on any medication? No? Okay, because I didn't think so, because he said to me before that he was getting very nervous—he was inclined to be getting a little paranoid."

"Yes. All of it is true."

"Again, these are all offshoots of fear. The fear is doing a number on him, and that's what I think now I understand what he means when he states, 'Someone else kills me,' because the 'someone else' is fear. Why, again, even though he takes his own life, is there something different about it?"

"Oh, there is, there is something different about it."

(*Sighs*) "This is what's driving me crazy. He keeps bringing it up, but he's not coming out to me and saying—like he just came out and told me about the fear. (*To Theon*) Now come out and tell me what it is. This is why I know it is not a suicide."

"Right."

"This other element of this 'taking of my own life.' Are you thinking of moving?"

"Yes."

"He just wants to let you know it's all right. It's like you don't—you feel if you move you're leaving behind. Or you're kind of 'terminating off' on him, and he says, 'No,' because there's also too much memory there. You might need a change of scenery."

"We've moved from the last place."

"Oh, okay. You're thinking of moving again?"

"Well, we were wondering."

"Oh. It's okay, because he talks about you changing residences. He just wants to let you know it's all right. But he says never to feel that if you move that you're leaving him behind."

"I believe that."

"You know that spiritually he's always with you, and that he is all right. He's home alone when this occurs?"

"No."

"But why is there the feeling of being alone—does it make sense?"

"Yes."

"He's telling me he is alone, so I assumed, Oh, he's *alone* at home. When you said no, he said, 'No, I'm home alone, but not the way you're thinking "home alone,"' because he tells me that he does *feel* alone. He's kind of closed himself in?"

"No—well, no. He had been . . ."

"Emotionally? Because again there's this feeling of somebody struggling here emotionally to a very strong degree."

"Oh, definitely."

"And I feel—was he getting some sort of professional help?"

"No, but he had—what can I say to you? He had gone beyond, he had examined himself and told us all—what you have just told us. It was actually like he was coming out of the darkness."

"Yeah, because he's telling me that he's—"

"He's leaving all of this awful stuff that he had been in behind, that he did it himself. He got it all out and was putting it all back together—"

"He admits going through the best of times and the worst of times."

"Oh, absolutely, definitely."

"But there's this incredible struggle within him, and yet his death is still an accident."

"Oh, God yes—absolutely true."

"But again, that's why he says that the stage is set, because he's going through this terrible struggle at times so you could think, 'Oh, this guy's emotionally unbalanced.' Then, all of a sudden, he's fine, or he's starting to work things out, and I keep hearing somebody saying, 'Surprise,' so apparently this comes as a surprise to him as much as it did to you all."

"Exactly."

"Without telling me, your son has a short name?"

"Yes."

"Okay, because when they have a short first name, they mean less than eight letters. Less than seven, too? Yeah, because he keeps telling me to drop. I've heard the name before?"

"No, I don't think so."

"It's not common."

"No."

"Hmm. It's a foreign-sounding name? Because he tells me I'm going to think I'm hearing a foreign language."

"Yes."

"Would it be a Slavic name or like this—"

"Close, but no—"

"I'm trying to think. I'm trying to think of a Slavic language, like German Slavic. All right, let's leave it go for the moment, okay. But it's a famous name?"

"Yes."

"He says that's a clue, that it's a famous name. It may be a clue to him, but it's not a big help for me. Now he goes to six and stops. It's less than six letters?"

"Yes."

"Because he goes to six and stops, and he says, 'Go down.' So there are less than six letters. The name can be translated into English?"

"Yes."

"Because he's telling me if I try to translate it, maybe then I'll think this is what it would be—"

"There's nothing—there isn't a name—"

"Oh, okay. Does his name have to do with colors?"

"No."

"Why is he showing me colors? Well, I don't know what it means, unless it's a very colorful name."

"It *is* colorful."

LESSONS FROM THE LIGHT

"Oh, I was going to say, unless it means that it's a colorful name by the way it sounds. It's funny—it's almost like your brother's name, Thad."

"Right. That's correct."

"Does that mean it has four letters?"

"No."

"Does it have five?"

"Yes."

"Okay, because he says to me that it's like your brother's name, Thad."

"He's right. He's absolutely right, but it's not."

"It's not Thad."

"Right, but—"

"But it's obviously five letters."

"Right, but there's no argument there are similarities."

"Is there an 'A' in his name?"

"No."

"I'm trying to figure out why he keeps telling me to think on 'Thad.'"

(Actually the a represented an "ah" sound that stood for "eon.")

"And it's unusual, very unusual—"

"Yeah, that's what I'm saying—if I can get Thad through—I never heard that name before in my life. If he would have said Thaddeus, I'd have said, 'Oh, I've heard that before,' but he's telling me now—I'm saying to myself, 'How can I draw a name through who is Thad, which I've never heard before, but I can't get yours through?'"

"Right."

"At the end, was he afraid somebody was after him or something? He keeps telling me about being frightened and paranoid, that somebody—it's almost as if he doesn't kill himself, that they will kill him."

"Yes. It's possible in this case."

"That's why he says again, 'Someone killed me.'"

"That's right."

"He pulls the trigger, but somebody's indirectly making him pull it, the trigger."

"That's exactly right."

"That could be all the emotion and the tension—it's like he's afraid somebody is coming to get him."

"Yes, that's exactly right."

"That could be why he says, 'I'm killing myself, but yet, it's not a suicide.'"

"Yes."

"Someone is threatening him? (*They acknowledge yes.*) Yeah, because definitely I feel threatened. And maybe now I think the key I'm looking for was his saying, 'It's a suicide—it's the taking of one's life—but it's not a suicide.'"

"Right."

"He admits to me that he's definitely afraid that somebody's going to try to get him and if they do, they mean business."

"That's right. Absolutely right."

"He admits that this person had tremendous capacity to get him, and yes, they would murder him."

"Absolutely. That's right."

"Because, even before, in the beginning, he started telling me he was murdered."

"That's what we feel."

"That's why I say to you, umm, that he takes his own life, but he doesn't kill himself, and he started saying to me, 'Someone kills me,' and starts saying he was murdered. And then I said—I can't remember what I said—but from what you answered me, I thought to myself, 'No, no, no, that can't be possible.' But, to explain it better, it's almost like somebody put him up to killing himself."

"We never thought of that, either one of us, but it's possible."

"Because, again, he's murdered but not by somebody else. But yes, by somebody else. Was he in some sort of legal upset or something?"

"Possibly."

"He admits that there's some sort of—he shows me scales of justice."

"That's exactly right."

"There must have been something sort of legal going on around him where somebody hit on him or something, or he felt there could be a hit on him and this was from this wrong crowd."

"Yes. There's a connection."

"There's a connection with this wrong crowd, he tells me. I keep seeing him going into deep water. He might have gotten in too deep. But he's a little on the naive side. He doesn't realize how deep he's gotten himself into this. And somebody's afraid he knows too much, or knows something, but he really doesn't. But for a period of time, he was genuinely frightened. Somebody's got him spooked where he's staying in. And it's almost like he's a self-inflicted prisoner because of this, again, concern of somebody getting him. Had he been threatened, though, yes?"

"Yes, but it's specific to a time."

"In the past? Because he admits being threatened."

"Right."

"Okay, so he had been threatened, so obviously somebody threatened him that night."

"Yes."

"Because he tells me he'd been threatened. Again, tension prior to this happening."

"Yes, that's all true—all correct."

"Now, wait. Is he at home, not with you all?"

"Yes, he's at home with us."

"He's telling me he's home again, so I just want to make sure he doesn't mean his own home. So he was at home with you all but—this happens at night?"

"Yes."

"Okay, but at an off hour. He certainly tells me that it happens when it's dark, or something, you know—in the late night or—could someone have gotten to him at night? I wonder if I mean more figuratively and not literally?"

"Oh, definitely."

"I feel someone gets to me that night, but I'm not saying they're in the room. There was a communication, telephone call—something like that? He keeps telling me that there's this communication prior to this tragedy. And I don't know if it's by phone message, or how, but some sort of ultimate communication, which puts him over the edge almost."

"Right."

"It's almost like somebody's found me—"

"Maybe—correct—but it's the circumstances."

"Yes, because it's a feeling that the paranoia's there again that somebody has finally caught up with me—whatever—and it's from the past, he says."

"That's the strange thing that happened."

"It's from the past, but it's an innocent involvement in his past. I mean—I'm not talking to a dope—but he's kind of naive."

"Very naive."

"But it seems like the fear just built up on everything. Like he was constantly afraid or depressed, whichever."

"There's the key."

"I mean not that he's blaming anybody—he still did this—but the point of the matter is there's still a *someone* involved. Even if it's indirect involvement."

"Oh, absolutely."

"Was he feeling frightened of you all or something?"

"No, not of us."

"But somebody else, like family? Or whichever—just a friend or something?"

"At that moment in time?"

"Yes. He says he's feeling frightened."

"He was. He was frightened out of his wits."

"Was he also worried about his health?"

"No."

"Well, he might have been, if you know, out of emotionally—"

"Well, he was in that moment. Are you talking about now in general?"

"That, yes, but more so at the time of his passing."

"That was sheer terror."

"Yeah, that's what I mean—the health—what he's worried about could be emotional."

"No, no."

"He feels that somebody was coming to him."

"Oh, yes."

"He keeps bringing up that at the time that he kills himself, he feels someone's coming to get him, and figures that this is the only way out."

"That's exactly right."

"This is a living person he feels is coming for him?"

"Yes."

"I mean, of this world?"

"Oh, yes."

"That's why he says, it's somebody he feels is coming for him and that communication that night convinced him that this person was going to come for him or they were going to get him or something."

"We didn't know that until after the fact."

"But does somebody literally come for him?"

"Yes."

"He says somebody is coming for him, I imagine that—they came in that early morning hour, that night or something, into the house?"

"Yes."

"So your home is invaded by a physical person?"

"Yes."

"He feels that they kind of caught up with him?"

"Yes."

"And obviously they were going to kill him."

"We don't know."

"He feels they were certainly going to kill him or do some sort of harm."

"That's right."

"He felt they were either going to kill him or do some harm, so, obviously, they had gotten into his room or his living quarters—I guess that they'd gotten in. It's almost like I'm not sleeping that night, or I'm definitely uptight and maybe I've been drinking to relax myself. So you're there, yes? But your home is invaded. He keeps telling me it's like you were there, and the home is invaded. Is this person approaching him? Or is he feeling that—because I feel like I'm doing it just—"

"They were there."

"It's like, you know, in the story *The Last of the Mohicans*, I can't remember the character's name—where she jumps off a cliff, because they're running after her. It's like 'I'm either at their mercy or I have to kill myself,' one or the other."

"That's right, that's it exactly."

"He's using that scene in the book as an example where I think—umm—I can't remember the one Indian's name, but he kills Humpkus—I remember—and then she jumps off the cliff because he's coming for her next, and she has no idea what is going to come. This is why he said he was so afraid."

"That's a good example, yes."

"It's out of this fear that 'They're coming for me, they're going to get me,' that he shoots himself. Were there legal upsets?"

"Yes."

"He keeps telling me there were legal upsets."

"You're very close to what happened before."

"Was he in some sort of trouble? Not unlike they're coming to take him to go to jail?"

"Yes, bingo."

"Yes—oh, that's what it is—because he keeps telling me that he is in trouble, but—"

"Right, but not really—"

"Yes, exactly, but he's not in trouble. Then I saw bars go up in front of me, and then I said—but did he think that somebody was going to take him to jail?"

"That's exactly what he thought."

"'Cause it doesn't seem like he would have been going to jail. He keeps telling me *now* he realizes he would *not have been*—but he was convinced they had him."

"Yes."

"But it is with legal officials coming for him?"

"Yes."

"That's the thing—it's somebody in uniform—that's why he's showing me the uniform. Okay. It just dawned on me now that that's why he showed me the uniform [earlier in the discernment]. And even though *he's* not in uniform, somebody coming to him is in uniform—obviously police or something. Were they accusing him of some sort of illegal stuff, which I don't feel he was involved with?"

"Right."

"He's telling me he is the—(*to Theon*) ah, thank you, you've taken the words out of my mouth—he's the victim, but he's not doing anything."

"That's right, that's exactly right."

"He's actually kind of embarrassed by it. Not only terrified by it, but embarrassed by it, because now he's coming out with it. He's telling me that before he almost couldn't tell me because he was embarrassed. He felt kind of ashamed. They were pointing a finger at him about a serious crime?"

"Yes."

"But he was not involved in these things and that is a fact now."

"Yes."

"And he felt there was no way he could get out of it."

"That's right, exactly."

"Was he under murder suspicion or something?"

"No."

"But something serious enough in any case? Yeah, okay. The thing is probably, again, he must feel, when he first got over there, that he might have felt in a sense that he was forced by someone to murder himself or something like this. Was there—was money involved?"

"No." (*Actually, yes, since the person breaking into the cars did so to steal, apparently for money.*)

"Oh—it seems like there was some talk of finance, or money involved— maybe there was at some point, but he just feels he has no alibi to defend himself or to prove he's not involved, and he just panics over it. That's what he must mean when he says he's toying with it, because he doesn't know if he is going to do this or not, to get out of the situation. And he's in a terrible state of panic, he states."

(*The police officer kept saying to Theon, "This is a felony, you're going to jail," over and over. Theon was not the criminal or doing anything wrong; he was the observer of the criminal acts of another person, who was drunk, trying to break into and rob the cars.)*

"That's true."

"And this is why—now, is that the key as to why this is not a suicide?"

"Exactly that."

"And that's why he says that you know this is the key I'm looking for, he tells me, because he knows why he's not taking his own life—"

"You already said it. He's going to jail."

"Yeah—it's like he's trying to keep himself out of the situation. I mean, he knew he was innocent here, but *they* didn't know. It's kind of the case where he felt they would not believe him, they didn't know; so it's like causing him to have almost like a nervous breakdown, you know, where he's losing, in himself, a sense of control."

"You mean at the moment, George. Is that what you're saying?"

"Yes—possibly at that moment he just—or beforehand—it's like things are building up—"

"It's like—all fear, I think."

"That's what I mean. It's something that's building up, he tells me, and so it could have been something from the past that's building up where—"

"When you say there's something from the past, you are right—there is something—"

"Yes, 'cause it's there. They were trying to link him with something in the past again?"

"No."

"There had been a problem in the past as such?"

"Yes."

"Maybe that's why he was afraid of a repeat of something of this nature."

"Oh, I know what you're talking about."

"Also, I keep hearing the name Erin."

(Erin) "That's me."

"Oh—he must be calling out to you then—good. He's calling out. Your name is Dan, you said? *(Daniel acknowledges.)* He keeps calling out, "Dan," he keeps calling out, "Erin," so obviously he's calling out to the both of you. Just there, he says he feels safe—you know he knows no harm will ever come to him again. There, he's safe. No one can do to him there what they were going to do to him here, or what he was afraid they were going to do to him here. He's kind of a 'no nonsense' person? You know, and he admits, yeah, he could have stayed here and worked out the situation, but it's like he didn't want to go through this again. He just feels he's totally at someone else's mercy. He is, but he isn't. But at the time there's so much on his mind, it's so much harder for him that he's not thinking rationally."

"Exactly."

"But as he states, he just wants you all to know, of course, that you didn't fail him in any way. So, he admits he makes this decision out of fear, and he's not blaming you, but, "*They* are the cause of my fear.""

"That's right. True."

"So someone actually does pull the trigger other than himself. The name Charlie mean anything at all?"

"We don't know."

"Your son keeps saying, 'Charlie is here with me now.' And just coming in and saying hello—whether it's friend or family he keeps stating that he's present. He keeps saying that 'Charlie is here with me.' Did either of you lose a sister?"

(*Erin*) "I did."

"He keeps saying your sister is here also. He keeps talking about your brother being there—that's Thad—and then he says there's also been a loss of a sister, but said not the one I spoke of before, so I figured one of you must have lost a sister— she is there with him as well. So there are a lot of people there definitely that are trying to 'be there' for him, like to help him out and help him to deal with what he's been going through. But he feels safe, he says. It's like his paranoia has left him, where he feels, 'I've gone to a place where now no harm can come to me and no one's going to come for me and bother me.' He just didn't feel safe here any- more. He was just so . . . he dies from *fear*. He's just so frightened that he just doesn't know any way out. And he'd started to feel too many people were out to get him you know—again, as he says, fear can be like anything that starts to snow- ball and it gets bigger and bigger, and though it might not be as big as you think, it looks bad. But that's why he's glad to be able to tell you that he definitely is all right and that the fear has left him. That he is all right, that he's not frightened anymore. He wasn't too keen on authority? (*They agree.*) Can't say that I blame him. Because, again, when he brought up the uniform before, I felt a chill within myself, and I didn't know what he meant, but apparently he was afraid of author- ities, uniforms, police, you know, agents—anything like this. Had he been in trou- ble before?"

"Yes."

"He admits there was trouble before, and he had a run-in with them where they'd left a very bad taste in his mouth."

"Exactly."

"And now when there's further trouble coming and it seems worse, 'I'm not going to go through this again.' So he just feels that—yes—he felt that in a way *they* were slowly murdering him because they wouldn't leave him alone. They were always going to be on his back about something. And he seems to have closed into himself, you know, became reclusive, because he doesn't know what other way to go with this constant fear and so forth. Not that he has a record, but I guess it's like someone who has a record where everything is okay, but if something happens, like a crime in the neighborhood, the finger would point at him, like he might have something to do with it. But something *had* happened?"

"Yes."

"He says that something had happened, and he was afraid they were going to come for him again. Did he have trouble with drink? Yes and no?"

"Well, I think that's right."

"But he's not an alcoholic."

"He drank to excess for him. But that was also changing."

"Yeah, and he might have been 'nailed' [arrested in the past because of it]. Did he have a DWI or something?"

"Yes, he did."

"He admits that he had something like that before, and this was his first run-in with them, so he feels the fear that they're coming for him. Like living in Nazi Germany, 'When are they going to come and get me?'—you know. That's the feeling—that they're always on his case. I will tell you one thing, and I can't blame him. It's not that he's afraid anymore, but he still has a freaking attitude toward them."

"Sure, I would, too."

"As he discusses it, I can tell that this is one part of him that has not spiritually progressed yet. It's just like, 'Well I have no use for those kind of people,' and he has no sympathy toward them. As far as he's concerned, anybody that wears a uniform in an abusive or harassing manner, whether they be agents for the government or for the local police force, he just has no use for those kind of people, he has no respect for them, no sense of dignity toward them. It's almost like I'm seeing those 'Proud of our Police' bumper stickers, and he's like, 'Oh, please! I have no use for these people.' And he admits this is a spiritual flaw, because he just rounds them up in one category—to him, they are beneath contempt. So he states, in other words, that he knows that he's going to have to work this out. But he really doesn't want to right now. He's kind of holding on to that right now because his fear on the earth has become annoyance in the hereafter—almost like, 'How dare these people, these little God Almighty's have done this to me?' Not that it's upsetting him over there, where he can't function and be happy, but he admits—right now he holds a grudge. It's just that he knows what they've put you through, and he knows that you have no respect for them either, and he says that he just feels that he was raped, and that you, too, were raped by the system. He says that he has not yet forgiven, and he knows it's wrong, but he says, 'I have to be honest with you, I just have no use for those kind of people.' His attitude is that every time they screwed him, it was always 'You're guilty. We got you, no matter what.' To make a name for themselves, it was at his expense and his family's expense. But in any case, does the name Bob or Robert mean anything? He does call out to friends, or people he thought were friends, because he feels that a lot of people kind of let him down, too. They were there for him and they weren't. He says no reflection on you—you're his parents and he loves you—but he says, 'I'm so glad to be away from here. It wasn't for me, it was a constant struggle.' You know, it's obvious as I'm talking to him, the guy is not a troublemaker or anything. He seems like a very nice guy to me, it just seems that he's the pawn in everybody else's chess game. This is the first time I've ever heard this, but he says he cannot in his heart and soul over there honestly ask you to forgive them, he says, 'Because I haven't.' "

"Oh, that's good. That's what I wanted to know."

"He says, 'I haven't' and he says he knows it's wrong. He says, 'I know it's a spiritual flaw, but I'm not ready for it yet.' He just cannot forgive them for picking on him to the point that they drove him to this. He says, as far as he's concerned, they murdered him."

"They did."

"And he says, 'I'm not going to deny this, they murdered me and they murdered the two of you.' He says, 'They ripped your hearts out,' by constantly putting him through this, and he says, 'I have not forgiven yet.' He says, 'Maybe someday I will, but not now.' He's not ready for it yet, and nobody forces you to do anything over there that you don't want to do. But on the other hand, he does say to you he is safe, he's free from fear and he says he is happy and at peace for your sakes. He says that, because it's true, and also to make you feel better. But he says, 'We all have an ax to grind with them, don't we?' And that hasn't changed on his part either. But again, he extends white roses to the two of you as a spiritual blessing and says that he's going to sign off because—you know, it's funny, now that I know what it's all about, I know why it took so long, because he wasn't even comfortable talking about it. Just to bring up the memory of those types again—'Do I have to?'—but he knew he had to, to put you all at rest and to help himself try to understand it even more so now, because you can feel he recognizes the value of it. One thing about him, he's not a liar. He'll call a spade a spade, and if he's not ready to forgive yet, I believe he's not. I agree with you all, I can't say I blame him. Some types of people are just the scum of the earth. They're useless, put in a uniform, and think they suddenly become important. Well, maybe someday they'll find out how insignificant they are, but in any case, he extends white roses, because he says he's going to sign off. But your parents, your brother and sister, your dad, different people, your grandparents and friends embrace you all with love, and they say not to worry, that he is all right. And he says that he is all right and at peace and freed from fear, but he says to continue to pray for him. Until we meet again, just know that he's with you and with that he signs off, the others do, too—there they go, and away he went."

WHAT SURPRISED ME about this discernment is how much free will we actually have in the hereafter. Theon, knowing that the "right thing" would be to forgive, is not quite ready and will deal with it in his own way. The Tomcheffs told me afterward that they were glad to know that he was still angry about his circumstance of passing. Right now their anger is all they have to pull them through their grief, and having Theon say "All is forgiven" would only serve to trivialize the agony they still endure. These are intelligent, aware people who understand that anger is like an acid that eventually destroys the vessel it is contained in, but, like Theon, they have the rest of their existence to learn from a difficult lesson and grow from it.

SENSELESS ACTS
OF VIOLENCE

WE LIVE in a violent world. The statistics tell us that someone is murdered across the United States every eleven seconds. I can't remember a single instance as a boy where I heard that someone in my town or neighboring areas was the victim of murder, but now it is commonplace to hear about neighborhood violence, and a new generation of people live with the very real possibility that one or more of their friends or family members will be murdered by another. We also learn from media, political circles and big business that, for the most part, the loss of lives is a "necessary evil" where progress is concerned, and we have slowly accepted this, on some unconscious level, to be true. Ask yourself how many times you have sat idly while the news program told you that thousands were massacred in Bosnia, a bomb blast killed hundreds in Israel or scores of people perished at a compound in Waco, Texas. Unfortunately for media and politics, murder has lost its appeal with people until it hits home and we have a loved one who is brutalized or murdered.

Murder does not just end the life of the victim. In the taking of the life of a loved one the entire family in essence has been murdered. This is one circumstance that the hereafter will concede that to understand and come to terms with a loved one who is murdered could take a lifetime, if ever, to recover from. There are so many overlapping issues of loss of control over one's life and vulnerability to strangers that it takes the very, very strong to understand that something will eventually be gained by this most cruel of lessons. The one thing I hear over and over from parents, spouses, siblings and friends of those who passed due to murder is what a senseless waste of a life was perpetrated by someone who can never really know how important was the life they destroyed to the ones who loved them. Nonetheless, the hereafter tells me that the taking of a life is a very complicated issue that has differing spiritual consequences for the murderer, the victim and the family.

I posed a question to the souls in the hereafter: If everyone in this existence has chosen their life here, who would decide to come back as a murderer? And what spiritual growth could possibly be gained by having life end so violently? Naturally we can only see from our own, rather myopic perspective here on the earth, and as much as I know from the souls in the hereafter about the Other Side, there are things that even I cannot know. Again it is a matter of faith that everything will become clear to us once our work here is done. But that does not help someone who is grieving over a senseless act of violence.

What I have learned from the hereafter is that while we choose the lessons in our soul growth here, we also can choose either unconsciously or consciously to veer off course and abandon our purpose for being here. It happens more often than you think, and I have seen this veering off-course in many who have come to see me. Some people have come to me and are so bitter at having experienced loss that they find themselves incapable of continuing on their road of understanding and learning. By having a tragedy and refusing to go on in our life's plan is a way of moving off our spiritual road. It is why the souls in the hereafter tell their loved ones over and over to "go on with your life." What they are saying is that we must move on from our setbacks and tragedies and continue again, to the end of our lesson on this plane. They also know that it is easier said than done. In instances where someone chooses a life of violence, something has gone terribly wrong in their spiritual lesson that not only can't they continue, they cannot even find the road. As these souls enter the hereafter having accomplished nothing good on the earth, theirs is a very long road to understanding in the hereafter, and they judge themselves to not be worthy right away of acceptance into the Infinite Light. It will be only after great amounts of work and redemption there that they will choose to move forward to the Light. But as random as these acts of violence seem, they still are part of an ever-changing plan of the Infinite Light to produce the lessons that we will suffer, learn, understand and then benefit from when it is our time to graduate into the peace of the hereafter. No matter what the circumstance, the time we are to pass is the constant, and only the method is the variable.

The souls in the hereafter who pass from violence are remarkably philosophical about the circumstance that got them there. This is probably because they have come to understand exactly why things happened the way they did and the lesson it was meant to provide for themselves and those who are now grieving their loss. In most discernments, these souls are reluctant to name their killer (if it wasn't already known to the family), because they don't see any real benefit in our knowing if it cannot change anything. There was a family who came to see me about three months after their daughter was murdered in her home. I know that they were hell-bent on knowing who the killer was because they had suspected a family member and wanted to see him pay for the crime. During the discernment, however, their daughter told them why it was not necessary for them to know. She told them, "If I told you who killed me, you would only ruin the rest of your existence trying to seek justice for something I have already forgiven and moved on with. You need to do the same." These wise words were something the family could understand, and it also helps to illustrate how carefully the souls in the hereafter work toward keeping us to our purpose on the earth without buckling under such tragic circumstances. There are other times, however, when the soul that was murdered will make a point of naming the killer, mostly because there is a greater purpose involved. This happened where a woman whose daughter's passing left her feeling that foul play had been involved, since her daughter had recently had a messy separation from her husband and was gearing up for a custody battle for their child. During the discernment, her daughter told her that her husband did, indeed, cause her passing and covered it up to look like an accident. Her purpose, she continued, in telling the information was because her child was at stake, and it was the child's spiritual path to live with the grandmother and not the father. Armed with this information, the woman had a second autopsy performed, where it became apparent that the inconsistencies were enough to classify her case as murder. The husband was convicted of the murder two years later. I don't tell that story to encourage people to seek me out when they suspect foul play (I no longer have the time to work on police cases) but to show that when a higher purpose is involved, the hereafter will trust us with the information that they know we will use correctly. It seems that whether they tell any information to us in instances like these is up to our ability to not have it change our spiritual path here. It is up to us.

What I find most extraordinary about the souls in the hereafter who pass violently is their ability to forgive and understand their attacker, and their request that we also forgive. Sometimes just by looking at how that information affects the family, I can tell that it is too tall an order for them, and it will probably never happen. But, nevertheless, the souls ask us to pray not only for them but also for their aggressors. They try to make us understand (as they do now) that no one escapes their own justice, and we are all accountable to ourselves in the hereafter. It is not necessary that we waste the time on the earth fighting for a justice that will never put things to right again. They feel that our time here is better served by trying to understand even if we cannot readily forgive. This is not to say that they don't understand how senseless it was for their aggressor to end their life. They just seem to have found a better way to channel their energies into finding good, even in people where it only flickers dimly. It is a model we can all benefit from. But no matter how profound the words from the hereafter, the simple fact is that having a loved one pass from violence is one of the hardest things to endure. The ending of a life that had so much promise leaves behind it a trail of broken dreams and lost hope for the future. But the souls there tell me that they have not lost anything at all, and life for them indeed goes on.

Most people who have a loved one pass violently become heartsick at the idea that their loved one experiences terrible pain or torture prior to passing. This is yet another experience where the souls in the hereafter promise me that they "never felt a thing." They tell me that, in the seconds before physical life is changed forever, their soul leaves the body without experiencing the physical pain associated with the violence. In that statement alone, I can see the color return to the faces of family members who feel so much better knowing that their loved one did not suffer prior to their passing. It is one of those graces of the hereafter that will be an eternal source of hope for us on the earth.

I MET PEGGY AND JOSEPH EDWARDS on a blustery October day in Syracuse. I remember the day well, because there was so much comedy around the hotel lobby that it almost seemed like a circus. There was a barbershop quartet convention going on, and you could not escape the constant crooning. During the appointment, I glanced out the window to see grown men dressed up as chickens crossing the avenue in front of the hotel. I knew afterward that there was a definite reason this couple was scheduled to come at this exact time, and that *someone* was working hard to help take the edge off the very tragic circumstance that brought the two of them to see me. That someone was their son, Corey.

Peggy and Joseph possess a type of quiet dignity and strength that is rarely found in bereaved parents. They are lovely people who, in spite of the terrible things that happened, remain convinced that life is still worth learning from—no small feat. No matter how much they have learned and grown after the passing of Corey, they are every bit as much victims of murder as their son, and helping others to understand violent passings by including their story, I hope, will be a way for them to continue to fight back, for their sake and for Corey's. At the bottom of a note they sent me, they wrote, "The defendant in our case took our son's life. We refuse to let him take ours! It's not what happens to you—it's what you choose to do about it." I could not find a better way to explain what the souls in the hereafter teach us than in that statement. Peggy and Joseph Edwards prove by their outlook that they are better than their circumstances, and their story is a tribute to a son who continues to do good on the earth through his example of hope. The following is written by them:

"When Joseph and I decided to have children, we made the conscious decision to have our two sons, Jay and Corey, be our number-one priority. I was a stay-at-home mom and Joseph worked to provide for the family. There was a peaceful existence in our upper-middle-class lifestyle. We carefully planned how we would raise our sons, teaching them the importance of God, education and morals. As African American parents, we instilled the importance of higher education. For Jay and Corey, it was not an option but a necessity for them to succeed in life.

"Our sons grew up to be caring and loving individuals. We taught them that when faced with an altercation, it was all right to walk away and never to resort to violence. Unfortunately, the values and morals we taught our sons only seemed to make them prey for people with no principles or respect for life. All too soon, it became apparent to us as parents that our circle of influence and our circle of control were limited. A parent's worst nightmare came true for us, the morning we received a knock at our front door. It was a state trooper who came to inform us that our son, Corey, at the young and tender age of nineteen, had become a homicide victim, one of the statistics of a senseless act of violence in a black-on-black crime.

"Corey was a very social person. That became apparent very early in his life. Neighborhood friends, nursery school classmates and teachers always enjoyed interfacing with Corey because he was so easygoing and compassionate to others.

Whatever he was involved in, be it school, sports or music, you could see his love of people. I recall an incident with one of his elementary school friends. Corey and his friend Jessica were invited to perform a clarinet duet for the local school board. Jessica's reed broke just prior to the performance, and she squeaked throughout the entire musical piece. Even though the piece was ruined, Corey took it in stride and tried to console and cheer up his friend. Throughout high school, he was an honor roll student, an Urban League Black Scholar and a member of the National Honor Society. His plans were to become a college professor, marry the love of his life, have children and continue the same lifestyle that he was raised in. He knew what was needed to be successful.

"Corey went to Baltimore to attend a local state university on a full scholarship. He entered college with the same mixed emotions as any other student—excited about meeting new people but reserved about leaving home. In the beginning of his freshman year he called home a lot, saying, 'I'm homesick, Mom.' But I told him how proud I was of him to acknowledge those feelings and that they were perfectly normal. I still thank God to this day that I was home to receive those calls when he needed to connect with home. Just as we expected, in a little time Corey was making friends. Because making friends was so easy for him, we would always warn him to choose his friends wisely. Corey would always share a dorm room with another student and was always so respectful of another's room space. He would not feel at ease until he had arranged his belongings in a way that would leave more space for the other student.

"On April 9, 1995, during his sophomore year in college, Corey and three of his friends decided to leave campus and go to a local club in town. The cab ride to the club provided time for the four friends to joke around and enjoy each other's company on an evening of some good clean fun. Once inside the club, Corey's friend, Jamal, spotted a female friend across the room and went over to say hello. She was engaged in conversation with another male patron. When Jamal stopped to say hello, the male patron became upset and asked him, 'Why are you stopping here?' Jamal replied, 'I'm just trying to say hello to a friend and get past to get to the bar.' The male patron began to argue with Jamal because he did not appreciate the interruption, but Jamal assured him that he meant no harm and continued over to the bar. The patron became so aggravated over this innocent encounter that he told the female, 'I am going to get him. I am going to burn him up when we get outside.' Alarmed by the threat, the female immediately went to warn Jamal. She suggested that he gather up his friends and leave. Our son Corey was unaware of what had happened since he was on the phone, talking to his girlfriend who attended another college. He had just asked her to stay awake until he could get back to his dorm room, because he had something to tell her. The four friends gathered again to leave the club. Upon leaving, a brief scuffle broke out between Jamal and his friends and the male patron and his friends, which was immediately stopped by the club bouncers. In an attempt to separate the two groups, the bouncer escorted the male patron and his friends out the club's front doors, and directed Corey, Jamal and their friends out the side door. Corey and his friends apologized to the bouncer for the incident and headed to the street to call for a cab to take them back to the campus. When the bouncer saw Corey and the friends waiting for their ride in front of the club, he strongly suggested to them that they wait for their ride farther down the street. It seems he was aware of the male patron's temperament. Jamal told the bouncer, 'That's all over.' These were the last words he ever spoke. The male patron had gone home to get his 9mm semi-automatic handgun and retaliated for the scuffle by spraying bullets into the crowd that gathered in front of the club. The male patron purposely aimed his semi-automatic weapon at Jamal and his friends. People began to scatter and hide to save their lives. Corey attempted to run back down the alley toward the side door of the club, but, because of the constant heavy spraying of bullets he was unable to reach safety before his body received four bullets.

"Corey died at the scene of the crime. There were gunshot wounds to his chest, back, thigh and buttocks. Jamal died four days later from gunshot wounds to the head. There were four other people wounded at the scene, and police recovered a total of sixteen cartridge casings. One bullet remains to this day lodged in the body of a bystander.

"The male patron, just nineteen years old himself, was arrested ten days later and charged with first-degree murder on two counts, as well as five counts of attempted murder on the bystanders also wounded in the spree. It took one year before our son's case went to trial. It was a year filled with trial dates made and canceled three times. We felt like we were being victimized all over again. The trial finally took place, and for seven days we had to look at this evil person and hear the testimony, reliving the terrible nightmare with detailed information about the death of our son and his friend. We thank God that justice prevailed, and the murderer of our son was found guilty of two counts of first-degree murder plus four counts of assault and unlawful use and carrying of a handgun. He is serving two life sentences consecutively with no parole, plus twenty years for the assault and handgun charge. Hearing the verdict did not and cannot erase the pain of losing our son. It did, however, give us some comfort in knowing that the person responsible for taking our son's life will pay for the consequences of his decision that April night.

"You cannot turn on the news or read the paper these days without coming across stories of innocent people caught in the crossfire of insanity. It can happen to any family. It happened to ours. We believe that the deterioration of the family unit produces the type of person for whom human life is valueless. Unless we can take strict measures in our community to restore safety, the day is not too far in the future when every person living will either know someone who has lost or will personally lose a loved one to a senseless act of violence.

"The devastation and pain of losing our son is beyond words. It is a loss we carry with us daily until the day we die, but our faith teaches us that life is eternal. We needed to make a spiritual connection with our son, and this desire lead us to George Anderson. It was comforting to learn from Corey that life is beautiful in his new world and that he has a job and a purpose in the hereafter. We were thrilled to hear that he has his own place there, for that is something he had always wanted on this side. The biggest comfort of communicating with Corey was his encouraging us to go on with our lives, knowing one day we would meet again. I used to feel guilty when someone would tell me, 'You're looking good.' I even felt guilty to laugh. But thanks to the communication from Corey, we are now living with a comfort that allows us to go on with our lives."

THE DISCERNMENT

"Well, to start, there's a male presence here—somebody who's just popped into the room. There's another male with him—two males, of different generations, I can definitely feel that. There's a lady, too, and another one. You've got four people in conversation over there. In the beginning I'll only hear bits and pieces of their conversation and, from that, start getting the clues. All right, I'll follow the way they do it. Umm—I don't know what this means, so don't explain, but I can overhear someone saying, 'Dad is here'—does that make sense? (*They nod.*) Okay, I assume it does somehow, so let's leave it at that for now until they explain better what they mean. There's a female walking around the room. There is a female close to both of you passed over?"

"Yes."

"And a male, too?"

"Yes."

"But a young male?"

"Yes."

"Because there are two males of different generations, and all of a sudden they seem to break out of their talking and seem to be walking around. All right—again, I don't know where this can go to, so just say to me yes if you understand. I'm overhearing someone talk about the loss of a child, does that make sense?"

"Yes."

"Now somebody said, 'Mom is here.'"

"Yes."

"I am going to assume what I am hearing—you are Mom and Dad?"

"Yes."

"Because whoever it is directs it at you now. I heard again, 'Dad is here. Mom is here,' and they seem to push it this way at you. There's talk of loss of a son. You did lose a son?"

"Yes."

"Okay, I just want to get over that threshold so that I can get going here. Your son speaks about, also, father or grandfather. Did one of you lose your dad?"

(Joseph) "Yes."

"Okay, that must be the 'Dad is here' also. It is your dad—your father, his grandfather. He said, 'Father/Grandfather is here with me.' Oh, that's probably why he said, 'Father/Grandfather'—his father's father. Wait a minute—someone is speaking about 'Mom'—your moms are still here? One has passed?"

"Yes."

(to Joseph) "Yours has passed?"

"Yes."

(to Peggy) "Your parents are still here?"

"My mom."

"Your dad has gone—okay, because there are, again, more people spinning my head a little bit, because they are all talking out, and somebody said, 'Mama is with me,' and I ask, 'Well, whose?' *(To Joseph)* So obviously it's your mother, and then somebody else who says, 'Father.' There's a flock of people back there all claiming to be your grandparents—so I'm assuming all your grandparents have passed on."

"Yes."

"And this is why I'm getting this confusion with parents, grandparents, father, mother—everybody's jumping in many different directions. The main focus, obviously, of why you're here is naturally to hear from your son. He knows that, but he says that he can't help it if other people want to say hello also (*they laugh*) so he says they're here, too. He says, 'We all live in the same community, so to speak,' so when it was announced that there was going to be an opportunity to discern, they get the word, too, and they want to let you know that they are near. One thing though, (*to Peggy*) your dad does approach you, and your father does feel that he could have been closer to you, is that true?"

"Yes."

"Because your father feels that you might have a little bone to pick with him, as they say. Your son steps aside because he says that your father has a need, and your father walked up to you and apologizes to you for not being closer. This is kind of a long overdue apology, but better late than never. Your father does feel that he kind of abandoned you emotionally, is that true?"

"Yes."

"Because he states that he's there and then he's not there, and as strange as this may sound, he wants you to know that he always loved you, even if he had a strange way of showing it, or wasn't there to show it. Your mom is still here on the earth, yes? Because he calls out to your mother and he states that your mother did not have the easiest life here either. He calls out to her—that she's come a long way, and has achieved, but he feels he could have been closer with her also. In her heart she still loves him, yes?"

(*She laughs.*) "I don't know."

"Because he calls out to her with love and feels that in her own way she still loves him. She might be a little 'teed off' with him, but, in any case, he says, 'Tell Mom you've heard from me, and he states—he just wants to let her know that he knows now that he was wrong."

"Okay."

"And your mother might relish hearing that."

(*Laughs*) "Yes—okay."

"That's why he wants her to know that he was wrong. He jokes—he says your mother could have her moments, too, but he takes more of the blame. It takes two to tango, but, let's say, he tangoed a little heavier."

"Umm-hmm."

"All right, your son—I'm sure you want to hear this, and I should not be cynical—your son declares he is all right. I'm sure as parents you want to hear that, but he says he's all right—and in a safe place, does that make sense?"

(*They are unsure how to answer.*)

"Well I guess it does, that he's in a safe and happy place. I'm sure you'd want to know that he is in a safe and happy place. He writes 'Tragic' in front of me. His passing is tragic, obviously, yes?"

"Yes."

"Now he puts up an umbrella and puts under the umbrella 'accident,' is that correct?"

(They indicate no.)

"Well, you see, he puts it under the umbrella of accident, which can have some different meanings, because he is putting 'accident' in quotes. But he does not pass in a vehicle-type accident."

"No."

"Because he's telling me that it's not what we would think of as an accident. He says, 'No, no, it is not that, but it is under the umbrella of 'accident.' It happens suddenly, yes?"

"Yes."

"That's why it's under the umbrella of 'accident,' whether it be something like that or a health problem, it happens like this *(snaps fingers)*. *(To the hereafter)* All right, all right—it's so much easier to just tell what they say. He gives me the feeling of breathing trouble. Does that make sense?"

"Yes."

"Okay, this is why it is so much easier to tell you, instead of asking, 'Did he have breathing trouble?' I'll tell you what *he* says, and then ask you. Am I correct in my assumption that something does affect his chest area?"

"Yes."

"Okay, because I keep feeling something's not right here *(points to his chest)*. He says, 'You could not save me.' Does that make sense?"

"Yes."

"I mean, you *couldn't*. It's like, you may oppress yourself at times thinking, 'Could I have done something here?'—but your son says, 'You could not save me.' Your son seems pretty much like a straight shooter—he's going to tell it like it is."

"Yes."

"He also speaks of visiting in dreams, so you obviously have dreamt about him."

(Peggy) "Yes, I have."

"Because he says, 'This is not the first time you are hearing from me,' and he also thanks you for the memorial."

(They laugh.) "Yes!"

"So obviously good things have been done in his name, and he tells you only because he wants you to know that he's aware of it. There was a planting also?"

"Yes."

"Because a tree grows in front of me, so there must have been two forms of memorials. Something is done in his name where others can benefit in his memory, but then the tree sprouted in front of me and he said that he thanks you for the tree-planting memorial also—that his name has been put in, in that arena."

"Yes, yes."

"There is strain to my heart. Does this make sense?"

"Yes."

"It feels to me as if my heart is giving out. Does that make sense?"

"Yes."

"Okay. Am I safe in saying that it seems like he's having a heart attack, but it's not a heart attack?"

"No, he's not having—"

"No, that's what I mean. It feels like that, but he's not having that. There is a jolt to his system though, yes?"

"Yes."

"Because he tells me—I'm feeling like my heart is bursting out of my chest, but it's not a description of any kind of suffering—it's just how the body is reacting. Something must have cut his air off, yes?"

"Yes."

"Because I keep feeling I'm losing air. (*To Joseph*) He draws to you, his dad— are you near to him when this occurs?"

"No."

"But he keeps addressing to you that you couldn't save him. Does this make sense?"

"Yes."

"That's why I'm thinking—your son just complained to me, he said, 'See, you went off the track and you went wrong.' He said, 'You should have said I am coming closer to him addressing that you could not save me, and does it make sense more to dad.' He says, 'Right away you ask if he was near to me when this happened and you went off the track—go back to doing it the way you were supposed to.'"

(*They laugh.*) "That's him."

"But again, that 'You could not have saved me' is directed more at you for whatever reason, and being his dad, it is as if, 'I should have been there, I could have done something'—that sort of thing, and he wants you especially to be at peace about it because, as he says, you suffer in silence a great deal over his passing. (To Peggy) I mean, not that you don't also, but he says that you know what he's driving at. That's all I need to know—I won't challenge him again and do it the wrong way. Now there is a falling feeling, does that make sense?"

"Yes."

"Okay, because I feel I'm—falling. I don't understand—your son is showing me a uniform, does that make sense? He wasn't in uniform, of course—"

"No."

"I don't understand what he's doing that for. All right, maybe it's something that I don't understand, but I'm not going to dwell on it, so let's leave it go for the moment. Your son describes his passing almost like in a sleep, does that make sense?"

(They are confused.)

"Maybe at the final moment it is like he just goes to sleep and lets go, because he's speaking just going into a sleep. I see St. Joseph appear, which would be significant of a happy death in spite of the circumstances. Your son does pass peacefully from this stage to the next. He keeps stating that in spite of the circumstances he does not suffer prior to his passing—"

"Okay."

"—and you have to know that."

"Okay."

"So he's emphasizing that without me even having to question it—he's telling me, 'They must know that.' The circumstances may look tragic and unpleasant, and he says, 'I want you to know that I do not suffer prior to my passing.' Something hits the chest?"

"Yes."

"There's a hit to my chest, and I keep feeling I'm all out of sorts in there, and I fall—obviously he goes down or collapses, 'cause I fall—and I'm hit to the chest, and then my whole system goes into a jolt. It's shutting down."

"Yes, yes."

"This again could be symbolic, so bear with me, but he is speaking of a weapon, is that correct?"

"Yes."

"There is a weapon involved."

"Yes."

"Okay—I'm hearing a bang—is the weapon a gun?"

"Yes."

"Okay, I just want to make sure, because a 'bang' may not necessarily be a gun. It could also be a 'bang' of something else, so I said to myself, let me tell you first what I hear. Because I almost slipped and asked you if it was a gun, and you could have said no. And your son said, 'Say you hear the bang first, then ask if it is a gun!' So obviously he is shot."

"Yes."

"To the chest?"

"Yes."

"And to the head, yes?"

"No."

"Why is there that dizziness. Was there any injury to the head?"

"No."

"Unless internally again from the shutdown, because I feel like my whole system is shutting—it could be probably what he meant before. That could be the injury to the head, internally, like the blood not going to the brain. Everything's going down. This could be another reason why I feel I'm falling—yes, he is falling, but also my internal system is falling because I'm getting ready to pass. This is why he puts it under the umbrella of accident—it's not an accident, but it's not a health problem—"

"Correct."

"—and he knows if he doesn't drift me away from thinking 'health,' I'm going to go in the wrong direction. Because sometimes if somebody suddenly becomes ill, they describe it over there like it's an accident, a sudden health problem develops like an accident, so he's very careful where he's directing me. I keep seeing that television show *Crossfire*—is he caught in the crossfire?"

"Yes, he is."

"Because that's how he describes it. Your son—I'm sure you know this—but your son keeps saying, 'This isn't my fault. I got caught in the crossfire.' He feels—*he's* all right and at peace—he feels more sorry for you all because you live in the shadow and the memory of it. He says, 'I'm fine, I've gone through it. I've gone through the crossfire and moved on.' That's why he's saying he's in a happy and safe place, because his life was threatened here because we live in an unsafe society. This isn't Disney World. And as he states, this is why he wants you to know that he is in a safe place. He says that now you all have to try to put your minds and hearts in a safe place as well. He gives me the feeling that he is basically at the wrong place at the wrong time—you know, he has a reason to be there, but almost like he shouldn't have been, or could have left sooner, or something. I'm supposed to be there, but I shouldn't be there. It's like somebody going to a job—I'm not saying that this is what it is, but only as an example—somebody goes to a job and maybe was supposed to get off at five o'clock but stayed until six. You know, they are there longer than they should have been, and this occurs."

"Yes, uh-huh."

"I mean this with politeness, but your son gives me the feeling he's inclined to be a little naive, would you agree? He's not stupid, don't get me wrong, he's street smart but he's a little too trusting."

"Yes, yes."

"A little too naive in some areas, like—he could run into someone who might . . . take advantage of that."

"Yes."

"I get the feeling that I'm talking to a nice guy that's bright, but a little too trusting and a little naive. And he recognizes that those virtues, as admirable as they are, kinda did get him into a little bit of a mess."

"Umm-hmm."

"And your son tells me to say to you that he admits now that he's a little on the headstrong side. (They laugh.) That you might have been trying to tell him that for the longest time, and of course he could not see the forest for the trees, and he says, 'Well, mom and dad were right.' Sometimes his own independence wasn't his best friend. Again, not that he's a bad person—but he kind of hangs out with the wrong crowd?"

"Yes."

"They're not bad people, but they are bad people. You know, I have a taffy pull with it—because I see a big tree in front of you with shade over us, which would mean they were 'shady' (they agree) but maybe, as your son puts it, maybe a better word would be 'misguided'—that's how he describes it. He keeps showing me shoes being fitted—he always wanted to fit in."

(Crying) "Yes."

"And that symbol seems to have more meaning than I understand, but you understand. That's why he's telling me, 'Say everything you see me doing or saying,' but he says that he always wanted to fit in, and yet he's independent. I keep seeing a 'cool cat' in front of me—you know, he wants to be in with the 'cool cats,' as we would say in my generation. But in any case he states—umm—I keep seeing things being tied up. He got tied in with the wrong things. And this is where he is a little naive and too trusting."

"Yes."

"These people are one step ahead of him, and he thinks they're cool. But also your son admits at times he felt like kind of an outsider."

"Umm-hmm."

"He might have felt like the outcast—maybe growing up he was picked on or he wasn't welcomed in or embraced into the—there's a lot of peer pressure, as they say. So he thinks he's in with the cool people now. In a lot of ways like me growing up—being picked on in school and made fun of because of the ability and all, but I still wanted to fit in and he did also."

"Yes."

"I will say this—he does come across as a very sensitive individual, but maybe at times he just doesn't know how to convey that sensitivity in the right direction. He also feels that at times he was at odds with you all. Is that true?"

"Yes."

"I mean, I'm sure as parents you had your ups and downs—that's normal—but he feels at times he could make it more downs than ups, and he does apologize for kind of giving you a run for your money."

"Um-hmm."

"Because there were days, he knows, that you wanted to throw in the towel— like, 'I don't know what else to do with this guy' (they chuckle), and I see that happened. You put hands up, like, 'Forget it—leave it in the Lord's hands—I don't know what else to do.'"

"Exactly."

"But your son has grown up over there. Here on the earth, he was grown up in age, but he was a little bit of a boy trapped in a man's body. And he states that in the hereafter he has grown up and matured himself of his own free will. He says, 'No force is exercised over here, nobody tells you what to do.' But he states that he found himself over there, which is . . . what he was trying to do here, but there were too many curves and he went the wrong way a few times. But it's all part of the fulfillment. Now, I'm seeing again this tree with the shadiness, so was there illegal activity going on?"

"Yes."

"Yes, because there must have been something—ah, yeah, yeah—that's why I was seeing the police uniform, meaning—not necessarily that the police were involved, but it could be my symbol of illegal things going on. Or against the law, or whatever. And your son admits now that he's more of a follower than a leader. At times, somebody might have suggested, 'Well, let's do this,' and you know—again I feel like part of this group or 'family.' He says that he learned one thing—if he had this to do all over again, this wouldn't be happening, because he would be going in the opposite direction. But again, as he states, and it's true—he shows me the final scenes of *The Wizard of Oz* where the good witch says to Dorothy, 'You have to learn it for yourself.' The scarecrow couldn't think of it for her, and the tin man couldn't feel it in his heart—she had to find the answers herself. And this was a rather rocky road to find it for himself, but he says, 'I've found it for myself.' You obviously pray for him, because he certainly thanks you for the prayer and asks that it please continue."

"Um-hmm."

"Yes, as parents, your son says no one is perfect, but you've always tried to do everything right. Especially where he was involved, and he recognizes that you always tried to do everything right, and . . . sometimes he could fight you all the way. *(To Joseph)* Toward the end, he speaks about you and he having a lack of communication, is that true? He feels toward the end that he could have been closer."

"Yes."

"Maybe in his rambunctiousness or rebelliousness—I feel he was always close to both of you *(they agree)*—but he was getting a little . . . distant? Not that he's not talking to you or anything, but becoming a little distant, maybe getting too wrapped up in what he thinks is his life or what he should be doing."

(Joseph) "I understand."

"He just wants the both of you to know that he always loved you and still does, even though he might have seemed a little independent toward the end. He's speaking about an argument. Was there an argument with this group that he was with?"

"Yes."

"It seems like—I keep hearing a scene out of an opera where somebody is singing '*Pace, pace*'—'Peace.' Was he trying to keep the peace, or trying to help the situation?"

"Yes."

"It seemed like his heart was in the right place—yeah, he's in with this crowd and yeah, there's an argument, and you know—you screwed me and I screwed you and all this kind of nonsense, but the thing is that it's ending up in violence. But it's almost like he's caught in the middle of it—again, the crossfire—he's trying to work this out and it seems that he recognizes that violence can ensue, and he's trying to be diplomatic or harmonize the situation—in some instance trying to keep the peace to a degree. It just seems like one big mess that got out of hand, and he happened to be there and got caught in the crossfire."

"Yes."

"I see what I think is an illegal substance. Was that going on?"

"Yes."

"Yes, because it seems like somebody was—drugs and money—that's what I see in front of me."

"No, there may have been drugs at the scene, but he wasn't involved."

"Oh—no, no—I don't mean *him*, but the other persons possibly were involved?"

"They could have."

"Because I see drugs and money, so even though he wasn't involved, somebody else might have been involved, or somebody feels they may have been cheated—but the thing is, not *him*, but somebody else there or somebody in his crowd. Somebody's got a bug up their rear end—something about shady activity, to do with drugs and money, and this is what he's trying to tell me. And of course this could have happened prior, it's building up, the eruption occurs, and then your son happens to be there. It's like you always knew that if he lived life a little bit in the fast lane, and this could happen, and you always worried about that. But again, as he says, you could tell him from your own experience with life what was the right thing to do, but he says he didn't listen. 'You might have wondered sometimes if there was anything between the ears,' he says. But you knew it was, and you knew that he was getting off the track. Because in his heart—I'm talking to a very nice guy—"

"Yes, he is."

"—I'm talking to a very nice guy, and hey—who of us doesn't have a skeleton in our closet. I do, and I'm sure you do—everybody does. He knows you're happy to hear that he's found himself in the hereafter. You probably just wish that he'd done it here, so that he could be here with you physically."

"Yes."

"And he says, yes, it can be very frustrating from him to say, 'I'm very close to you spiritually,' because he recognizes that maybe at times it's not much compensation."

"Okay."

"Particularly again—he jokes that you talk out loud to him, so you must think he's still around."

"Yes, I do."

"Plus, with holidays approaching, naturally, you start to feel it a little more. You almost dread Christmas and Thanksgiving coming because it brings to mind that there's something missing. The two of you have come a long way in life, yes?"

"Um-hmm."

"You definitely have worked hard and gotten to where you all have gotten and you've surmounted many obstacles—and again, you wanted to do everything right. Yes, again, he thanks you for praying for him and asks that it please continue. Not a religious young man, but spiritual in his own way. Again, as I said, his heart's in the right place. As a matter of fact, I see Jesus appearing behind you saying, 'Peace be with you, and peace be with your son also.' Because of the tragedy of the passing, you just want to know that he's at peace in the hereafter, and he is. One thing I will say about your son, he's very bright and independent. I mean, no matter where he goes, he'd make friends and have a job in ten minutes—"

"Exactly."

"So that's really the least of your worries over there. Because even if you never got to meet me and hear that confirmation, in your heart you would have known that with life after death, your son found his way. I mean, if this guy moved to Mongolia, he'd find a way to fit in and survive (*they laugh*), so I'm not the least bit worried about him in the afterlife. He says that the greatest triumph over there was doing his life review, seeing where he fulfilled and where he could have fulfilled his soul growth here, and maybe where he got off the track. But the main thing was, through that life review—through that teaching experience, like watching yourself in your own movie as the observer, which makes it more effective—he says *there* he was able to find himself and move on. Also—(*to Joseph*) your dad feels he could have been a little closer, is that true?"

"Yes."

"Because he just wants you to know that he always loved you, even if he had a strange way of showing it. He and your mom seem to have become closer in the next life. He says that they've settled out their differences over there. Your mother jokes that your father finally grew up, ha ha. Not that she's putting the blame on him, but it's just that . . . both your dads really did not have an easy life here. (*They agree.*) They admit it was not an easy life, and this of course could cause them to go in directions to try to make things easier. (*To Joseph*) Your father feels he was a little hard on you, is that true?"

"Yes."

"Mentally, a lot. He might have made you feel that, you know—there's a right way and a wrong way—he just feels that he put a lot of pressure on you mentally and emotionally, and he does apologize for that. He doesn't want to take the credit for it, but he says, 'Look what you've turned into—look at the person you have become. I keep seeing the Virginia Slims ad—*You've come a long way, baby*—and you have, and he is very proud of that. Your father admits, even if you don't agree, that he could have been a little on the domineering side—he could just maybe bring the pressure on you mentally that could bring a sense of dominance with it."

"Hmm."

"It sounds like I heard the name Al or Alan, but that doesn't mean anything, does it?"

"His middle name is Alan."

"Your son's?"

"Yes."

"Good, I'm glad you said so, because it sounded like his voice, and it sounded like he said something about his name. (*To the souls*) Okay, you gave me your middle name, now how about your first? I thought I'd give him the hint. He does seem to like to play games, too, your son. (*They laugh.*) I have to admit he seems to be—there's a little twinkle in his eye of like, he's busting my chops a little bit. But he's doing this also because you will know that he's back to his own self. There's talk of a support group. Do you belong to one?"

"Uh—no."

"But you've thought of it?"

"I've thought of it."

"It's not a bad idea. You know, you do suffer in silence a great deal. It might help you just to be around people who unfortunately know exactly what you are going through. You're a little shy, he says, about it. He says speaking out will not only help you but also could help somebody else indirectly. But it is also, too—he apologizes that people might have cooled it with you a little bit. It seems like some people have distanced themselves. You know they could be friends or family, and not because they are being mean to you—it's just that they don't know how to handle the situation. But yet, your own family seems to have been very supportive."

"Um-hmm."

"Now your son singularizes himself, which could have different meanings, so let me share the meanings with you first—that could mean he's the only son, he's the oldest or the youngest. Do any of those apply?"

"He's the youngest."

"Okay—which is another reason it hits home so bad. So he has brothers—oh wait—brother?"

"A brother."

"He just corrected me. I said brothers and he said brother. Wait a minute now—he's speaking of a female. Does he have a sister also?"

"I had a miscarriage."

"Oh, okay, I think you would have had a girl."

"Yes."

"Yes, because he's talking about a female that he's close with, and then he said, 'I have a sister.' (To Peggy) So apparently had the cycle of birth continued, you would have had a daughter. And your daughter—his sister—is there with him. Apparently they've become good pals over there. Yes—you did have a miscarriage where you feel you lost a daughter?"

"I lost a daughter and a son."

"Okay—oh, maybe that's why he said he had brothers/brother. He corrected me first, but now I understand why he said it that way. He has a brother here on the earth, but a brother in the hereafter."

"Correct."

"Technically, in that case, you can elaborate and I'm glad you did, because I can be confused by what he means. So obviously his sister and his brother are there with him, but he has a sister and brothers—one that's still on the earth—who he was close with."

"Yes."

"He calls to his brother also, 'Please tell him you've heard from me.' Because his brother suffers in silence over the passing, too."

"Yes."

"Again, it's bad enough to be bereaved parents, but bereaved siblings sometimes don't have an identity. People will think, 'Gee, it's not as bad on them, it's worse on the parents,' which it is, but it's just as bad on them, too. So whether your other son believes in this or not, he says, 'Tell him you've heard from me' and he sends his love to him. Your son jokes that he doesn't have the patience with people believing or not believing, because sooner or later everyone is going to have to come here and find out he's right. 'Eventually, everyone is going to have to graduate to here,' he says. Now without telling me, he's speaking about the first part of his name, and I guess he's doing it, as I say, rear-end backward. Because he said, 'Alan,' which is his middle name, but—also, was there someone else he was close with, like as a father figure?"

(They are unsure.)

"Was there an uncle he was close with?"

"Yes."

"Did this uncle pass?"

"Yes."

"Because he's talking—wait a minute, let me get this straight—obviously you are his biological parents, right?"

"Yes."

"Okay, because he started saying to me about having a father figure over there, and I say, 'Well, what do you mean—these are your parents,' and he said, 'Yes, it's not my father, but it's like a second father.' Someone he was close with, and then when I addressed it to you and you seemed confused, he said, 'Tell them it's my uncle.' This is how you would know who he is referring to."

"Yes."

"Obviously this uncle is there with him as well, and he's like a second father. I don't know if they knew each other on the earth, but I guess they did. It seems like they hit it off and then hooked up over there, and there seems to be a nice harmonious relationship."

"Yes."

"Now, if this is an uncle to him, is it the brother to one of you?"

(*Peggy*) "My brother-in-law."

"That's fine, because there's a brotherliness with him to one of you, and that would be brother or brother-in-law. His wife is still living?"

"Yes."

"He calls to his wife and family. So that would be your sister, then."

"My sister, yes."

"So if you think she can deal with this, he calls out to her and just wants to let her know that he is all right and at peace. He calls to her and his family. He must have passed young by today's standards, too, yes?"

"Yes."

"Because certainly you don't look ancient, and I would assume he's not either, so that's another tragedy of the loss of a brother or son in the family, too."

"Right."

"Did you have a stillbirth? Did you know it was a boy?"

"Yes. They lived just a day or so."

"Okay, so that's the thing—they passed in infancy. Your son speaks about his brother being there with him—who obviously was there before him."

"Yes."

"Because he talks about his brother being one of the souls who welcomes him into the Light. His brother was always like his guardian angel while he was here on the earth, so his brother and sister were with him. Now without telling me, he's giving me the feeling that his first name is short, is that correct?"

"Yes."

"It's common, yes?"

"Yes."

"Well, he's showing me eight. Now I'm going to assume it's less than eight letters."

"Yes."

"Now he's showing me seven, and it's less than?"

"Yes."

"He's taking it slow, so he's going to screech to a halt at any minute, I'm sure. He's showing me six now. Is it six?"

"No."

"It's less again? It can't be any less, so it must be five then. He showed me six, and I thought, 'Do you want me to go one less?' but he really didn't answer me. When you said no to six, then I thought, okay, it's got to be five. It's obviously less than six, and he was cutting me down. (*to the hereafter*) Okay, if you can tell me that and you can tell me your middle name is Alan, you should be able to tell me your first name. Wait. You can shorten his first name more?"

(*Peggy*) "I have."

"Yes. Maybe it's not traditionally done, but it can be."

"When I talk to him, I shorten it."

"For instance, let me use as an example—if somebody's name is Brian, you would call him *Bri* once in a while, even though you really don't do it often. He also extends white roses in front of the two of you and speaks of birthday. (*To Peggy*) Is your birthday coming up?"

"My birthday is coming up."

"Okay, that's what I figured, because he's standing in front of you with white roses—just holding them—and then he states that he's speaking of birthday. So he wishes you a happy birthday and extends white roses to you. Your son would be the younger of the sons?"

"Correct."

"Is there a David, someone he knows? (*They are unsure.*) Because there seems to be a tremendous show up at his wake and funeral, so—"

"Yes, there was."

"Okay, let me just leave it with you. It could be a friend or whatever that he's calling out to. Also—he's showing me five letters again—and now he says to me 'A-B-C-D' and he stopped. I'm going to assume that the first letter is after the D in the alphabet."

"No, it's not after the D."

"It's before it? Okay, that's probably why he said 'A-B-C-D' and stopped. He's telling me to halt and he's surrounding me—it's not the D, so it must be A, B or C. So much for my assumption. I'm glad I told you what I heard first, and then asked. With the first name, he gives me the feeling of watching my spelling. Would you spell his first name differently?"

"No, it's just that between the two of us we spelled it a little differently than the traditional way."

"Oh, maybe that's what it is. I wonder if he's saying the name into my subconscious and my brain is thinking that that's not the way to spell it. I wonder if he showed me a clue and I overlooked it. He probably realizes that if I hear the name I will say, 'Well, wait a minute—that would be spelled *this* way,' and I think he's trying to condition me to recognize that it's not going to be what I think it is. He's being very careful about it. So obviously it begins with C—I think he realizes that my brain is going to fight him—he's telling me to distract myself, so maybe other messages will come in. (*To Joseph*) There's talk of retirement. Are you retiring?"

(*Laughing*) "I think about it."

"Oh, I don't know, because your son extends golden roses to you and says that you will retire, and congratulates you on retirement—even if it's a year or two from now. But I don't feel that you fully go out to pasture. I think you'll still work. Let's say, for instance, that you work for the Post Office and you retire from that, you'll still work at something else, even if it is part time or temporary. Also, he speaks of a move for the two of you. Up ahead you could be investing in property, and your son just wants to let you know that it's all right. The reason that he's bringing it up now is because years from now if you decide to do this, you might get hit with a little guilt and think, 'Oh my God, we're leaving him behind,' and that's why he wants to let you know it's all right. He doesn't want you to feel that your life can't go on, or your life has to be stuck now because you'll think he's disappointed in you that you're leaving him behind, because this area is where he originates and you all do, too."

"Um-hmm."

"Now your son circles a Y. Is there a Y in his name?"

"Yes."

"Wait a minute. Y is at the end?"

"Yes."

"He's got a movie star's name?"

"I don't think so."

"The second letter is a vowel."

"Yes."

"Don't explain, but the movie star I saw was Cary Grant. Now his name obviously isn't Cary, but is there an R in the name?"

"Yes."

"That's what he's doing. He showed me it again, and I said to him, 'But your mother said that your name is not a movie star's name,' and he said to me, 'You're not looking close enough—look at what I'm showing you.' He just said to me, 'Change it to C-O-R—make the A in the name Cary an O, the next letter would be R'— oh, Corey. Simple as pie—he did it beautifully. Because he said, 'Go back to looking at the movie star'—and that's why I said, 'His name is a movie star's?' and he said, 'See, you did it wrong—you should have told them what you see, and then start to listen to me.' So his name is Corey, and at times you called him Core."

"Yes!"

"That's why he's telling me the nickname. His actual name by baptism is Corey but he says, 'The family calls me Core.'"

"Yes."

"I mean this with respect. But your son did have kind of a weird sense of humor?"

"Um-hmm."

"Because he admits he lives life in the fast lane to a degree, and he says, 'Figures, I'd go out with a *bang.*' (*They laugh.*) But I think because you were so looking forward to hearing from him today, he wanted to do it so perfectly and so carefully, and he wanted for you to leave here knowing that you've heard from him. That's why he said, 'I had to give you my middle name, Alan, and then build on the first name, Corey.' To give you double proof that he's in the room. It's funny—at times, was he ever called Corey Alan?"

"Yes, Alan called him Corey Alan."

"Because he says that you would use *Core,* but that you would also call him Corey Alan at times, and that's another reason that he's given me both names emphasized. This is his code to you to let you know that you are both hearing from him."

(They sigh, becoming emotional.)

(To Joseph) "He speaks of your back. Do you have back troubles?"

"Not really—"

"Lower?"

"Sometimes."

"Yeah—he just tells you to watch—now I notice you walk with a cane so you obviously have leg trouble or something, but at times your lower back or your hip may bother you—"

"That's true."

"I'm not telling you something you don't already know. As your son says to me, 'You have to live with it,' and you have lived with it, but at times as you get older you may feel it more in the lower back or such. But as your son says, 'So what else is new. You've gotten this far with it, and you'll make it to the finish line.' You all are traveling soon, too, yes? He's wishing you a happy trip and encourages you to go."

"Okay."

"Because he says, both of you at times kind of put your life on hold."

"Yes."

"It's like you feel irreverent if you go on with your life and be happy, and your son says that you want to know that he's there and happy and going on with his life. He says, 'Why can't you do the same?' Yes, it's a little harder on you. You're in the shadow of the aftermath of this tragedy, but he says that one of these days the undertaker is going to come for you, so you might as well make the most of it while you're waiting. He says that it's like sitting in a doctor's office—you might as well read or do something to occupy the time. I see palm trees around you—so you may be traveling to where they exist, within our own country or close by. As he states, go on with your life, take a trip—don't be so afraid to be happy again or to live. He won't think you don't love him anymore if you don't bury yourselves alive. I see you shrouded in black—that you may feel that you have to stay now in perpetual mourning—but as your son states, his life was not terminated, it has continued. It was terminated in the physical, yes—that we know. But it was not terminated in the spiritual. He says that it has continued elsewhere, as if he moved to a foreign country. And with his independence, as he says, he could have packed up and moved somewhere else. He could have moved to Australia, he could have moved to Greenland, he could have moved to South Africa, he could have gone to South America. You don't know where your son's life could have taken him if he had been here, so you can't think that he would have always been there. He would have had his own life to fulfill. He speaks of work. Was he working when this occurred, or was he near his job?"

"No." *(George has confused his symbol of career. School was Corey's career.)*

"Why does he talk about work then? There was social life though—yes?"

"Social life?"

"Yes. There were people around at the time?"

"Right."

"Maybe it was social and work—people might have been working as well as having a good time. It's just that he knows it was the worst day of your lives when you got the news. And he says that you've been through so much in your lives to begin with. Now you've been through this. As far as you're concerned anything else would be like nursery school."

"Correct."

"He knows that in your hearts—there are nights that you go to bed when you're very down about this, and you just wish you would die. But as he says, he's checked your records and you're still supposed to be here on the earth. He says, 'Someday you'll have to come here, things will come full circle, and we'll be back together.' *(To Peggy)* You also are employed?"

"No."

"Were you thinking of it?"

"Volunteering."

"Okay, as long as you have something to occupy your time. Even if it's not paid employment, where you'll still be doing something. Your son says that if you have too much time to dwell on this, you will constantly dwell on it, and he just doesn't want to see you suffer and make yourself crazy over it. It's better to have something to occupy your time, even if you're doing something as a volunteer. He's glad that in a way you have turned a lot of your grief into useful work, which is good. Again your son states that he's all right over there and in a happy place. Does someone pray to Christ on his behalf?"

"We both have."

"Yes, because again I keep seeing Jesus appearing behind you, saying, 'Peace be with you and peace be with your son, Corey,' now that I know the name. So obviously you have prayed to Jesus on his behalf, and certainly continue to do so, because he is all right and in a safe place. One thing you can be assured of—no harm will ever come to him again. No illness, no harm, no unhappiness, no sorrow—he jokes that this is a permanent vacation over there, where everything is pleasant and harmonious. He made a joke. He says, 'We don't have a rainy day like you do.'

(*They laugh.*) 'We're in perpetual light—it's like the perfect summer's day.' But even though you might feel that his life was cheated because he didn't get a chance, he says that it continues *there* and says his life here was fulfilled. He feels a sense of fulfillment with his life. And he says, 'You have to remember—it's my life—you have to see it from my point of view. I feel fulfilled.' And he impresses you both to go home and get a good night's rest. Because with the exception of this tragedy, your lives are pretty normal?"

"Yes."

"I mean, I'm sure you have your ups and downs—everybody does—but even before the tragedy you had the usual ups and downs, and this really takes a big piece right out."

"Yes."

"Also, there's talk of a pet. Did you lose one or did he lose one?"

"No."

"Did he have one? Because he keeps talking about the pet passed on being there with him."

"Oh—yes. Okay." (*They laugh.*)

"It was the family's pet."

"Yes. (*Laughing*) The fish."

"And he states that as strange as some people may think it is, that which has experienced love and felt love survives in the hereafter, because love can never die. So he says—he loved the pet, and the pet loved him, so he says, 'The pet is here with me.' It's funny—because your son is there with family but he likes his independence, which I don't think will surprise you."

"Um-hmm."

"He tells me he has his own place—it's funny—I see a little pond at his place, and there's what I see now as the pet fish as you told me. Again, you'd much rather have him here, but as long as you know he's all right and in a safe place, it makes it easier."

"Um-hmm."

(*To Joseph*) "There's a uniform around you. You don't work in uniform, do you?"

"No."

"Okay, a uniform is changing around you, where you kind of step out of it. This could be my symbol that you retire or start to change within your work—something is going to change. There's finance around you. You're signing legal paperwork involving finance. Maybe concluding, but again not fully concluding. (*To Peggy*) And even up ahead you may work for money or salary because there is some—you've got some ideas in your head about ways to keep your mind occupied. So up ahead you may decide to get a job, or start to go on a little bit, and your son just wants to let you know that it's all right. You have to go on with your lives. He's not going to come and give you a line of bull, but he says that you have to go on with your lives just as he has. You have to *try* to be happy again. Yes, you are going to have your bad days, but that's all right. There are going to be days that you feel like you're ready to rip your hair out, but it's okay. It is normal. It's okay to have those feelings, but don't let it be your downfall. Up ahead, though, I wouldn't be surprised if you joined a little support group. It's funny, because you meet friends there. Not only that, but you'd be amazed at how your simplicity can help someone else."

"Okay."

"Because as he says, 'It's the simple things that turn out to be the most profound.' That's what you have to keep in mind."

"Um-hmm."

"All right—he's telling me he's going to let me go, so—he worked very hard at this, but he did a nice job. I can't complain. At one point I got so frustrated and thought to him, 'Look, I don't even want to know what your name is if it is going to sound as if I'm fishing,' and he said to me, 'No, no, just follow my instruction.' (*They laugh.*) And when I didn't, he came back and said, 'You're not paying attention. Tell them you see Cary Grant and now follow.' But he embraces the two of you with love, and his brother also, and friends. Obviously he had friends that he was close to that he calls out to. Your parents are doing the same. It's obvious that you came to hear from Corey, but they are here also. And they all ask that you please remember to pray for them. But your son, Corey Alan—Core—keeps stating that he is all right and at peace. But, in any case, he's embracing you with love, also his brother, girlfriend also. Your other children are also embracing you with love—your son and your daughter—to let you know that they are there as well. Three of your children are in the hereafter, your parents, your dad—doing the same. They say, 'Pray for us until we all meet again,' and Corey says, 'Just know that I'm all right and at peace, and go on with your lives until we see each other again.' And there they go."

. . .

VIOLENT CRIME, in any form, is a difficult process to come to terms with and learn from as a spiritual lesson of the earth. The families of those who pass through another's violent actions have to reckon not only with their own lives but also the life of the otherwise complete stranger who has entered their family in the most horrible of ways. They become intimate with a person they would never want to know, yet now know personally. The only benefit, if there could even be a benefit of violent crime, is that it would eventually be possible to forget, at least temporarily, about the miserable life of someone who killed a loved one. But what happens when the killer is *not* a stranger but someone whose life is already tangled into the fabric of the family's life? The pain of losing a loved one to the violence of a family member is the hardest loss of all to reckon with, because in most cases the killer is someone who was trusted, cared about and intentionally brought into the family fold. It is also the most profound destruction of trust that anyone will ever have to endure on the earth.

Beverly Jones has what most people seem to want. She is a woman who is well-heeled, beautiful, successful and has overcome many adversities with great strength. Beverly also has what *no one* would ever want—she is the mother of a murdered daughter. I admire Beverly's strength and vigilance in a situation gone completely out of control, and her perseverance in finding answers to her daughter's murder and protecting her grandchildren against whatever odds might surface. I think her story serves to prove once again that no matter how difficult the lessons we will have to face here, we are never unprepared spiritually and the tools we need to accomplish our goals are always within us. Beverly recounts the incredible story that led her to fight for the rights of her daughter, the victim of a senseless act of violence:

"LITTLE GIRLS are the nicest things that can happen to people. They are born with a little bit of 'angelshine' about them. Kerry Lynn was the newest thing in the world—a beautiful, perfect daughter, my darling little girl. She weighed in at seven pounds and eleven ounces . . . seven-eleven, I thought—she would always have luck with her.

"Kerry was born to me fourteen months after my son, Kevin. Although also a beautiful child, at six months of age he was diagnosed with cancer, and the outlook was dismal. After several surgeons refused to operate because they felt it was too risky, we finally found a wonderful surgeon who restored Kevin's health. Kevin loved his little sister and often insisted on sharing his most prized possessions with her.

"Our lives were filled with smiles, laughter, fun, tears, comfort, curiosity, happiness and love. But Kevin's illness returned, and the following months were filled with constant trips back and forth to the hospital. I prayed, I comforted him and I loved him, but his life was coming to an end. He died on May 19, 1962. He was eighteen months old. I buried him on May 22, one day after my twenty-first birthday.

"And now I had Kerry. I loved her with an intensity that life had not prepared me for. I had gone into shock after Kevin's death, but we had to go on with our lives. Now I planned for Kerry's future and dreamed of a life full of love for her, free of struggle for her. I never dreamed of Paris or Rome for her. I wished for Kerry her own adventures and happiness, friends and love in abundance. I wished for her what she had given me—wonderful children to reach for her, who love her as she loved me . . . such joy!

"As Kerry grew, so did our affection for each other. We spent all of our free time together. In 1967, when she was six years old, her brother Trevor was born— a very quiet, placid child. Kerry was much different—always on the go. Her smile was infectious, and her personality was electric. She was filled with energy but was the most delicate, gentle soul. Her joy was in making those around her happy. An achiever, and yet even if I undoubtedly overloaded her with expectations, never did she disappoint me—what a wonderful, kind spirit. She was not just special to me—she was *special*. We are bound to one another—a bond stronger than life itself.

"Then she met the man she wanted to marry. She loved him and she wanted a life with him, babies, and a home of her own. She was a most beautiful bride, and I wanted to make everything right for her. I wished I had money enough for the things she dreamed of, but I gave her what I could—I passed on the gift of love.

"Very soon, Kerry had her own home, a wonderful career in the cosmetics industry, and became a gorgeous, classy, self-assured successful lady. Then came a bigger home in the suburbs and a beautiful baby daughter. Although she returned to work, she still found the time to be an extraordinary mother to Courtney. I had observed how much alike my daughter and I had become, but most of all I was proud and happy because Kerry appeared so happy. A few years later she had a miscarriage, and then a short time later came a son, Jeffrey, almost five years younger than Courtney. To the outside world it was the perfect family—two beautiful children and a nice home.

"I had started a new business and I was in the process of opening a retail store. It was to be a business for my two children. Although both of my children are well educated, I thought it would be wonderful for them to have their own business. Kerry chose the name for the store, 'Exemplar,' which means 'the best example,' and we planned on opening November 1, 1994. But in May of that year, Kerry came to me in confidence to tell me that she was ending her marriage. Since I had left my husband, and my children came from a broken marriage, I tried so hard to shield them from hurt and asked her if there were a chance that she would stay. I was completely surprised by her reaction. She told me that she thought I would understand more than anyone and became terribly upset. She confided to me that things were really, really bad. Over the past twelve years she had given her husband many chances, but things never changed. Now it was over. Kerry no longer wore her wedding ring, and she told me that her husband, Rob, was to leave the home sometime in January 1995, after the Christmas holiday.

"I had noticed a change in Kerry. She became very distressed, and the intensity of this upset overcame me. It was understandable to me, though, because this was a young woman who was not only very responsible but also vowed that she would never break up her marriage, knowing what it was like to come from a broken marriage herself. Sometimes we give of ourselves so much that we forget that a relationship is made up of *two* people. I should have told her to go easy on herself and not to think of this as failure, but I didn't. What I did say was that she was my daughter and I loved her and that I was on her side.

"During the summer that followed, I offered more dinners out and took photos of Kerry's husband and the children because I knew that since their marriage was ending, there would be few more opportunities. Kerry worked outside the home part time and went on buying trips with me for the new store—all happy memories. We became even closer as we prepared for the store to open. Also through that time, Kerry opened a new bank account under her maiden name and began buying things for her new home as she looked forward to the start of a new life. Even though she worked almost all her married life, her husband would not allow her to decorate their home—something she wanted to do badly. Now she looked forward to new beginnings and new dreams. During Thanksgiving weekend, we spent many hours together having our hair done and enjoying lunch after Kerry found a birthday gift for her mother-in-law. She showed me the notes that her husband had given her a few weeks earlier that promised her he would give her no trouble with the children and would leave the home as promised. Kerry never seemed happier. Later that week, Kerry, Rob and the children had a family portrait taken at a studio. I called her and arranged to meet her at her job. She was so happy. We hugged, we laughed, we planned. That was the last time I saw my daughter alive.

"At about midnight that evening, I got one of those calls that every parent wishes to God they never get. It was Rob, my son-in-law. He said, 'You better get over here.' I asked why, and he just said, 'You better come over.' I started becoming agitated, and again asked why. 'Kerry is gone,' he told me. Knowing they had problems, I asked him where Kerry had gone. Then he said, 'Kerry is dead.'

"I don't remember the drive to her home. I remember my friend asking if it was okay if we stopped for gas. My next recollection was walking through her doorway and meeting people. I wanted to see her and asked where she was. Her husband told me she was at the hospital. I wanted to go, but he told me that I shouldn't. When I asked him why I shouldn't go, he told me that I wouldn't recognize her. 'Why wouldn't I recognize her?' I asked. 'Her face is a mess,' he told me. 'Why is her face a mess?' I asked. 'She fell and hit her head,' he told me.

"I was told that Kerry was exercising on a plastic step (something she had done regularly) and when she fell, she hit her head and died. Kerry was thirty-two years old, in wonderful condition and very healthy. Rob said that he went out to the store for a few moments, came back and found Kerry dead. Then came all the lies—she drank a bottle of wine, smoked too many cigarettes and was anorexic— the lies went on and on. Something was wrong. I went home for a few hours and returned early the next morning. When I arrived, her husband warned me, 'Things are going to change.' I kept asking questions while I was taking care of the funeral arrangements. I felt something was wrong.

"That Sunday, Rob called me back with the results of the autopsy. Kerry died of a fractured skull and asphyxiation. How could this be? Also, there were the stories I was told the day before that I couldn't believe. They were impossible. I began to suspect my son-in-law. He had arranged to have her cremated in a hurry, and in my state of shock, I had been talked into this. He had also called me early that morning, instructing me to tell everyone that Kerry had died of an aneurysm. When I asked him why I should lie, he told me that he didn't want to answer questions people might have. I told no one what I suspected.

"As I was preparing for the funeral service before going to see Kerry's remains at the funeral hall, the phone rang. It was Terry, a friend of Kerry and Rob, and he was anxious to talk. Terry confided in me that he had arrived at the house and had seen Kerry on the stretcher that dreadful Friday evening. He told me that his first reaction when he saw her face was, 'Oh, God—he's killed her.' Terry wanted a second autopsy and consulted a doctor for his opinion before approaching me. I learned that unless foul-play is suspected, an autopsy will be very basic and routine. We agreed that morning to ask for a second autopsy.

"Picking up the phone to call the coroner was one of the hardest things I could do. It meant having to admit to myself that my son-in-law may have killed my daughter. I knew his character, and I knew that he was a controlling person, so I had to be sure what I was doing. You see, I have two beautiful grandchildren, and I knew Rob would refuse to let me see them. But I thought to myself, 'What would Kerry want?' I knew what I had to do. I had to know how Kerry died. She would have done no less for me. As hard as it was to make that phone call, there was nothing that prepared me for the outcome of that decision.

"The coroner contacted the police, which is standard procedure, and then made the rest of the family aware of a second examination. I pointed no finger or blamed anyone. I just wanted to know how Kerry died. Even before anyone knew of a second autopsy, Rob's mother stood outside the glass doors of the funeral hall, shaking her fist at me. She was agitated that I had spoken to the coroner directly. When the news of the second autopsy became known, all hell broke loose. I thought that people closely related to Kerry would support the news of a thorough autopsy, but I was wrong. When he found out about my request for the second autopsy, my ex-husband began screaming at me, blaming me for wanting to know how a healthy young woman in excellent condition could be found dead on the floor. He shook his finger at me and said, 'You did this.' I told him, 'Yes I did. She's your daughter, too! Don't you care how she died?' I stood up and lifted Rob's sleeve, exposing the scratches on his arm, the ones Terry had seen the night Kerry died. 'Don't you care?' Rob's father also screamed at me, 'If my son is charged, the same thing will happen to you!' He went outside and threatened my friend with the same thing. After dinner that evening, Rob's parents didn't bother coming back to the funeral hall, but his brother did. He took my son to the privacy of a lower level and tried to get him to convince me to call this off. All I wanted was to find out what happened to my daughter, and for this my life was turned upside down and even threatened. If it had not been for Kerry's wonderful friends, I don't know what I would have done. Even though they themselves were in so much pain, they offered me support. Kerry touched so many lives in such a big way, and even in death we drew strength from her and became Kerry's voice.

"After some time had passed, Trevor and I opened the store in Kerry's memory—both of us wanting to continue building Kerry's dream. Those concerned spoke with the police without pointing a finger, expecting them to do their job, but that didn't happen. I called the police two weeks after Kerry's death and was handed over to a detective in charge of the case. When I asked how the investigation was going, to my surprise he raise his voice at me and said, 'This is not a murder. Rob was a poor grieving widower! There's no criminality here, and as a matter of fact I am just going in to check the autopsy reports in a few moments.' Even though several times I tried to interrupt him and was told that he 'had the floor here,' I quickly realized what I was dealing with. I apologized for bothering him and told him that I wouldn't call again, and I didn't. This was like a nightmare. If ever I could have gone off the deep end, it would have been at that moment. This officer hadn't even seen the results of the autopsy, which he admitted to me. It turned out that the second autopsy results would not be available until months later. Again someone is screaming at me because I want to know how my daughter died. My daughter was dead and nobody seemed to care. The evil, the immorality, the incompetence—I wanted to shake them, to scream out, '*Help me! Why won't somebody help me?*' My beautiful, sweet, gentle daughter, so full of dreams. This delicate little soul that was so kind. '*Isn't anyone listening?*' She would have listened to you if you reached out to her. '*Doesn't anyone care?*'

"I decided to hire professional help. I hired a private detective, a criminal lawyer and a family lawyer. I also saw an excellent psychiatrist, which was a very good move. Before this I never dreamed that I would ever need a psychiatrist, but today I thank him for keeping me together. As expected, I was now forbidden to ever see my grandchildren. I couldn't call, send gifts or visit. During the investigation, Rob denied any problems in the marriage. Rob also aligned himself with my ex-husband and his wife, and then together they told anyone who would listen that I had gone 'off the deep end.' They prepared court documents to try to keep me away from my grandchildren. I don't understand the hatred and the evil in them and I hope I never do. What I do understand is that I have two beautiful grandchildren whose mother was full of love and shielded them from evil. I wanted for those children what their mother wanted. I wanted them to grow up knowing what a very special and wonderful mother they have, and most of all I wished for them what their mother would have wanted for them—peace. By Christmas there was an application before the courts seeking to grant me visitation. I was denied Christmas with my grandchildren. Their father's lawyer had convinced the court that I would tell my grandchildren that he killed their mother because I was investigating. In April, another application was submitted to the courts, and I am now allowed to have visits with my grandchildren every second Sunday. Not for long periods, but I thanked God for anything I could get.

It had been six months coming. Each time I see my grandchildren I tell them how special that day is to me. I tell them how much I love them. Their father controls the gifts that can be accepted, but I am thankful for what I have and pray for more.

"As the investigation continued each month, my counsel was given a little bit more information regarding the autopsy. The private investigator is now convinced that Rob was involved in Kerry's death. The coroner who performed the second autopsy believes there are many unexplained inconsistencies and has labeled it a suspicious death. The head coroner instructed police to reopen the case. On March 17, 1995, I found out that the coroner found a large sampling of Rob's DNA under Kerry's fingernails. It was a breakthrough. In the late spring, my investigator met with the same detective that has been in charge of Kerry's case. He was given copies of what we had found and any other information that would be helpful, yet still nothing happened. Later, when the detective was called by one of my attorneys, he said he was busy investigating other homicides, indicating once again that he did not consider this a homicide. I directed my counsel to speak with the coroner to have him replaced. After two months of waiting, I was pleasantly surprised to discover that two new detectives had taken over the investigation of Kerry's death. They were genuinely eager to find the truth.

"I have been told that Rob will be arrested and charged for the murder of my daughter, and they are making certain that this time there are no mistakes. They have given me an idea of time, but they will not warn me before it happens. They will call me when it is over and then continue to keep me informed. As for the first detective, he phoned and left a message on my answering machine, but I could not bring myself to return that call. I was told later that he should never have made that call, that he was out of line. He apparently wanted to apologize. Each day I wait for the phone to ring telling me that the nightmare is over. The police have warned me that it will get worse before it gets better, and to plan on another two years before it goes to trial.

"Over that year, I was reminded time and time again that the victim has no rights. I was also in an abusive relationship, and there are many of us. How many of us have to die before things change? How many deaths of young women have been overlooked? How many murderers are walking free? I never for a moment thought that my daughter was in physical danger, probably because we never expect danger to come from people we know. I believe now that whenever our daughters tell us that things are not working, we have to listen with our hearts because they will most likely never say how bad things actually are. Abused women are ridiculed if they tell about the violence they have endured. Teach your daughters to leave abusers. If they stay, they are only helping the evil grow. Tell your daughters when they are young, and tell them often. It is too late for me. Fortunately I had the funds to fight back. How many cannot? If it were not for the professionals I hired to help me, I truly believe Kerry's death never would have been investigated.

"Over the months of this investigation I lost myself in books trying to find comfort. I found the book, *We Don't Die*, about George Anderson, and then read the other two books about him because they fascinated me. I had to meet him, and after tracking him down through the book publisher, my son and I were able to see him. Our meeting was delightful—Kerry is at peace and she explained through George how she died. The facts were as we expected. She also expressed to us her concern for her children. Hearing her words, I knew in my heart that I had done the right thing so many months ago.

"As for Kerry—her dreams and her future on the earth were stolen from her that night, but her love will live within us. Her spirit will live within her children. Dear sweet daughter, you have the love, the love that links us—take it with you. No one can steal that."

THE DISCERNMENT

"Of course whatever I say, just answer yes or no. Let's see—first of all, there's a female presence, and there's a male, and another female. There's a young female, and definitely another couple, but older, of another generation. Somebody back there speak another language?"

"Yes."

"Yeah, because I hear something else. I don't hear English, I know that, but I don't know what language it is. Don't say it, but I definitely hear another language in the background. But there is a female close to you passed over?"

"Yes."

"A young one and older one, too? (*She is unsure how to answer.*) Well, I'm going to say yes for you because I'm sure that there is, even if it's from another generation that you just don't recall at this moment. Somebody else is present as well. And a male also. There's a strong fatherly presence. Did your dad pass?"

"Yes."

"Okay, because the male claims to be your father. His mother has passed over, too, yes?"

"Yes."

"Okay. And you all are family?"

"No." (*This response was from a good friend of Beverly, who accompanied her and her son to the discernment.*)

"But does your dad know these people?"

"Yes."

"Because he is saying hello to all of you. That's what's making me wonder. Your daughter is passed on, too?"

"Yes."

"He talks about your daughter being with him."

"Yes."

(*To Beverly's friend*) "And you know her also, yes?"

"Yes."

"Yeah, because she kind of made a wise crack, like, 'Don't say nobody knows me here' or something like that. Obviously then she's family to you all (*indicating Beverly and her son*) but if she's not family to you (*Beverly's friend*) by blood, she certainly is family by choice and that makes the difference. So you and she are not family by blood, but you are like family."

"Yes."

(*To Beverly*) "You've dreamt about her, yes?"

"Uh-huh."

"Because she says that this is not the first time you are hearing from her, that she has come to you via dreams [or in something like an altered state of sleep], where you've actually had a visit with her—where she's communicated with you before. You obviously pray for her and she certainly thanks you for it and asks that it continue. She says to me that she is much better than she was before, over there—that she's more tranquil. I don't know—possibly when she got over there she might have been a little upset?"

"Yes."

"That, or uncertain, but she says she's more tranquil at this time. Her dad is still living?"

"Yes."

"She keeps bringing him up—whether you have contact with him or not I don't know, but she keeps bringing up her father. (*To Trevor*) You and she are brother and sister?"

"Yes."

"Okay, because she's coming to you as a sister. I didn't know if she meant by blood or emotion, so in this case it is both. *(To Beverly)* Now your mom is still here?"

"Yes."

"Because your daughter is calling out to her. So then the couple that are with your father must be his parents. Did they speak French? Would it sound like that to me?"

"Well . . ."

"It's funny. French is being spoken because that is what I'm being told, even though that might not be his native language."

"No, but he could speak French."

"Okay, because I definitely hear French in the background, so obviously that's another language he's able to speak."

"Yes."

"Your daughter talks about passing tragically, that is true?"

"Yes."

"And it certainly is beyond her control."

"Yes."

"There's a pirate around you, so apparently something nefarious is taking place with her passing."

"Yes."

"She was having upset in a marriage?"

"Yes."

"Because she is talking about trouble in a marriage, but you didn't know about it?"

"No."

"I feel like I'm keeping it to myself."

"Yes."

"There's trouble in the marriage, but it's *inside.*"

"Yes."

"Is there an Arthur passed on or living?"

"Yes, living."

"Does she know him?"

"Yes."

"Oh, okay. She's asking how Arthur is. Were they close?"

"He's my friend."

"Okay, because she keeps saying, 'How's Arthur?' She's asking for him like somebody would do to be polite. And also, this Arthur—his dad is passed on?"

"Yes."

"Because someone is hanging around in the room claiming to be his father. And also a brother, too. Did he lose a brother?"

"No."

"Brother-in-law?"

"Well, I don't know too much about it."

"I'll have to leave it with you, because there's talk of him. His dad is here, but somebody else claims to be brother or brother-in-law. It's somebody you may have to ask him about."

"Okay."

"Your daughter has children?"

"Yes."

"More than one, obviously—yes?"

"Yes."

"Because she's saying *children*. She keeps calling out to her children—who you do see?"

"Yes."

"Is there always like a struggle with it?"

"Yes."

"Because there's a feeling that you are seeing them, but I'm getting my chops broken for the privilege."

"Yes."

"Obviously the children are with their father."

"Yes."

"Because it seems that they are—it's like you have what I'd call visitation rights?"

"Yes."

"And yet there's always a *song and dance* connected with it."

"Yes."

"Your daughter commends you that you keep persevering, that you continue to see them, and she is very happy about it. One of your grandmas is passed also?"

"Yes."

"Yes, because somebody is hanging around you claiming to be your grandmother, and it seems to be one that you knew very well."

"Yes."

"There's a feeling of you growing up with her. She certainly is an influence in your life in younger years, that obviously she lived with you or lived nearby, because you certainly recall her. It's obviously the one that you knew better, because it's somebody that you do pray for and she claims she's around you like a guardian angel. It shouldn't surprise you because it seems she played that role when she was here on the earth. The name Carrie mean anything to you?"

"Yes."

"Passed on?"

"Yes."

"Is that short for Catherine?"

"No."

"Is that your daughter?"

"Yes."

"C-A-R-R-I-E?"

"No—K-E-R-R-Y."

"Oh, *Kerry.*"

"Yes."

"Oh, okay. Obviously you don't come from New York so I'm thrown off by how she said it. It sounded like she was saying Carrie. I just pronounced it wrong. Your daughter passes from loss of air?"

"I understand that's—"

"That's how she says she passes. I feel as if I'm going to sleep, but my oxygen is being cut off somehow."

"Yes."

"Did someone try to make it look like she took her own life?"

"Umm . . ."

"Because she claims that she didn't."

"Yes."

"So somebody might have thought that could be a speculation, but she emphatically claims that she did not take her own life."

"Yes."

"She smothers?"

"I believe so."

"She's telling me she's smothering, although it looks like something else is involved."

"I thought perhaps that might be the case."

"Because she's telling me she's losing consciousness from lack of oxygen, and I feel—I'm not saying this is what happened—but I feel almost as though there's a pillow over my face."

"Yes."

"As if I'm being smothered, and yes, there is some other circumstance playing a role."

"Yes."

"Is there a weapon involved in her passing?"

"No."

"Not in the traditional sense—not a gun or a knife, but something else must have been used to cause her death. Let's say for instance she was smothered with a pillow—the pillow would be the weapon."

"Yes."

"There is a weapon involved, she tells me, but not a traditional weapon—not what we'd normally think. There is distinct evidence that there's some sort of foul play involved in her passing."

"Yes."

"Because there is—it's unquestionable. It's not a speculation—in other words, the police would say to you, yes, there's foul play involved in this."

"Yes."

"Okay—she's telling me the same—yes, there is foul play involved in her passing. Obviously some situation of foul play has taken place, and I keep seeing somebody sweeping tracks—so apparently somebody has covered their tracks, covered them very well."

"Yes."

"This happens at home?"

"Yes."

"Was there finance involved?"

"Umm . . ."

"Or did somebody think there was?"

"I believe there might have been."

"There's something going on with—money has been taken. Now I'm not saying that she was robbed, but since she's passed on, something shifted with finance."

"Oh really."

"And it might be something that you obviously were not aware of."

"Yes."

"There's a considerable sum—I'm not saying millions, but there's a considerable sum of finance involved. I feel as if once she passed on, money was shifted, something else was done with it, because I keep feeling I'm taking it from one place and putting it somewhere else."

"Okay."

"Somebody has covered their tracks very well."

"Yes."

"I keep seeing Agatha Christie in front of me, so somebody obviously planned the perfect murder. Because every little detail has been attended to. Yeah, I keep seeing that character Miss Marple from the Agatha Christie novels—like you'd need somebody like her to get to the bottom of this. You have an investigator on this?"

"I did have, yes."

"Yes, and he did come up with something? Because there's talk of an investigator almost, in a way, confirming your fears."

"Yes."

"But again, the lack seems to be proof."

"Yes."

"This is what your daughter says. You can point a finger, you can assume, you can do anything you want, but if you don't have proof, you have zero, you're back where you started from. And she talks about that this was neatly planned out. At this point, there's somebody involved, and I feel that there's more than one person involved."

"Okay."

"If somebody opens their mouth, then obviously you have something to go by."

"Yes."

"Was there any injury to her throat at all?"

"I don't think there was."

"Funny—again that feeling of—I'm not saying she was strangled, but I feel as if I'm strangling."

"Yes."

"So there must have certainly been a cut-off of air somehow. Again she brings up the money bit that plays a significant role."

"Really? I'm not surprised."

"Do you know for a fact there was any large sums of money involved?"

"No, I don't know for a fact."

"There must be something—money or something of value involved, because it's something that feels enclosed. Like it's secretive and it must have been taken from one place and put somewhere else."

"Uh-huh."

"See, because again—now I'm seeing money in front of me. Money can represent what I see, but it can also represent something of value. If someone did something with real estate, it's money but not cash. Something of value has been transferred—maybe that's the better thing to say because I'll make you think I'm seeing literal cash, but something that would be worth a considerable sum of money has been altered."

"I'll check that."

"And it's funny—I see green fields—I don't know if that represents property or not. It could be something in real estate, money could have been put into real estate. It's almost as if this could possibly—you might feel you hit another dead end, but it could give you a lead, because something has been moved somewhere else and it involves a considerable sum. And it must have happened recently, because it doesn't seem to happen before her passing and it doesn't happen immediately after her passing. I feel when things cool down it happens, when the attention is off me. Is this still an active case?"

"Yes."

"Because that's what she says—that it is still active."

"Yes."

"Her husband under suspicion?"

"Yes."

"But he has an alibi, yes?"

"Well, yes."

"Funny—yes and no."

"Yes, that's right—yes and no is right."

"Because he's there, but he's not there."

"That's right."

"I keep seeing somebody walking down a two-way street—I'm here and yet I'm there."

"Uh-huh."

"And I'm sure he doesn't know how to *bi-locate*, but—because he claims to be out of the residence when this occurs? There's a feeling of him being out, but not being out. Being out, but possibly coming back and going out again."

"Yes."

"I keep seeing a revolving door. Somebody has come in one side and gone out another."

"Yes."

"Was he seeing somebody else do you know?"

"I don't know that."

"Presently now?"

"Perhaps yes."

"Funny, I see a triangle—that there's some sort of romantic triangle going on."

"With him?"

"It could be like, him, your daughter and somebody else. Like in other words, he's married to her but also seeing somebody else. There's some sort of triangle involved. But your daughter gives me the impression she's not the type to bring her problems home to you."

"That's right."

"So she's not going to come home and tell you, 'I suspect this' or 'This is going on' or whatever."

"Yes."

"Did you and she work together?"

"No, not work together."

"It's funny, because she's talking about work contact. Were you in the same type of line together?"

"No."

"I don't know what she means by work contact."

"Well, she worked and I had her children." (*It did not become apparent to Beverly that Kerry was talking about the store they had made plans to open together.*)

"Maybe that's what she means, because she keeps insisting you and she worked together, and I didn't know how—I thought she meant like a nine-to-five job. But in that case, if you served that purpose for her, that could be where there's work contact as well as friends. This happens at night?"

"Yes."

"Because there is darkness. Late at night?"

"No."

"Why does it seem exceptionally quiet then?"

"It was early evening."

"Because everything seems so quiet. Everything's quiet, and yet I feel I can get caught up in the shuffle. It's almost like he claims to be out of the house at the time that it occurs, but yet I don't feel somebody actually saw him out of the house."

"Yes."

"Could there be another male involved?"

"I guess—anything is possible."

"Yeah, because it almost seems like another male is involved. Now to what degree, I don't know. Did the other male do the harm or did the other male know what was going on. Did your son-in-law work with finance?"

"No."

"You don't know if he had large sums or—"

"I don't know what he had."

"There's something financial or of value involved. Unless it was with your daughter or something. You don't know if she had any personal funds or anything like that?"

"I know that she didn't have a lot. I know just the house."

"That could be the real estate. Because again—is this real estate worth a considerable sum?"

"Yes."

"She keeps bringing up the green fields—that's a sign of real estate. Something's gone on with real estate where something's been switched. I mean that could be a deed of a home, changed from one name to another. Something has happened."

"That's possible. He could have changed it into his name."

"It's almost as if I hear an argument going on prior to her passing, over money."

"Yes."

"Money and real estate. I keep feeling I'm cornered, so obviously someone feels cornered by it."

"Uh-huh."

"This is perhaps maybe the only possible link that you may have that there's a new lead."

"Yes."

"Were you thinking of getting another investigator?"

"No, I wasn't thinking of it."

"It's funny, because I keep seeing a female in front of me investigating the situation."

"A lawyer—another lawyer."

"You find out she does a lot better job than maybe a guy did."

"Uh-huh—that wouldn't surprise me."

"Because it seems that there's possibly a sincere interest on her part."

"Yes."

"It seems you're pursuing but reaching a dead end each time."

"Yes."

"But something about this transfer—your daughter says that if there's wrong-doing here, which there seems to be, sooner or later the person has to mess up."

"Yes."

"Because I see a circle—that's a symbol of *what goes around comes around*."

"We hope."

"I mean, it may not happen tomorrow, but eventually it has to. I'll be honest with you, she basically has put it behind her, but she knows you haven't and you're really not about to."

"No."

"So, for your sake—not that you're looking for money or anything like that—you just want to get to the bottom of it."

"Yes."

"Do you feel her husband had something to do with it?"

"Yes."

"Because she gives me the feeling that he did. To what degree, I don't know, but I'm definitely feeling he knows something or he's involved or he committed the act. She's not making judgment on him—but he seems like—too *charming*?"

"Yes."

"Also, too, he's been caught in lies before?"

"Yes."

"Because she admits—and she's not saying this in judgment—but she gives me the impression he's kind of like a pathological liar."

"Yes."

"He's convinced himself that he's telling the truth."

"Yes."

"It's actually as if he has some sort of psychological disorder, where he can make up the story and it can come across very convincing like he's telling the truth—and he's actually lying but doesn't think he is."

"Yes."

"He claimed to have gone out that night?"

"Yes."

"And somebody did see him out?"

"I don't know that anyone saw him. He went to the store."

"He can back up his alibi?"

"Yes."

"It seems, though, the time is a little off. He's out, but he's back sooner than he claims he is."

"Yes."

"It's like, he'll go out, he'll come back very suddenly, possibly do whatever happened or be involved in it and then leave again."

"Really?"

"Again, the revolving door—I'm in and I'm out."

"Uh-huh."

"Yet he makes the discovery?"

"Yes."

"Yeah, and then I come in one way again. Could he have exited by another means?"

"Uh-huh."

"Because it seems he's not using the main—like he could have gone out a window, another door, something."

"Yes."

"He makes a very—I don't want to sound dramatic, but it's almost as if he's going out a secret passage. There's another exit way, where obviously he exited very easily. Because, technically, the store is not very far, true?"

"That's right."

"That's the feeling I'm getting. Kerry's giving me the impression that if somebody had to do it, they had to do it damn quick. I mean that somebody had to literally be watching for the opportunity to get in."

"Yes."

"Was there a forced entry?"

"No."

"Yeah, because that's the thing. It seems like somebody gets in."

"Uh-huh."

"The only thing I could say is, unless he went out and left the door open or something like this, there's an obvious—was her head injured at all?"

"Yes."

"She got cracked in the head or something? Because it feels like somebody's coming from behind me and belting me one."

"Yes."

"I don't mean to be graphic, but it seems like your daughter didn't even know what hit her. But she's hit more than once, yes?"

"Yes."

"To the back of the head."

"Yes."

"It's coming from behind. Because she tells me that, in all essence—she gives me the impression she does not see who kills her."

"Uh-huh."

"She *literally* does not see, although I feel she knows it's him."

"Yes."

"She might have found that out later on. The children were there?"

"Yes."

"She claims they were in the house, but obviously asleep or something like that."

"Yes."

"Yes, because it seems they are not—it had been too perfectly planned. It's like nobody saw a thing."

"It's planned?"

"It's almost like a feeling of it being planned. And even if it was planned very abruptly, it could have been that he decided he was going to do it that day, but he knew exactly when the perfect time would be."

"Uh-huh."

"Had there been an argument that day? Or you may not know."

"No."

"There's a feeling that there was some sort of argument or falling out that day. Yeah, he feels overwhelmed by finance, or something must have been going on where they felt a sense of financial pressure of some sort."

"Well, they were separating."

"Because again there is trouble in the marriage, so if they decided on separation, he might feel that he's going to get screwed in the deal, and that's why he's reacting accordingly. To be honest with you, I see a time bomb in front of me—apparently he is capable of—he's too calm, which actually makes it scary."

"Now?"

"No, at the time. It just seems he might have taken things with too much dignity where actually the wheels were already rolling."

"Uh-huh."

"Really, in all essence, I keep seeing John Barrymore in front of me. Apparently this guy was a good actor."

"Yes."

"He plays the role very well. And I take it the police did suspect him, yes?"

"I don't think at the beginning."

"But they do now."

"Yes."

"Yeah, because maybe in the beginning he gave them a good line, but it seems there's no other possibility. Could he have reentered the house by this other exit or entrance?"

"Yes."

"Because it seems he is not coming back in the way he originally leaves. Is there a lower entrance, like a garage entrance or a basement entrance—something like this? I feel like I'm coming in from an alternative entrance and I could enter the house very quietly from that. Because again, you would expect him to come in the front or main door, or the back door or something. Is there a garage?"

"Yes."

"Possibly he could have entered from there?"

"Yes—either that way and back to the front—there are two doors."

"He definitely does not reenter the way he exited to go to the store. Was your daughter supposedly watching television or something?"

"It's possible."

"Her mind was apparently occupied on something at the time, because I keep getting the feeling I am not aware."

"She could have been exercising."

"Obviously he's come back into the house and something is occupying her mind where she doesn't realize that he's reentered. And she's doing something— watching television, exercising, whatever—she's doing something that has her mind occupied. And unquestionably he must have come—whoever it is—he must have come from behind."

"Yes."

"If she exercises, was she in that attire?"

"Yes."

"Would she have had the music on?"

"Yes."

"See, that's the thing. And she would do this daily?"

"Yes."

"This is her routine?"

"Yes."

"See, obviously he knows it—perfect timing. I'm going to the store, bingo—if he took the car, he could have gone around the corner and then could have come back in again. I keep seeing like the 'private eye' in front of me—all is not what it seems. He took a vehicle to go to the store?"

"Yes."

"Because I feel like I've turned the corner, waited for a few seconds and could have come right back. So, in other words, I have to then go back to the vehicle. There was never a weapon found?"

"No."

"Yeah, because that's the thing—there's a weapon involved but apparently not one found. That's probably why she said that there was a weapon involved. But does it seem to be a blunt type of instrument?"

"It's possible."

"She definitely passes from a blow to the head."

"Yes."

"Because that's what I'm being told. She passes from blows to the head. There was injury to the mouth as well?"

"Yes. There are marks."

"Yeah, because it feels like I've been struck there also. Were any teeth knocked out or anything like that?"

"No."

"There's a feeling of injury around here *(indicating his head)*—scratches or something."

"Yes."

"Yes, it's almost like I'm being struck with the butt of something. But it leaves gashes in the head?"

"I haven't seen the autopsy reports directly—I haven't been allowed to—but I understand she had marks on the head."

"Yeah, it's not like somebody did it like Lizzie Borden, but definitely there are blunt strikes to the head. Also, too, did your son-in-law know the right connections?"

"Connections?"

"Like he knows who to get for an attorney or I don't know—there just seems to be a cover-up through connections as well."

"Yes."

"He's not stupid—that's a fact. He might come across that way, but he certainly is much smarter than you think. There may come a time up ahead, as your daughter encourages, even though this is on your mind and you're pursuing it— you may want to let it sleep for a while, if only to see other things develop. She gives me the feeling that you are missing the forest for the trees because you are so wrapped up in one direction."

"Yes."

"But the one thing I can tell you is she certainly seems fine. She's fine over there, and she's all right and she keeps insisting that she's put it all behind her. It's not something that's pressing her or tormenting her over there. She certainly is in a safe place. Also, too, is he moving?"

"He's supposed to be."

"Again something is going on with property, real estate in more ways than one that is very interesting. There's talk of him changing residence also."

"Yes."

"It's almost as if in the future he's trying to make it more and more difficult for you to see the children, so eventually you'll just give up out of sheer exasperation. But your daughter says he doesn't know you that well. You are not about to give up that easily."

"No."

"At this point it seems that the police are pretty convinced he's the one?"

"Yes."

"But it's like, *I know he is but I can't prove it*—that's the feeling I'm getting. Because there are no other motives otherwise."

"Uh-huh."

"You know that nobody else would do it. She's giving me the impression she really doesn't have any enemies or anything."

"No."

"And I think there was a great deal more tension going on between the two of them than you are aware of."

"Yes."

"She's not the crybaby type."

"That's for sure."

"He's having trouble with jobs?"

"Yes."

"Because your daughter keeps telling me he was losing jobs. Again, there was definitely financial strain on them."

"Uh-huh."

"And I get the feeling that she might have felt she was carrying most of the load, or at least trying to keep things together."

"Yes."

"Because it seems he's kind of like screwing up—he's losing jobs—did he have drinking troubles or something?"

"No."

"Funny, it's like somebody who has a drinking problem. He's being very irresponsible. I guess then it's something symbolic. He's having trouble with jobs, there's definitely financial pressure on them. Unquestionably I get the impression he feels cornered, and if anything happened, he definitely would be the one who's going to lose out on the deal."

"Uh-huh."

"He seems very protective of the children, but almost *too* protective."

"Yes."

"There's a feeling of everything falling neatly into place, as if a plan was there—the kids are in bed, they're asleep. They didn't really hear anything, did they?"

"Not that I know of."

"There's a feeling of them not hearing anything. She gives me the impression—doesn't it seem strange? He goes to the store, she dies in that span of time, and he comes back and finds her. I'd say his alibi is good, but I wouldn't say it is solid."

"Yes."

"It's got some cracks in it. But again, psychologically he knows how to handle himself under questioning or whatever. He's very, very shrewd. Again I feel like I'm working with two parts of my brain—one part of him may recognize that he did it, but another part has convinced him that somebody else has. So pathologically he's lying because his psychological problem has convinced him he's not the one."

"I believe that."

"It's almost like he has a split personality, like a Jekyll and Hyde. Your daughter does report that you do pray for her, and of course she thanks you for it. She tells me that however you handle this situation is your business. She's not telling you what to do, she's just telling me that she's put it behind her. But no matter what, she wants you to keep a channel open with her children. That's all she really cares about, that her side of the family is always present, and that they know you're still there for them. That's the one thing she says for up ahead—he'll do everything to fight you tooth and nail to keep you away, but that's where you'll have to hold your ground, and you certainly will. As your daughter states, it's true no matter what—what goes around comes around. Even if he gets away with it in this lifetime, he won't get away with it in the one to come. She's just more concerned about her children at this point anyway. Again, she brings up—you have to look into this real estate business, or this financial exchange, or a combination of both that will show itself. Whoever this woman is [Beverly's new attorney] might be very shrewd about finding something out in a very indirect way. There's a feeling again of somebody slipping up, so eventually it may come to pass. He might have been the one who does it, but somebody else knows or suspects. I keep seeing scenes from *Gaslight* with Ingrid Bergman, where the husband is very shrewd in the way he handles himself. But as your daughter states, you have to handle it in a way that you think is right, but she again impresses you to maybe lay low for a while and let things happen on their own. Maybe sometimes you become wrapped up with it too much, and you might miss the forest for the trees. She's come in dreams to you, too, yes?"

"Well . . . not really."

"Well, unless you genuinely don't remember. I know I dreamt last night but I couldn't give you a detail. But she does talk about coming to you in dreams."

"Good. Tell her to keep coming."

"Is there a wedding coming up or something?"

"Perhaps. My son-in-law's brother."

"Because there is talk of marriage and it's connected on the husband's side of the family—or even with him. And she says not only is there a marriage in the traditional sense but also a 'marriage' as a merger of two things figuratively. Maybe this real estate thing, but there's a merger of two things and there's a marriage. And again, this could also play a role—he might think he's out of the range of fire now although he is still under suspicion. He might start to do things that eventually seem just a bit out of the ordinary. Yes, he's waiting for the smoke to clear and he probably thinks it is starting to clear. That's why he's doing things now. Did your daughter keep any type of diary or something?"

"Yes."

"Is it missing?"

"Yes."

"She keeps talking about it. There's obviously evidence in there, or something has been written because she's talking about writing or keeping a journal. I keep seeing *The Diary of Anne Frank* in front of me, so obviously she is keeping a diary or journal of what's going on in her life, and he must know about it."

"Yes."

"I mean, as much as the Gestapo would have wanted to find Anne Frank's diary to keep quiet what was happening in Europe at that time, the same thing is happening with your daughter. It's funny that it was missing beforehand or certainly disappeared not long after her passing. And certainly somebody doesn't break into a house to steal a diary. The diary is a key piece of evidence. There is definitely documented evidence that she might have confided in the diary about marital troubles, finance—you know, things going on."

"Uh-huh."

"It seems he doesn't know about it, and then all of a sudden he finds out about the diary. So I wonder if he found out about it after she passed on, and maybe that's why I feel it's missing beforehand—because she's keeping it in a safe place. He called the police right away, yes?"

"Yes."

"Because, again, he plays his cards right—he calls the police right away but obviously there's time afterward to search through some of her personal things, to make sure. I see fire, so I'm going to assume it's been destroyed—I'm not saying that it was burned—that could be my symbol that it has met with destruction. It could give evidence against him that he's unpredictable. It didn't look like the house was robbed, true?"

"That's right."

"As far as I can tell that's the only thing she seems to speak about that is missing. There's always talk of him going off on jobs or something, but they don't work out. There are definitely a lot of problems going on."

"Uh-huh."

"And she's trying to keep it together, but after a while, like any sensible person, she's had it up to *here*."

"Yes."

"And then she figures, *okay—I want out.* It seems like financially for a time she was carrying the load."

"Yes."

"I feel like he's getting a free ride, but she leaves, the holiday is over and he's on his own."

"Yes."

"The name Martin mean anything?"

"Yes."

"Living?"

"Yes."

"Connected with her?"

"Yes—and him. It's his cousin."

"She keeps bringing up Martin. Did they speak French also?"

"No."

"Somebody said *Martine*, but that could also clue me to the name Martin. Are he and his cousin very chummy?"

"Yes."

"I wonder what's up with them, because she gives me the feeling of Martin kind of being involved. Now, I don't know how involved—maybe not involved in the actual crime—but maybe he suspects his cousin did it or he said something. He might be someone else you might want to keep in mind and keep an eye on if you can, just to see. Because sooner or later somebody has to mess up. And when it comes to abandon ship, we all know it's going to be 'every man for himself.'"

"Uh-huh."

"Is Martin kind of shady?"

"Yes."

"Because I keep seeing him under a shady tree—that this is somebody who is a shady character."

"Yes."

"So there may be something he knows. I'm not saying that he was involved directly, but he might have found out or he might know something is going on. Maybe he *is* involved, who knows, but there is a feeling of involvement, so there must be something loose there. I guess with this she is going to fade—she seems to be fading down. But the last hurrah was about Martin and she shows him under a shady tree—a symbol that he's a shady person. Again, she's not making judgment—just telling the facts. Has he been involved in illegal troubles before or something?"

"Not that I'm aware of. It's possible."

"It's almost something you might want to look into a little bit. People can be involved in things and not have gotten caught either, but this is somebody you may want to look into. I see somebody pointing a finger, which is usually a symbol to keep your eye on that person. I get the feeling you don't trust him either."

"No, I don't."

"Something could certainly be up. But for the time being there may be a 'sleeping period.' You may feel you have to lay back for a while or lay low and just let things fall into place. At one point you may think it's better if the smoke does seem to clear. But, in any case, they're telling me they are going to withdraw, because your dad and the other people that were here are signing off. Your daughter is going back also, but most particularly she says her main concern is that you always keep your channel open with her children. She wants all of you to know—to have the assurance—that she certainly is in a safe place. But with that she withdraws with love, and says to just know that she is all right. She says, 'At least I know I'm in a safe place and no harm could ever come to me again.' They understand spiritually over there as she now knows—if he is the one, sooner or later he has to reconcile this. What goes around comes around—it must happen, and it's inevitable."

"Yes."

"Even if you don't see it in your lifetime, the person sooner or later has to face up to themselves. But in any case, she sends her love to the three of you and to her children also, and she just says, 'This is Kerry signing off until we meet again.' And there they go."

(In April 1997, Beverly's former son-in-law was arrested and charged with the second-degree murder of Kerry. Because of the extensive DNA evidence, his conviction seems imminent. Beverly still has limited visitations with her grandchildren and hopes that after his conviction she will be granted custody of them.)

Eight

LOSS OF
A PARTNER

THERE WAS A WOMAN who came to see me in South Carolina one February. She had lost her husband, a military man who, in communicating during the session, reminded me very much of my own father. Three months later, in Cincinnati, a gentleman who communicated from the hereafter to his wife during a session seemed so familiar that after the reading I felt compelled to tell this woman that I felt like I knew him. "Oh, you do," she told me. "You met him three months ago in South Carolina." Since I hate doing discernments for people who have been to see me less than a year before (there is no challenge, either for me or the souls in the hereafter), I asked her why she would come so soon after having had a discernment just three months prior. "You see," she explained, "I was married to that man when I was sixteen years old. That was fifty-three years ago. He is the only man I ever knew, and we have never been apart. It seems only natural to me that he would want to visit with me as much as he can." At first hearing, this could almost sound comical, but in a very real way she believed and understood that not even physical death could separate her from her husband. I wish more people had that strength of conviction. She was right, though, because the souls in the hereafter tell us constantly that *love* is what survives of our physical bodies on the earth, and it is a gift that cannot be taken away. No matter what divides us on the earth, our spiritual bond is permanent and enduring. You have to be connected to someone that strongly to know what that feels like, but it is there. Those who have lost spouses have told me that they do not necessarily need *me* to maintain communication with the people they held so dear on the earth and now in the hereafter. That is absolutely correct and is a real indication of true understanding of the way things work in the hereafter—love is a bond that cannot be broken. Sometimes it is a bond that survives *in spite of* itself, as in relationships that were rocky or abusive. But the love is the common thread, and it remains with us here and hereafter.

In discernments that I have done for both husbands and wives, I find it interesting that the souls there say that it is harder to be a widower than a widow and for different reasons. While all loss is tragic, I have been told that the wife is the heart and soul of the home and very often assumes the role of housekeeper, financial director, health care provider and moral supporter. With so many roles that wives fulfill for their husbands and families, more than just a lifetime partner is lost at the wife's passing. I have also been told by the wives in the hereafter that no matter how much the bravado of the husband, men in general have the greater need for nurturing—something that wives do without even thinking. When it comes to the widow or widower here, it seems that different lessons are to be learned by the loss of a spouse, depending on if you are a widow or widower. During discernments where a husband has passed, they seem to encourage their wives' newfound independence and help them to be strong. They also tell their wives that they were glad they passed first, because they could not have been as accepting of loss as their wives in the same situation. During the discernment, men in the hereafter will admit (probably for the first time in their lives) that women are indeed the stronger sex and are in a better position to cope with loss and still move on in their life's journey.

The one issue that is raised at almost all the discernments of a spouse who has passed on is the issue of remarriage. In a group session that I had done for a bereavement group in Queens, New York, there was a man who had lost his wife. His wife came through in a discernment to tell him that it was perfectly all right to go on with his life and *new* love, and that if he loved this woman, then she would, too. He broke down and cried. He told me afterward that after five years of loneliness after the loss of his wife, he began to date a family friend primarily for the company she provided. His relationship blossomed, and he called his children together to discuss the possibility of his remarrying. They were angered by his involvement and have since become estranged. They felt that he was sullying their mom's memory by getting involved again, and he admitted that at times he felt the same way. By hearing from his wife that she not only approved of his "going on" with his life, she helped him understand that she also would love the person that brought her husband peace and joy on the earth. She had also mentioned that sooner or later the children would come around and accept his choice with her help from her unique vantage point. What discernments like this help me to understand is that the power of love in the hereafter is far-reaching and is not mired by jealousy or single-mindedness. When we pass into the hereafter after having more than one spouse, we become a community of love of the spirit, and we are not bound to the convention on the earth that each person can only love one other person. In the hereafter, true love is of the soul, and, removed from the physical, it has no bounds. The only way the souls can help us to understand this concept on the earth is to think of our relationships with people we truly love but are not involved with physically, such as having a spouse as well as best friend that we love equally in the heart. It is also not uncommon that souls who had the same mate on the earth due to remarriage have told me that they have become good friends in the hereafter—after all, they already have so much in common.

Spousal loss is hard when you consider that the spouse you lost is also your best friend, or sometimes even a sparring partner. In one discernment for a woman who had lost her husband to cancer, the soul from the hereafter told me that although life was not always easy he still loved her even if at times on the earth he had a strange way of showing it. To illustrate his point, he showed me a scene from the old television show, *Friday Night Fights*. Even though times are not always easy on the earth, the spouse in the hereafter still loves and cares for their beloved here and tries to help guide their spiritual road here until they are reunited again in the hereafter.

There are some times when, no matter how much people love each other, the relationship crumbles on the earth. Hindsight being 20/20, the spouse who has passed on begins to understand completely the problems that persisted and is in a position to help the surviving spouse. They know that in spite of the terrible things that may have been said and done, they love us and forgive, and hope that we can, too. Even in circumstances where violence or infidelity has marred or even destroyed a relationship, the profound feelings of love endure from the here-after despite the hardship that was caused or done. Many admit that they learn, sometimes for the first time, how they could have been a better spouse, and part of their spiritual lesson in the hereafter is to learn to feel and show love, no matter what the circumstance. They do this in an effort to help their surviving spouse learn to love again and without reservation and, in time, to forgive and move on. One of life's hardest and most productive spiritual lessons is that we must love someone even though they have caused us to suffer.

Deborah Scholes knows firsthand the damage that can be done by spousal abuse, both physical and mental. Yet in spite of the terrible things she endured both before and after the passing of her husband, John, she remains remarkably philosophical about her life and the man she continues to love and still hopes to understand. After everything that has happened to her, she still holds fast to her memories of a man who had the capacity to be as kind as he was sometimes brutal. It takes a strong conviction to stay centered about the meaning of life and lessons in this dimension when you have seen the worst it has to offer, but Deborah still sees John as the husband he *could have been*. I don't think that there is a better example of unconditional love and forgiveness. Deborah allowed me to use her story to help others understand that love survives no matter how badly it is beaten and that, in the end, people are the sum total of their capacity to love without condition:

"YOU CAN NEVER SAY what you would and wouldn't do in a situation until you find yourself in it. It is so easy to say, 'I would never let someone hurt me. The first time it happened I would be out of there.' That's what I always thought. You see programs on television about abused wives and you think they are stupid for staying, but you never count on what the power of love does to your thinking. It makes you see beyond all the bad in someone and see the hurt in them. Something in you *makes* you stay, good or bad. Sometimes situations get better and people change—but mostly they don't and things get worse. All you can do when you find yourself in an abusive relationship with someone you love is to hope they get better. Hope is all we have. My hope is that people who think I was crazy to stay in an abusive relationship can see it from my eyes and know that I loved John *in spite of* himself.

"If I had to pick the one thing that drew me to John when we first met, it would have to be his eyes. There was something so familiar to me about his eyes— they were so blue and beautiful, and when I looked into them it was like looking into my own soul. We met at work where we both worked in a factory, and in 1983 we went on our first date. We started dating while I was separated from my husband with whom I had two children—a girl, Amie, and a boy, Chris. John was the type of person that everyone loved for his teddy-bear personality, and my children took to him instantly as he did to them.

"As our relationship progressed, there were some things about John that I started to notice. I didn't see it as a problem at first. I just thought that John was a little *different*. We would go out somewhere and John would have a few beers, and then his behavior would become erratic. He would sometimes get a little out of control. I didn't know what to think because I wasn't a drinker, and thought maybe that if he controlled the beer his moods wouldn't change so much. My mother and father noticed the sudden changes in his behavior and thought that it was because of drugs. I defended him by telling them that if he was doing drugs I would have known about it. He wouldn't be able to hide it from me. They were right, though. John did confide to me later on that he used to do drugs—crank and pot. But that was in the past, and for most of the times that we went out together things were very nice and very enjoyable.

"As we became more involved, I noticed that John had trouble dealing with his temper. He would be annoyed or angry about something, and then have a beer or two and then just go off the deep end. He started hitting me when he was angry, and a few times I had to be hospitalized as a result of getting hit. The worst was when he saw my ex-husband's car in the driveway after he dropped off the kids one day. John saw someone come out of the house and, thinking it was my ex-husband, threw a beer bottle. It was actually me that John saw, and the bottle shattered the side of my face and cut my temporal artery. When my ex-husband drove me to the hospital, John followed in his car. He came into the emergency ward, found my ex-husband and began to beat him. The police had to be called again. I never thought I would *ever* let someone hit me, but when you love somebody and know not even *they* understand why they have these episodes, something makes you want to stay and help them. There was no dealing with him at all during these episodes until he slept it off and calmed down. There were a couple of incidents like that, but when he did calm down and for most of the time, John was very good to me and wonderful to be around.

"We decided to pool our resources and save some money by having his car on my insurance policy, but because he was drinking again I told him that I was going to have to take him off my insurance. He found out about it and got so angry that he came to my house and trashed it. He broke down the front door, put holes in the wall—he just went crazy—all because he thought that by telling him to get his own insurance I was trying to break up with him. At that point I had enough and called the police and had him arrested. When he calmed down, he told me that he was afraid that I was going to leave him, and that dropping him from the insurance was the first step. I told him that I only did that because I wanted him to be more responsible. But now I realized that I did want to separate my life from his because I had just turned thirty and didn't want any more of the chaos of the last two years with him. I had myself and my children to worry about, and it just seemed that once a month he would go crazy over something. I used to kid him that he had his own menstrual cycle—he would be great all month, but then for two days he would be irrational and impossible to deal with. I wanted a normal life with him, but I would never know when those two days were going to pop up and ruin things. I guess that I should have left him when I first started seeing trouble, but there was something about John that I just loved, and I saw a good man in him in spite of the once-a-month episodes. He had so many wonderful qualities, and I just thought that it must be his age and that he would grow out of it.

"But he was arrested that night, and I decided that things would have to change. A counselor at the jail called me the next day and asked me if I knew that John took methamphetamines. I insisted that he didn't, but she asked me if I ever wondered why his moods would change so dramatically or why he never seemed to have much money. It really began to hit me. I had never put it together until that moment, and I felt so stupid for not seeing it sooner. She asked me if I loved him, and I told her that I did, very much, but I couldn't put up with any more abuse. She asked me to meet with her, which I agreed to do, and she told me that he would be going to Northwestern Hospital to battle his addictions.

"At the hospital, part of John's counseling involved coming to grips with the fact that he had a very bad relationship with his parents from years of growing up in a dysfunctional household. There was even an incident at the hospital where his parents lied about inviting me to John's birthday party there. He was so angry that I didn't come, but when I visited him afterward he found out that his parents never called me like he asked them to. He flew into a rage over this, and it was a major setback in his rehabilitation. After seeing his rage over that incident, the counselors there began to see a pattern developing in him.

"They began to understand that a lot of John's problems stemmed from the way he was raised and the lack of values in his family. There was so much lying and deceit in his family, and John grew up with no morals. When John got in trouble as a young boy, his father would constantly bail him out, never admitting that John could do anything wrong. One time when John was suspended from school for three days, his father devised a plan to make it appear to his mom that John was getting ready for school as usual, and when she left he would go back into the house. There was a lot of lying and a lot of secrets in the house. John would later tell me a story about the time when he was a little boy and he watched his father steal tools that he needed from the store because John's mom wouldn't give him the money to buy them. He also told me about a time at a picnic that his family went to when he realized that his father was the object of everybody else's ridicule. He was so embarrassed to find out that his father was considered a loser by the people who knew him. But his parents never taught John how to take responsibility for the things he had done as a child, and they made it worse by defending him even when they knew he was guilty.

"One night after drinking, John hit a street light and did a lot of damage to some property, and his parents stood up for him and even helped him get out of trouble. They constantly made excuses for the things he did and never made him take responsibility for his actions. John came to the realization that he despised his mother for all the things she had done to him growing up and for belittling his father. There was never any control in his life, and that lack of control followed him into adulthood. I think that both parents had emotional problems, and in a big way they helped create the monster that was in John.

"By 1986, John had served four months in jail for the night he destroyed my house, and he was continuing his rehabilitation. I started seeing someone else that year, but we ran into each other again at a Narcotics Anonymous meeting that I also attended to help be supportive of his recovery. He didn't see me come in and didn't know I was there. When it was John's time to speak, he talked about the things that had happened to him and he admitted all the horrible things that he had done to someone close to him who really tried to stick by him and try to help. I was so moved by that, and we talked afterward. We started seeing each other again after he promised me that he would never touch beer or drugs again, and I believed he was sincere. We moved in together, and although he was still trying to deal with his anger, he never drank or took any drugs. A few months later, my children and I were in a bad car accident, and John took care of us. He really showed us that he had changed and wanted to be a good person. We married in October 1987.

"After we married, John never hit me again. He was clean, sober and really trying to make things work, and they did. But one thing that he still couldn't shake was his temper and his rage over the smallest of problems. It would be for the most insignificant things. He would get frustrated and something would balloon into a major upset for him. But other than his anger, things were really going well for us, and we learned how to work around these moods. I was working in an auto salvage business, and John came to work there a while later. We eventually bought the company in September 1989, and things started going very well for us. John finally found something he was good at and was a wonderful businessman. Owning his own company gave him a sense of pride that really helped him feel good about himself. He started accomplishing goals in his life that he thought he'd never see, and the business was successful. During the years we were married, my children looked to John as a real father, and he was really in love with them. He would introduce them as his own children rather than stepchildren, and he was really there for them as a father. The children really grew to love him. Even though the children witnessed the times when he went crazy because of his temper, they were never afraid of him because none of the anger was ever directed at them, and he would never hurt them. His parents never acknowledged our marriage, and there came a time when even his counselors recommended making a split from them because they could never accept anything in his life that they were not a part of. In the nine years we were married, they never saw the inside of our home.

"In February 1995, John fell and herniated two disks in his back. It was devastating for him because he was always so proud of his accomplishments and the fact that he was so strong, and now he was in constant pain and not able to do much in our business except answer the phone. No matter how much he tried to compensate for the fact that he could no longer lift any of the auto parts, he was not able to accept the fact that he couldn't do his job. He had surgery to alleviate some of the pain, but he never got to the point where he could work the way he wanted to. After his fall, the problems we had before started coming again. He was humiliated and sometimes would break down and cry. The doctors had given him painkillers, but they were so strong that he couldn't do anything at all when he was on them. He started taking Valium instead, but he started taking more and more of it. We tried to restructure the business to give him a way to work without lifting anything, but he was so depressed. We bought a mountain home that September, and I hoped it would be the answer to our problems—he could relax there in a gorgeous setting. He started going up there more and more frequently to fish, but he would go without me and seemed to get lost in himself. I was losing my husband. It was like he just turned me off in his life. We were becoming less and less part of his life, and I know that he felt he was a failure and wanted to be alone. I tried to give him as much space as I could, but the isolation started to fray our marriage. I started to feel lonely and did something I thought I would *never* do—I had a relationship with someone else. John found out about it and we were able to work it through as best we could, but John's downward slide continued.

"On the morning of December 2, 1996, I got up and helped the children get ready for a family reunion they were attending. I had gotten the sewing machine out to finish a valance I had made for the mountain home. John came out and started getting upset that the children's rooms were not straightened up, and I told him just to forget it—they would get to it when they returned that night. But John couldn't let it go and became very angry. He threw the sewing machine to the floor and I started to leave, but he grabbed me by my hair and dragged me across the floor. As I got back to my feet and ran out the door, he followed me out to the driveway and started slashing the tires of my car. I went back into the house to just wait out this episode. I knew from experience that there was no trying to talk this through, and the best thing to do would be to hope it blew over soon. I got a phone call from a friend who needed some information that I had at work, so I decided to walk there since it was so close. When I returned, he was changing the tire he slashed and I could tell that he had calmed down. I went back into the house, cleaned up the mess he created throwing the sewing machine and finished the valance. John was calm now and even complimented the valance I made.

"By one o'clock in the afternoon, John was watching the Philadelphia Eagles play on television, but then came out to me and told me he wanted a tool back that he had loaned someone. I told him that Jeff had the tool (Jeff was the man I had the relationship with during my marriage) and I could already see John's mood darkening. John told me that he was going to get the tool and tell Jeff what he thought of him. I started to get scared that he would hurt Jeff or me or both of us, and I called Jeff to warn him before I left the house. But when I spoke to Jeff, he told me that John never said a word—he got his tool from Jeff and went home. I was out of the house all day, figuring that I had better let John calm down before I tried to come back, but I got a call on my cell phone from my children telling me that they had come home early from the reunion. I asked them how John was, and they told me he was fine. I was relieved, because I had tried to call him a few times, and he wouldn't pick up the phone. Even though the children were home, I decided to stay away a little longer to make sure things had blown over. I knew that John would never take his anger out on them, and it would be better for all of us if I waited until he was more calm. What I didn't find out until many weeks later was that John had been taking Valium all day.

"About eight o'clock that evening, my daughter called me to tell me that John had gone up to our mountain home looking for me. The home security printout showed that he was at the house for about fourteen minutes before he reset the alarm, which would bring him back to our home at around eleven o'clock. At that point I don't know how much Valium he had in him, but when he got back he was angry to the point where he started scaring the children, yelling at them and asking if I had called. They lied, telling him no because they were becoming afraid that he would find me and do something. He had come into the house with a beer from our garage that was about two years old (nobody drank beer in the house anymore) and began screaming at the children. After he asked them again if I called them, he told my son, 'If you are lying to me, the last thing you will see is a bullet.' It was the first time ever that he threatened the children, and they were scared. My daughter called me to tell me what had happened, and I sped back to the house within five minutes and left my car in front of the house rather than in the garage in case there was any trouble.

"When I came through the front door, John was sitting on the sofa with four beer cans on the end table next to him. He asked me where I had been and I told him I was just driving around. He told me that he was at the mountain house earlier and even complimented the job I did hanging shelves there. I could tell he had been worried about me and this was his way of making up for before. Everything seemed fine now and I was glad, because I didn't know what to expect. I looked again at the empty beer cans, but I didn't say anything because I didn't want to provoke him. I asked where the kids were and he told me that they were in their bedrooms. I walked about twenty-five feet from him, through the hallway and into my son's room to make sure they were all right. My son was in his room shaking. He was really upset, but I told him, 'Just get in bed. Mommy's home and everything will be all right.' When John heard that, he bolted from the sofa to right next to me in the doorway of the bedroom and said, 'I tell you what I am going to do. I am going to get a gun and I'm going to kill you, your kids and myself!' He was completely out of control from the beer and, as I found out later, the Valium. I was terrified now because this was something that I had never heard John say before. He ran down to the basement, and I told my children to hurry and get dressed so we could get out. As we got to the front door to leave, he came back up the basement stairs with a loaded gun. The front door was open, but he stopped us by blocking the door. When I saw his eyes, there was no doubt in my mind that he was going to kill us, and I became hysterical from fear. He had the gun aimed at my daughter's head and said, 'Just to show you I'm not bluffing,' and he opened the screen door and shot the gun. It sounded like a cannon. He aimed the gun at my daughter's head again, but she shoved him. I thought I was going to collapse from fear. He got up and punched her, knocking her to the ground. I gathered my courage and walked over to him, putting both hands on his shoulders, telling him, 'John, this is not what you want to do. Please, stop.' He aimed the gun toward the ceiling, and I told the children to go sit on the sofa, away from where we were. I told John that I had to go to the bathroom badly, and he let me go. Instead of going to the bathroom, I went into my bedroom and got my gun out and brought it to the bathroom with me. I was still shaking while I tried to load the gun in the bathroom, but I jammed it. After I tried to fix it, I wasn't sure if it was now loaded or not, but I put it in my pocket and got out of the bathroom. When I came out, he was sitting on the sofa adjacent to the children with the last beer in his hand. He was a little calmer now, but I could tell he was irritated. I asked him where his gun was, and he told me, 'Don't worry about it.' I asked him again, but he would not tell me. I told him that he shouldn't be drinking, and he let me take the beer out of his hand. I went to the kitchen and put the beer in the sink. I went back to him and said, 'John, please let the kids and me leave and we will talk tomorrow. He agreed to it, but I noticed that he had his hand down in the sofa between the cushions. I thought he might still have the gun in his hand because his hand was covered. I told the kids to get into the van and gave them the keys. I started to feel a little better—that he would just let us go and he would have time to get a grip on himself again.

"The children started out through the kitchen to the garage, but he jumped up and yelled, 'They're not going anywhere! I'm going to wreck that van and I'm going to kill them!' The children started to run but he bolted after them. My daughter tried to get the garage door open, but he ripped her back and she fell partly down the basement stairs. There was such rage in his eyes, and he started toward me. I was cold with terror. Like a robot, I reached for the gun in my pocket and shot him. He stopped cold in surprise. 'You shot me!' he said. He was so close to me that I realized that I shot him in the stomach. He fell down but then started to sit up. I thought he was coming at me again, so I shot him again. Suddenly I realized that I had shot him—I had shot my husband. I broke down and got hysterical. But when I looked at his hands, there was no gun. When I was in the bathroom, he must have gone back to the basement to put the gun away, and I never knew it—he wouldn't tell me where the gun was when I asked. I screamed to my daughter to call an ambulance, but she was too terrified to dial the phone, so I got up from where I was with John and called the police for an ambulance and gave them my address. Without realizing that you are supposed to stay on the line,

I hung up and ran back to John. They called back and my son handed the phone to me. Even though he was on the floor and in pain, he looked all right. He wasn't really bleeding. He kept saying to me, 'Debbie, I'm going to die,' and I kept telling him, 'No you're not. You're going to be all right. You *have* to be all right.' I was beyond hysterical as the reality of what I did started to settle in. He asked for something to drink, but the police on the phone said not to give him anything to drink and to roll him on his side. They asked me if he was bleeding and I told them that he wasn't really. We were able to prop his head up until the police arrived.

"The first policeman to arrive was a good friend of John's. He came in and asked me where my gun was. I told him that it was on the shelf above the phone. I turned to him and said, 'There is another gun.' I turned to John and said, 'John, you have to tell him where the gun is.' John told him that the gun was in the safe. I didn't see it, but this policeman went down to the basement and came back a few minutes later. When the emergency technicians arrived, they told me to go to the other room. John must have died just a few minutes later, because they brought him to the ambulance and started CPR on him. At 1:23 A.M. they pronounced John dead.

"Even though John didn't appear to be bleeding much after he was shot, he was bleeding profusely internally. I thought that the fact that he didn't feel cold (which is what I thought happened when people are dying) meant that he would be all right. I made all sorts of promises to God that if he could be all right, we would work on changing everything that kept going wrong. I was taken to the police station for interrogation when I found out that John didn't make it. They needed to know everything because it appeared to them that I just came home after a night out and blew my husband away. I was at the police station until one o'clock the next afternoon trying to sort out what happened that night. They let my children go home with my parents so that they could sleep, but they kept me there while they searched the house for John's gun. The police did find credibility in my story because the children (who were also questioned) saw what happened, and they also filled in some of the facts I didn't know, like when John went back down to the basement to return the gun to the safe while I was in the bathroom. The police went through everything but could not find the gun. The first policeman, John's friend, was alone in the house for five hours before it was officially searched, but I think that someone may have taken the gun. They asked me for the combination to the safe, which they told me was locked. I told them that the safe was only two weeks old, and since John didn't really know how to lock and unlock it he never locked it. The combination of the safe was in our bedroom drawer, but when the police unlocked it, only the gun box was in it. I told them that the safe and the room were never locked, so somebody locked the safe and the room. Because they could not find the gun, the District Attorney could not close the case as a justifiable homicide.

"It became obvious that the gun was taken from the house. They administered a polygraph test on me, which I passed, and they polygraphed the policeman who was John's friend and the first to arrive at the house. He failed it. After talking to the children again and administering polygraph tests on them, the District Attorney was inclined to believe that perhaps there was a gun and somehow it is now missing. It is very difficult to accuse anyone, let alone the police, who were the only ones in the house after me, of taking evidence, but the gun remains missing, and to this day has not been found. I think at this point it would be better just to let "sleeping dogs lie," since that evidence was not necessary to prove my story. On December 16, two weeks after John died, I was cleared of wrongdoing. Even after a lot of counseling to pick up the pieces of my family's life, I still have to deal with the fact that I ended John's life and that this incident had made front-page news. Our lives have been changed forever by this loss, but I know in my heart that John, from the hereafter, helped the truth come out and saved me from potentially going to prison. I still have to live every day knowing I killed someone I loved with all my heart, but I know that this is my lesson in this life. But in spite of everything that went on during our time together, I know that John loves me and the children and understands that no matter what happened, I still love him and always will.

THE DISCERNMENT

"Okay—well, first of all a male presence has come into the room, and a female. Another male and another male. One of the males seems to stay in the background so he may be of another generation. A female comes in and stays in the background, too. They talk about family, so I assume they all are family somehow, or family connected. There is talk about the younger male that passed on. Does that make sense?"

"Yes."

"Who is family, yes? Umm—"

(She begins to motion, no, but thinks about it.) "Yes."

"Yeah—I was going to say—through love or marriage, whatever. I saw your face and something told me to look away. I could feel the emotion [from him] so let's leave it alone. He does say that he's linked to you as family, is that correct?"

"No."

"Well, I'm going to go with it anyway, and I'll say by emotion then, if not by actuality. Passes young though, yes?"

"Yes."

"He claims that he comes to you in dreams. Is that true?"

"Yes."

"Because he said that this is certainly not the first time you're hearing from him. He comes to you nocturnally, which means in your sleep. Where you have actual visitation. This puzzles me—without explaining—why does he bring up dad, did his dad pass?"

"No."

"It must be that his dad is on the earth then. He must be *calling* to his dad. He keeps bringing up dad. I don't know if he and his father were close, but he calls out to him, 'Tell dad you've heard from me.' If they weren't close, maybe he's calling out due to a lack of communication. Now, this puzzles me, but it could also be a unique clue—this young male puts a big sweetheart valentine in front of you— does that make sense?"

"Yes."

"Am I correct in assuming that there is romantic involvement?"

"Yes."

"Okay. This is your spouse? (*She nods.*) Legally or emotionally?"

"Um-hmm."

"Okay, because he keeps saying that he's your spouse. Well, he just corrected me. He says, 'Well, I'm her *spouse*—legally *and* emotionally.' But the big sweetheart in front of you can be my clue that this person is romantically involved with you, *was* at one time, it could be my symbol of your being sweethearts, so I had to be careful. Once you shook your head yes, he saw the acknowledgment. And yes, he's not your family by blood, but he *is* your family. You're linked by marriage and by emotion. The term *family* makes sense. Now, again—his dad is on the earth?"

"Yes."

"He and his dad have kind of a crummy relationship?"

"Yes."

"Yeah, again he calls out. He's probably wishing that could have been corrected or changed. He's asking for his father. I don't know whether you have any contact with him, but I don't think it would really matter even if you did. He calls out to his father, but there must be some reason for it. Maybe something's up with the father that he must be aware of. Mom is here, too. His mom is on the earth?"

"Yes."

"Funny—close and *not* close?"

"Yes."

"That's the thing—they're there, but there's no relationship. They're close but they're not close. They're there only in the sense that they are his parents, but a relationship doesn't exist otherwise. Funny—your spouse is very close with your parents?"

"Yes."

"Yes, if I didn't know better, I would think *they* were his parents."

"Yes."

"Your folks are both on the earth, I take it?"

"Yes."

"Yes, he keeps calling out to your parents, and states that your parents are the parents he always wanted and never had—*your* parents are the family. He's the son-in-law, but he's more their son emotionally, and he asks me to ask you to tell your parents that you've heard from him, because he looks upon them as his parents. And he just wants to thank them for being so good to him while he was on the earth, being like parents to him and treating him like a son and loving him as a son. Whether they believe in this [mediumship] or not, he could care less—it's the message that's important, not the belief system. He just wants to let them know that he's all right and at peace, and just thanks them for embracing him into their home. It made a difference to him, and it may not have been a big deal to your parents, but your husband says that it's the simple things that are the most profound. Now he speaks of family. You do have family?"

"Yes."

"Now he means children, I take it."

"Yes."

"Wait a minute—why did he say *child* and then said *children?* You have children? Do you know what he's doing?"

"Yes."

"Because I don't understand why he says 'child, children.' Did you lose a child?"

"No."

"But you know what he means."

"Yes."

"I better leave it. You have more than one child?"

"Yes."

"Okay. Now he says there are two. Do you have two children?"

"Yes."

"You never expected to be a young widow, however, you might not like to hear this, but your husband says, 'If one of us had to go first, I'm glad it was me.' He never would have wanted to be a widower. But you do pray for him in your own way, yes?"

"Yes."

"Because he certainly thanks you for the prayer, asking that it please continue. Not a religious guy, but spiritual in his own right."

"Yes."

"Plus, you might even feel as if you'd had an apparitional experience as if you'd see him. You could have sworn he was there, and he was. Their world runs parallel to ours. It's not millions of miles away. It's here, just not physical. You glimpsed beyond the 'veil' for a short span of time, but long enough to feel that you have seen him in the next life. And as he says, someday you and he will be together again, because eventually you have to show up there. It goes without saying. He says that you have a while to go yet, so apparently you have a full life ahead of you. He knows that part of you just wishes you could die, but you're not supposed to be there yet. There are still things here that as an individual you must accomplish and achieve on you own. You are moving?"

"Thinking about it."

"He just wants to let you know that it's all right. It's like—you know you have to go on with your life, but part of you is so sentimental, you don't want to pick up and move on. But he says that it's okay to go on with your life. He says, 'Go ahead. Go on with your life.' He wants you to be happy. Why does he—he says there's one marriage—you've been married once?"

"More than once."

"Were there children from another marriage?"

"Yes."

"That's why he said, 'child, children.' He's trying to clarify that he has two, because he's brought it up again. You've had one marriage before this one?"

"Yes, they're from another marriage."

"Okay, because he's saying one marriage—he probably means that there was one marriage before him. When you said that you were married before, he brought up the children again, so apparently there was a child from another marriage. You might find this hard to believe, but you may have a third marriage. You may marry a third time, or certainly be involved in a relationship that would resemble one. Not right away, but there is a feeling of a third marriage. And he just wants to let you know that it's all right. It's almost like part of you has to have closure with him, and once you have the closure with him, it will make it a little easier for you to go on. What you and he shared is very special and will never change, but at least it would help you to move on with your life. He does talk about romantic involvement. Are you involved now?"

"Yes."

"Because he's glad you are. He wants you to be happy and go on with your life. You are taking baby steps, he says. But that's okay. You're handling it the way that's right for you. You and he had a good marriage. You're friends as well as husband and wife?"

"Yes."

"Because that's what he states. I'm sure you had your ups and downs in your marriage—everybody does. But he wants you to know that he always loved you and still does. But you certainly did have your ups and downs."

"Yes."

"He shows me nuts, which is my symbol that he could be a tough nut to crack. But he doesn't want you to think that he ever stopped loving you, even if it might have seemed that way. It seems at times he could get wrapped up in his own life and anxieties, and it might seem you were cast out. He just doesn't want you to think that anything was wrong. At times, though, he wasn't the happiest guy here?"

"Yes."

"He admits that he really didn't like it too much here. No fault of yours, or anyone else's—just telling the truth. He just admits that he wasn't the happiest guy here."

"Right."

"'Cause at times it seems he was close with you and yet he's very aloof. You know, you might have felt that your marriage was on the rocks and that you did something wrong, but he seems just to have gotten caught up in his own anxiety. He also apologizes. Was he kind of tuning you out near the end or something?"

"Um-hmm."

"It's almost like you're there and you're not there. Do you know what I'm saying? It's not that he's being hateful, but he's reserved or he's being the typical male and kind of tuning you out and in his own world. He had a lot on his mind."

"Um-hmm."

"He describes his passing as tragic. That's true?"

"Yes."

"But also puts it under the umbrella of 'accident.' Does that make sense?"

"Um-hmm."

"He does *not* pass from a health problem."

"No."

"That's why he has to put it under the umbrella of accident, otherwise I'm going to go in the wrong direction. This puzzles me. He contributes to his own passing?"

"Yes."

"So he admits. He takes his own life?"

"No."

"But that's the thing. He contributes to his own passing, but he doesn't commit suicide. That's why he's putting it under the umbrella of accident. He contributes to his own passing in his behavior, but he's not giving you a kick-in-the-pants suicide. He says he overdid it. Does that make sense?"

"Yes."

"Did he overdo it drinking-wise or drug-wise?"

"He was drinking that night."

"Oh, maybe that's what he means. He's saying to me that he overdid it with substance, drinking—"

"Yes. He had taken pills, too, but—"

"Oh, that's why he said drinking and drugs, why he said he overdid it with substance. There was a bad reaction with the combination. He said he fell. Does that make sense?"

"Hmm."

"He falls out of consciousness? That's what he means—like he's 'falling asleep' or going out of consciousness. Why does he show me a vehicle? Was there one involved?"

"No."

"What the hell does he mean by that then? Because he tells about a lurching at the heart—did anything affect the heart?"

(She is unsure how to answer.)

"Well, maybe this combination could have—let me just leave it alone. But he passes on from overdoing it, is that correct? That's what he states, but he also brings up a weapon involved."

"Um-hmm."

"Maybe there's too many things going on here. This is why I'm getting confused. He's saying to me that the drinking and the drugs or medication—then he says he falls, like into unconsciousness. Then he says there's a lurching at the heart from the drinking and drugs and then says that there's a vehicle involved. What does he mean by vehicle? Then he says that there is a weapon involved. Is that the vehicle that brings about the actual death? He may have just used the wrong word. He said 'vehicle' and when he saw I was confused he came right out and said 'weapon.' I heard a gunshot. Gun involved?"

"Yes."

"Yes, obviously that's the weapon. This is why he calls it an accident. Yes, he contributes to his own passing, but it's an accident. He is not in the right frame of mind. He's out of control. He's fallen into disrepair with himself. He's gone out of control where he's not able to control what he's doing."

"Um-hmm."

"It's funny. He shoots at a funny angle?"

"No, but I understand."

"Does that make sense then? He says that he shot at a funny angle and when you said no, he said yes, and to ask again—ask if it makes sense, that he shot at a funny angle. He was threatening toward you?"

"Yes."

"Because that's what he states. He shot at a funny angle, so he must have tried to shoot you first or—"

"Threaten."

"But he was threatening toward you, that's what I mean. He might not have intended on harming you, but he did it in any case. Wait a minute—there's another gunshot, though. Does that make sense?"

"Yes."

"I'm not trying to be funny, but I'm seeing Annie Oakley. He shot at you and you shot back?"

"Um-hmm."

"Actually, you shoot him."

"Yes."

"But in self-defense."

"Yes."

"Because he's stating that he shot at a funny angle, but he's out of control—you can't take the risk that he's playing games."

"Right."

"That's what he recognizes. And that's what has to be understood. Somebody can say, 'Well, you killed your husband, but it legitimately was in self-defense.' He's pointing the gun at a funny angle, but he's out of control and might have missed you, but it's like, what is he going to do next? It's funny—you feel you murdered him, and he says, 'You didn't murder me—you released me.' He does not feel it's necessary, but he recognizes that you do. He says, 'I forgive, if that's what you need to hear. I forgive.' I'm curious. He's hanging laundry in front of me. That's a sign that he's not going to 'hang your laundry in public.' Apparently this is between you and him. He seems to be a pretty private person, and this is between you and him. This may sound strange, but between you and him—he says that you did him a favor. He was not happy here, he was out of balance here, he felt he was failing, plus he felt that he was a tremendous burden in your life. You might not have felt that way, because he knows that you love him in your own way and still do (and vice versa). This was not an act of anger or vengeance or hatred by you. This is a genuine act of self-defense. It's like, if you don't take care of yourself, he's going to blow your head off. And he admits that night, even though he shot at an odd angle, he was still out of control and anything was possible. Plus he admits that he was being abusive. I keep seeing scenes out of the movie, *The Burning Bed*, so apparently you understood that anything was possible at this point. He had been abusive before, yes?"

"Yes."

"You went through an ordeal though, since this has happened?"

"Yes."

"But it's clear now, yes?"

"Yes."

"Because I see clear water in front of you, and he apologizes for the ordeal you went through. Believe it or not, he was actually helping you from the hereafter so that things would clear. Because the system's trying to nail you."

"Yes."

"But he does state that he was helping you to get the water clear again. He always loved you and still does, even if he had a strange way of showing it. And it's funny—he came from a screwed-up home, so that was his way of showing or giving love, and he didn't know any better. I see an overhaul. He's done a complete overhaul with himself in the hereafter. And this is why he's able to talk. I do feel I'm talking to a really nice guy."

"Yes."

"His heart's in the right place, he's a sensitive guy—maybe sometimes a little too sensitive, where his sensitivity makes him defensive or lose control. But he's done an overhaul on himself with that and his life review, and this is why he's able to talk clearly—that it's okay. This is between you and him, he states. How someone else judges you, and people have—"

"Yup."

"—he says, is nothing more than the sin of pride, thinking they know better when they know nothing at all. And that's what you have to try to tell yourself. Again, he realizes that you are living in the aftershock. There's also lack of communication with children?"

"Yes."

"Yeah, because—I don't mean to be impolite, but I see the *you know what* 'hitting the fan'—so apparently it's involving the children. Still, the bulk of the mess has been cleaned up, but there's still a mess to be cleaned up. I do see fingers being pointed, so apparently you are being blamed—by children?"

"Well—"

"It could be a blame almost in a subdued way. I feel like you're being blamed, even if it's not being vocalized. Is his family giving you a hard time?"

"Um, no."

"He says something about his family giving you a hard time, but maybe that's what *he's* feeling. Thank God they didn't, and maybe he's surprised that they didn't. Maybe I'm just taking it the wrong way. But as he states, 'I forgive and hope you do, too.' Remember, it's a two-way street. He owes you an apology and also needs your forgiveness as well. You always loved him no matter what, and, ironically, he always loved you, too, no matter what. He was like a big boy trapped in a man's body, and he was losing control all the time and throwing tantrums like a spoiled child. It's not like you didn't try to help him to help himself and understand, and, for a while there, he was making progress. Things were well, and then all of a sudden he went downhill again. His life was a roller coaster—up and down—and he doesn't mean to be impolite, but he says that he just couldn't get his *you know what* together here. Over there, he's gotten it together. So, as he feels, in a lot of ways you did him a favor—you released him into the hereafter, which freed him from a lot of the torment here, and he had to snap to attention there. He had to look upon his life as an observer and not a participant and be able to pull things together. I see the immaculate heart of Mary over your head. Does that mean anything to you? Have you prayed to the Blessed Mother on his behalf?"

"Yes."

"Because Mary appears over your head as the Immaculate Heart, and he tells me that you have prayed to her on his behalf. So he asks—and he's not religious, but he is spiritual—he asks that you pray to the Immaculate Heart of Mary on his behalf, to help him continue to find himself in the hereafter. But he is much happier there. When he first came in, he told me that I was discerning him as he is *now*. But he is all right and at peace. To him, what happened in the past is water under the bridge for you and for him. That's what the feeling is from him now since he's progressed. So, yes, an ugly trial is brought to a happy ending. You have children by him?"

"No."

"Why does he keep calling out to children? Oh, your children from another marriage, I keep forgetting. But they were like *his* children?"

"Yes."

"That's what I'm getting at. In his heart, they are his, and he keeps calling out to his children. Again, there's a stigma attached to this, and people will judge and say the wrong thing, and kids can say nasty things. I keep seeing scenes from the movie *The Night of the Hunter* where the kids are getting harassed because the father had gone to jail, and I feel that your children have probably gotten their knocks from people with vicious tongues. Your husband says to tell them he's near as a guardian angel, because he does love them and knows they love him, regardless of the horrible way this has turned out. But you *had* to defend yourself, and he says that with all sincerity. You *had* to defend yourself, you had no choice. I'm not trying to be cruel, but he gives me the impression that it was 'kill or be killed.' And at that point, he did not know what he was doing. He jokes that he was foaming at the mouth, like a mad dog. And people judge *you*—they wouldn't trade places with you and be in that situation, and if they were they would have done the same thing. And again he emphasizes, 'This is between you and me.' He speaks again about moving. You're thinking of it?"

"I am."

"He seems to encourage it. A change of scenery—I feel like I want to start all over again, and he's encouraging you. There's the birth of a child in front of you as a symbol of starting all over—a new beginning. He's glad you are seeing someone. You're going on with your life but you're still a little afraid, and that's why he's trying to tell you to let go of the fear. The Blessed Mother again appears behind you in a compassionate sense, telling you to try to let go of your fear. Your husband knows that you feel you've made a mistake somewhere, but you didn't. Let yourself off the hook, as he puts it. Be happy again and go on with your life, because you are entitled to it. This is an unfortunate tragedy that has occurred, but you had no choice in the matter. And that's why he contributes to his own passing. It's almost like he's daring you to do it. A part of him wants out, and I don't mean to sound cruel, but it's almost like he wanted to kill himself but didn't have the chutzpah. Maybe it had to go this way for whatever reason. As he says, 'As long as you understand you're not a bad person, you're not a cruel person, you're not a valueless person and you're not a person who lacks in compassion and love.' You have all of the proper attributes that a person should have. People don't realize when they make comments how much this has bothered you, that you had to be reduced to this, because you're not that type of person. And then you have to deal with the system—trying to investigate—and it's a nightmare. But the worst is over. There may be some repercussions now and then, but the nightmare is over. There's talk of a courtroom. Did you go to trial or something?"

"No."

"Or close to it?"

"Well, I had to go into the courtroom to get my stuff back."

"Oh, okay, that's why I'm seeing the courtroom. Because I keep seeing fly paper as a symbol of things being sticky, but it's cleared away now."

"Yes."

"Also the name John passed on."

"That's him."

"Oh, because I'm hearing this all from John. Some people have faded from your life, though?"

"Yes."

"Because he says not to take it personally. Some people judge and some people just don't know how to handle it. Some people also become frightened. But as he says for anybody who talks big, they wouldn't have changed places with you under any means. And he could be physically abusive."

"Yes."

"And, again, I'm seeing *The Burning Bed*. Abusive, paranoid—anything could have set him off. And he knows now that the more you tried to do everything right, it only made things worse. It was never good enough. But he admits that the night this tragedy occurred, he had gone mad. I keep seeing Norman Bates—like we all go a little mad sometimes. He had been physically abusing you, too, though, yes?"

"Yes."

"Because I feel him coming at you, trying to strangle you or something. He had a drinking problem, yes?"

"Yes."

"Because he admits he had a pretty pronounced drinking problem anyway. That, plus the combination of the drugs, made the situation worse. Have you been having trouble with your health?"

"Somewhat."

"Physically, though? Because it's stemming more from emotion. I'm sure that after what you've been through, you aren't going to go out and whistle 'Dixie,' but the thing is, he states that you've been having some trouble with your health. Make sure you get enough rest, too. It's like, even though this is over, you still sleep on edge or live on edge, and it's almost like at times you feel you're going to be haunted. He keeps telling me that it isn't the case. Maybe that's why it's a good idea to move. He's glad that somebody is in your life, though. It has made a difference. He says that he's tried to steer good things in your favor. He does have a good heart. His heart's in the right place. I think that when he went to the hereafter and did his life review, he saw and understood what happened. It's almost like he sat there and thought, 'What an ass I am,' and then tried to correct it and make it better for you. I feel that he's very childlike and not that he's blaming, but a lot stems from his upbringing. He did not come from a *Leave It to Beaver* house."

"Right."

"He extends white roses to you as a spiritual blessing but also as an offering of peace and love between you and him. He says that he knows it hurts—what other people say and think. And he knows that letting it go in one ear and out the other is easier said than done. Remember to tell yourself when that happens that this is only between you and him. 'This is our business,' he says, and 'Don't punish yourself for what you did in self-defense. I forgive, I love you and you love me, and that's *all* that matters.' He also says, 'I'm glad you forgive me also.' I see ice breaking in front of me—it breaks the ice. That's why he does encourage you to pick up, brush yourself off and move on. It's all to your advantage, and there's nothing really holding you here anymore. He shows me Disney World. Are you going there?"

(She laughs.) "Oh, it's not likely. It was our favorite place to go."

"Maybe that's the reason why he's showing it to me—because it's significant to you beyond just going there. He loved it as much as you did, and you had happy times there. But he speaks about going there again in the future. It's funny, but when you went there you'd get your batteries charged again and things would always seem to be better. It's like the kid in him would come out."

"Yes, yes."

"And this is probably a symbol to you that it's John you're hearing from—it has specific meaning now and in the future. He had an overwhelming sense of failure on the earth."

"Um-hmm."

"I think he might have locked it up in himself, but it seems as if he felt he was failing. You also say the rosary for him?"

"Yes."

"Because I see white rosary beads over your head, again with the Blessed Mother. Apparently you say the rosary for him, and he doesn't want you to think you are wasting your time. This has helped him to help himself in the hereafter because you are embracing him with love through the sacred hearts of Jesus and Mary. He wants you to know that it is not in vain. Someday when the children can understand this better, talk to them about it so that they know that he loves them as he always did. Again, if I didn't know better, I'd swear they were *his* children—in his heart, they are. Plus he apologizes to them for turning their world upside down and scaring them. Again, like in *The Burning Bed*, where she also had children. I'm sure you can relate to that movie."

"Yes."

"And he keeps showing it to me to summarize it all for me how it was for you. It also describes how his parents were supportive to him but didn't see the wife's point of view. There must have been days where you feel you've been ready to scream because everybody is pointing the finger at you, like it's your fault. He knows that as long as you know that he forgives, you forgive, he loves you, you love him, then the case is closed. He wants you to leave here in peace, and go home and have a good night's rest. Let yourself off the hook. He just wasn't getting it together here on the earth. It was getting worse and worse, and he was just getting into a terrible state again and again. And you just want to know that he knows you still love him, and he says, 'I know that.' He loves you and he knows that you love him. He does have a good sense of humor though, yes?"

"Oh, yes."

"Because it seems that he could be the greatest guy in the world sometimes.

And he jokes with me from the hereafter, 'Yeah, it takes getting over here and seeing myself in a movie [the life review] and seeing that this is where I *blanked* up.' Why is there pressure to the head? Was he shot to the head?"

"No."

"Oh, wait a minute—I just realized something. He was shot to the chest. That's why I'm getting that lurching at the heart that I felt before. Possibly after the bullet hit him in the stomach or the chest, apparently the heart started to give out. I felt pressure in the head, like it was spinning, and that's what made me think it was a shot to the head. But apparently he was just so out of it that his head must have been spinning."

"Yes."

"You live out of New York State?"

"Yes."

"Funny, he says you are heading west. Now I don't know what that means. It could be west of the state you live in, or in the western part of that state. But he says that you want a fresh new beginning though, yes?"

"Yes."

"I wouldn't be surprised if this year or next year—up ahead you may be going in a new direction. He is glad for the opportunity that the Infinite Light gives him so that you and he can have this closure so that you can move on. This happened in your state?"

"Yes."

"Again he asks that you tell the children you've heard from him. Just know that he always loved you and he knows how much you love him. That will not change. One thing he admires about you—you are always very quick to forgive. He says that most people in your shoes couldn't do that. He admits that he was wrong, something he wouldn't admit too often when he was on the earth. Especially when he was in that state of mind. Okay, he does tell me that he is going to withdraw. Was there something you wanted to know?"

"I wanted to know who took the gun out of the house."

"It's been—disposed of?"

"Somebody stole it at the scene, out of the house."

"It was a handgun?"

"Yes. The gun he fired was missing."

"It's never been found or heard from. It's funny. He shows me a uniform." (*Deborah believes that at the time of John's passing, his friend, a policeman, took the gun in an effort to cover up the murder attempt on her and frame her for murder.*)

"Yes."

"You're pretty sure that it was one of the cops who had taken it."

"Yes."

"Well, the minute you asked, he showed me a uniform and I felt—it was a valuable gun?"

"Not really."

"But a nice one."

"Yes."

"It's funny, the key here is the *collection*. (*She doesn't understand.*) No, no—I wonder if the person who took it has a collection. That's the thing. He tells me that the key here is the collection, whatever the heck that means. I'm assuming that's what he means, unless he means something else."

"Okay."

"You know, this is the strangest thing. I'm waiting, but I don't seem to get a name. I just thought of something. He may not know the name. He may just know that it was one of them that did it. But one knew him?"

"Yes."

"Personally?"

"Yes."

"*You* know what the name is."

"Uh-huh."

"You know, in a way I think—funny, but I keep seeing the movie, *Dead End*. I don't think he wants to be a squealer, because he keeps showing me the scene in that movie of the Mark of the Squealer. I don't think your husband wants to be a squealer. However, he says about the uniform, says it was a cop, and said, 'The one who knows me, and knows me well.' He said that you know his name and you know who he is talking about, but as he says, does it really bother you that much?"

"Well, yes."

"Well, I leave it in your hands—this is your life and your business—but he is giving me the impression for you to let it go. But that's your choice." (*It is not common for the souls to "name names" from the hereafter with regard to crimes unless there is a clear reason why we must know.*)

"But he helped me through it anyhow."

"I see sleeping dogs in front of me, which is my symbol of letting sleeping dogs lie."

"Okay. Is that what he wants me to do?"

"Yes, because as your husband stated before, it's water under the bridge now.

He says, 'What will this do for you? Ask yourself.' He knows that you need something to remember him by, and he says that there are better things coming. Was your husband on the force? Why do I see a uniform with him, too?"

"He wore a uniform to work."

"Oh—okay, that's all I need to know, because I felt I saw someone stand in front of you and extend white roses to you, and he looked like he is in some type of uniform. Again he says that this person that took the gun is almost like a brother, but again I see the sleeping dogs. Let sleeping dogs lie. You have to do what you think is right. I see a hornet's nest, and it's like you don't want to open up a hornet's nest with this. Especially since things are behind you."

"Yeah, they are."

"You'll be raking over old coals. And again he says that it isn't worth it. All right, in any case, he tells me to let go. He likes to talk, but that's good. I can feel that he got a lot off his chest and a lot settled between you and he in *privacy*, and that's what he cares about."

"Just tell him that everybody is—"

"He knows, and he says that he is closer to all of you than you can imagine. Just know that he knows that you love him and he loves you and the children. He calls out with love and tells you that he is near. In a lot of ways he is glad that there has been a happy ending to this ugly tragedy. And with this, he signs off and sends his love. There are other people in the background, but it's obvious to them who you had the need to hear from. So your husband, John, signs off, calling out to Earl and the children, asking that you tell everyone that you've heard from him. Again he says, 'Let sleeping dogs lie. Just go in peace and be at peace until we meet again.' With that he signs off, and away they go."

THERE ARE NO MORE POWERFUL WORDS to hear from the souls in the hereafter than "I forgive," and it is perhaps one of the greatest lessons we will endure on the earth to have the courage to say to them, "I forgive, too." It helps us to remain true to our goal here to love, no matter what the circumstance. It is not necessarily true that you "always hurt the one you love." Some marriages are actually like ones in a storybook—two people who are soul mates, friends and lovers. Losing a spouse who was all of these is a life-altering experience that can ruin lives if it is not put in a perspective of hope. One good friend mentioned to me that losing her husband was like losing an oar to a canoe—she felt destined to spend the rest of her life traveling in a circle with no distance gained. The only words of wisdom that the souls in the hereafter can offer is that love never fades, and that the splendid reunion of soul mates in the hereafter will be worth the agony of separation for a short time on the earth. In the meantime, though, we are left only with our hope and our memories to keep us going. Spouses in the hereafter are the most insistent that we not lose heart in our struggle to continue with our lessons on the earth. They promise that the benefit far outweighs the pain.

IT WOULD BE VERY HARD for me to confine a woman like Roxie Strish to a description of "widow." Talking about her husband, Larry, who passed on in 1995, Roxie still gushes like a teenager in the cloud of a first love. It is evident to anyone she speaks to that her love for Larry still burns in her heart, and you have to admire that kind of passion. Even after suffering such a crushing blow to her life, Roxie still possesses the soul of a "hopeful romantic" and the unshakable conviction that it is only a matter of time before they will be reunited, no matter how much it hurts to be separated. Roxie helps me and others to understand that nothing really separates us from our loved ones, and that absence truly makes the heart grow fonder:

"MY HUSBAND LARRY was born with his gaze skyward, his passion to soar in the heavens. At the age of fourteen he began his flying lessons and what would be a lifelong love affair and storied career in aviation that included 160 combat missions in F4 fighters, fourteen years in 727s with the airlines, four years of international travel in a Nigerian Tribal Chief's Lear 25 and flying the race circuit in a Chicago-based Indy Car team owner's Lear 24.

"I grew up a stone's throw from the Indianapolis Motor Speedway, and after getting Mario Andretti's autograph as a ten-year-old little girl, dreamed of the day I would race there. At age twelve I began racing quarter midgets and began a twenty-year pursuit of competing in the Indy 500. My racing continued into Formula Fords in the United States and England, Formula 3 in England and Super Vees back in the United States.

"One March morning in 1992, the sweet song of an Indy car testing lured me to the Speedway for a visit. It had been a dark winter, with my dad passing on from lung cancer in February, and the race track always cheered me. Other than the team itself, few people are allowed access to the pit and garage areas during a private test, but as a wannabe driver, I, too, was welcome. But this day there was a new face, one that would change my life forever.

"Mario and Michael Andretti were testing, and Larry had flown some of the crew members into town. Tan and handsome with an infectious smile, I was drawn to Larry instantly. I introduced myself, and quickly it seemed as if we were long-lost friends. The tan forty-four-year-old stranger had captured my interest. In only hours, Larry was flying off, but it seemed our destiny together had begun.

"May brought Larry back to Indy, and now, with thousands of people milling on the grounds and no planning on our part, we again found each other. We spent the day surrounded by the masses, in our world of only two. It seemed we had *long* been together, separated for a time, and now reunited. We nestled into each other's being as if we had forever shared our heartsounds. We fell in love this day.

"His job had him flying in and out of town, but we spent hours on the phone together each day. By mid-May we had our *first* date away from the track; he proposed after dinner. Having had a few drinks, and given that it *was* our first date, I gave him a 'definite maybe' and asked that if he was truly serious to please ask again when we were both totally sober. May 28, just twelve days later, on bended knee at the airport, he asked again. This time the answer was a 'definite yes'!

"We'd have married that very day, but Larry had a better idea. He suggested we wed in October, on what would have been my mom and dad's forty-forth anniversary. 'Let's carry on tradition,' he said. 'This way, Rox, your mom won't just have to be sad on that day; she can have some joy for us.' Larry's caring and romantic nature was unending.

"Other than the business trips he flew, Larry and I were hand-in-hand inseparable. We went to all extremes to be together. He airlined me to the races so we could be together, and when the boss wasn't looking I rode first class in the Lear with him. He actually put me in the cockpit and gave me some hands-on flying experience the first time he sneaked me on board. The power of the Lear pushed me back, making me one with the seat and what I'd guess to be like holding a tiger by the tail. It was difficult to know which of us wore the bigger smile: me from the thrill or Larry at seeing my joy.

"We maintained both his apartment in Chicago and my little mobile home in Speedway, Indiana. With any two-day break in his schedule, we would return to Indy and the small-town lifestyle we both preferred.

"Larry was supportive of my racing goals and even tried to help me secure sponsorship, but as our days together turned to weeks and then months, I realized the unimaginable: I no longer had the heart to race. That which had defined me for twenty years had lost its importance. I now saw clearly the dangers and didn't want to risk losing one precious second with Lar. My racing days were over.

"On October 17, 1992, surrounded by our racing and aviation 'families,' we were married at the Laguna Seca Raceway in Monterey, California—the last Indy car race of the season. Mario Andretti walked me down the aisle as the love song Larry had written for me was being played. This was the happiest day of my life and would always be the most treasured day of the year to us. Alone together, with family or surrounded by friends, our world remained only two. It grew increasingly difficult for us to be parted, even for a day-trip of flying. Lar didn't see them, but I couldn't stop the tears from rolling each time I watched him blast off without me.

"There seemed but one logical solution to the only thing that brought us sadness, and so I asked what Larry had obviously been waiting to hear: 'How long would it take for us to be able to fly as a team?' His smile was huge as he answered, 'Three years . . . maybe less.' I was so naive about the licensing requirements for flying and terribly disappointed to learn I couldn't just go straight to Learjet co-pilot school. Lar patiently told me it would mean starting at ground zero in little piston planes and working my way up, but even that first day he encouraged me to believe that we could make it happen. My flying lessons began immediately, and by April 1993, I had my Private Pilot's License.

"In May, Larry shocked me by asking my opinion on his resigning his position. Larry *lived* to fly. He *loved* his Lear and the Indy car circuit. The amazing thing was that *he loved me more*. He didn't see it as a sacrifice when he left his position to concentrate on our goal . . . getting my needed ratings to allow us to fly as a team. Others only saw it as an unbelievably foolish risk, but to us it made perfect sense. We would now live off credit cards, the belief in our dream and a most passionate love for each other. By using a military-profile, highly intensive flight training program, I had the needed ratings on December 31, 1993. Now we could find our dream job.

"Our hopes were high going into the new year. We pursued numerous job leads but faced repeated disappointment. Larry had over 23,000 flight hours, but my 300 total hours didn't help our efforts. We continued to hope and to believe. We even worked to *create* our position, by trying to convince people with a true need, to *buy* an aircraft. Our hopes rose and fell over and over again, and soon 1994 was but a memory.

"Early in 1995 we watched a television program in awe, as a most-tested psychic gave comfort to those who grieved with words of love and reassurance sent by their loved ones on 'the Other Side.' We both had tears streaking our faces. I wrote the man's name and the title of one of his books on a tiny piece of scrap paper. I tucked it away, saying to myself, 'If anything ever happens to Lar, I *will* find this man.'

"As we continued our job search, our conversations became more profound and soul-searching. We discussed life and death, life after death, organ donation and even someday being scattered to the winds. God forbid, but if one of us were called Home without the other, we promised, if able, to let the one left here on earth know we *were* still near to them. Our credit-card debt continued to grow and so, too, did our extreme oneness. Larry wouldn't allow me to feel guilty for our plight. His faith shined brightly, and together we felt invincible.

"In late May 1995, after seventeen months of searching, we landed our dream position. We were hired to fly a corporate jet, Sabre 80, for a businessman in West Virginia. (We named our bird *Flipper* because of the resemblance to a massive dolphin.) Together we attended Flight Safety school in June, and on the twenty-ninth we both passed our checkrides, making us each Captain-qualified in the Sabre and allowing me to be an insurable crew member despite my low hours. On the fourth of July, Lar, our cat Fred and I moved from Indy to Huntington, West Virginia. We continued to unpack and settle into our beautiful new house on a hill, between the many trips we were already flying; we had never been happier.

"Seventeen days after our move, at approximately 4:55 A.M., I was awakened by pure panic of the heart. I found Larry on our bathroom floor . . . unresponsive and not breathing. I worked desperately on him for over forty minutes while the ambulance struggled to find our home. My forty-seven-year-old husband, the light, love and joy of my world, had suffered a massive heart attack; he did not survive it.

"Larry improved the quality of life for over 100 people through his gifts of organ (corneas), bone and tissue donation. The doctors assured me that I could not have saved my Lar—that even if it had happened in the hospital, the outcome would have been no different. His first-class medical in April had failed to find the severe blockages and enlargement of his heart, but even if it had, his days might not have been any longer. They certainly wouldn't have been as happy. Had they known, and performed surgery, and had he survived it, Lar would have been a candidate for a heart transplant. His flying days would have been over, and though he wouldn't have complained, his heart would have been broken.

"These reassurances brought me little comfort. All understanding of the world left me. I was numb with shock and overwhelmed by a wracking grief. While not once would I question God or ask 'why?' I couldn't fathom that He hadn't called me Home, too. I was grateful and thanked Him for each and every precious second He had given us to share together on this, His earth, but with every breath of my being I begged Him to let me follow and to be reunited with Lar. The pain of separation was unbearable.

"From that first day, there were reasons to believe that Larry was doing all that he could to keep his promise and to let me know that he *was* still near. I wanted so badly to believe but wondered if I was merely on the verge of madness from my sorrow. For his family's sake, we held a proper Catholic service in Pennsylvania and then a memorial service in Indy. The U.S. Air Force presented me with a flag and three spent shell casings, symbolic of 'Duty, Honor and Country.' (Later, they would send me a plaque in Larry's honor.) As he wanted, he was cremated. I knew where, when and how the scattering would take place, but that would be later. With each of Larry's wishes that was fulfilled, I hoped and prayed the call Home for me would come.

"I returned to West Virginia unable to comprehend the future. I didn't eat, and when sleep came there was no rest. I cried nearly without stopping and sobbed aloud my words to Lar. I pleaded for him to still be near, to still love me. I was terrified that he would get a 'head start' on me in Heaven, and that when I did get the call Home he would be too far ahead for me to be with him. I begged him to wait for me.

"My thoughts turned to that tiny piece of scrap paper. I couldn't remember the man's name, where he was located or the title of his book. Then, as if prompted, I opened one of our as yet unpacked boxes. There it was. The tiny paper and the name I was frantic to recall: George Anderson, *We Don't Die*. I didn't believe I would survive the wait, but I did, and the discernment encouraged me to write about one survivor's tale and a love story that transcends all. Maybe, just maybe, we, too, can help another broken heart to trust that love doesn't die when we do.

"Perhaps some would say we should have known it was too good to last, but Larry and I recognized a love so perfect as a bond of souls that even the veil of death does not, cannot, will not, sever. I will always be grateful to God for blessing this trip and to George Anderson for sharing his most precious gift. Having lived, loved, laughed and cried with Larry and me, you should not be surprised to find that our love for each other is truly without end."

THE DISCERNMENT

"Was there a recent passing around you?"

"Yes."

"Yeah, 'cause St. Anthony is standing behind you, in black, and has his hands on your shoulders. There's been a recent death. There's been a loss. It has nothing to do with religion—it's a symbol for me. Umm . . . yeah, besides your dad, there's another male close to you passed over?"

"Yeah."

"'Cause somebody's behind you. It's another male, obviously a young male, too, yes?"

"Yes."

"Were you romantically involved?"

"Oh, yes."

"Because there's definitely like a big heart, a Valentine heart in front of you. So you must have been romantically involved, were married!"

"Yes."

"I mean romantically involved, yes, but as he said married. You know, you're married as husband and wife but you're also *good* pals."

"The best."

"'Cause as he said, we're married as husband and wife and friends also. 'Cause, unfortunately, you not only lose your husband, you lose a *very* good friend. Umm, as he states, and I don't mean this to be crude, his death has like really screwed you up."

(Crying . . . answer almost inaudible.) "Yeah."

"That's the best way I can put it. Because he tells me, to tell you, that he's so sorry his time came or however he passed on, or both. Because he says, it's like *blanked you up* bad. You don't know whether you're coming or going."

"It's true."

"It's actually like frightened you, his death, and—"

"I don't think frightened."

"Well, frightened almost in the sense of, you can't believe like this has happened. You know, in that sense. 'Cause obviously he was a young man, yes?"

"Yes."

"Certainly by today's standards. You have children?"

"No."

"Did he have any?"

"No."

"Why's he talking about children? Were there children in his family he was close with, or anything?"

"No." (*Notice that George doesn't sway. Eventually, much later, this makes sense.*)

"What, nieces, nephews—anything like this?"

"Well, lots of those."

"I'll go with it then, 'cause he's calling out to children and he won't back off. So he must be calling out to his nieces, nephews, something of this nature. Your husband passes tragically? In the sense of his age, I guess, yes?"

"Tragic to me."

"And in the sense of age as well. . . . He knew he was going to pass on?"

"If he did, it was a well-kept secret."

"Yeah, 'cause he says he's not shocked by death. So when the time came, he must have gone very quickly."

"Very quickly."

"Perhaps, maybe why he thought that. He have health troubles?"

"No."

"Anything in his chest area?"

"Well, that's what got him."

"Ah, ah, I was just going to say don't say anything, 'cause that would be health problems. Did he have health problems? You said no. He says, 'What about my chest area?' He *have* a heart attack?"

"Yes."

"Yes, he says he drops dead of a heart attack. I'm like finding it hard to believe, as you must have been, because to be honest with you, I feel like I'm talking to somebody who's young and healthy."

"He was . . . I thought."

"It's funny, though. He might not have felt well a few days before, and he might have thought he was coming down with something or . . . I *feel* not right inside, but I'm not even paying attention to it or I don't know what's going on."

"He wasn't scared, was he?"

"No. Because he tells me that . . . He seems to be a pretty down-to-earth type of guy, like if you're going to go, you're going to go."

"That's exactly—"

"He says to me, if I weren't supposed to pass on, I wouldn't have passed on. He says, as difficult as this is for you to accept, apparently it was his time to let go. It was his time to pass on. He always was in a hurry?"

"No."

"It's funny, it's like he said to me he hurried to get his work done, but I think—"

"I think he's not talking about—"

"Work?"

"Yeah. I think he means—"

"But see, work doesn't necessarily mean your nine-to-five job. He might have felt his spiritual work here, he might have been in a hurry to get that done—knowing in the back of his mind he was on his way."

"Can you tell me his name?"

"Not as of yet, but don't say anything, we just started. We've got a while yet. He just got here. Well, actually, he's been here from the beginning. He got caught up with your dad and your grandparents. But he says he's there. That's funny, because your father kept talking about the loss of a *son*, but I realize, it's his son-in-law. You know, it just dawned on me, how dumb, I overlooked it. That's why I started pushing the brother thing. You know, did your father lose a brother? Why is he referring to somebody as the son? But it just dawned on me, it's his son-in-law. Were you afraid he died alone? Because he keeps saying he didn't die alone. Physically, yes, he might have. But spiritually he did not. 'Cause you feel you didn't have a chance to say good-bye to him. But, as he says, would we say good-bye to each other anyway? He says, I don't *think* so. He says, I'm not coming here to say good-bye to you; I'm coming here in this manner to say hello to you. To let you know I'm still with you. 'Cause you do seem to have a very positive, loving relationship. And he says—"

"The best."

"And he says, *I'll never say good-bye to you*. He says, I haven't left you. Physically, yes, spiritually, no! he says, and someday we're going to be together again. You dream about him, yes?"

"Not often enough."

"He claims he comes to you in dreams. But even if you've had a few, maybe you just don't remember. He claims he comes in dreams. That this is not the first you're hearing from him, nor will it be the last. There's also times he's given you other signals. Like, you could swear that, you know, suddenly you're thinking of him and a song comes on the radio to relate to him."

(Roxie chuckles over this.)

"Yes."

"I feel like I turn my head and I could have sworn I saw him standing there. He definitely has given you evidence that he—"

"Yes, yes!"

"He is certainly near to you, besides this particular discerning experience. Did he have block—well, you don't know. Did he have blockage near his heart?"

"Yes."

"'Cause I keep feeling like I've got blockage near my heart."

"Yeah, everywhere."

"And again, he basically thought he was in pretty good health, yes?"

"Yes."

"Yeah. I mean, he might have thought so. He was kind of live and let live?"

"Yeah."

"I mean, he's not like some kind of radical. But again, his feeling is if you're going to go, you're going to go. I can't say I—"

"That's *exactly* how he was."

"I can't say I disagree with him. He's right. I mean, you could have the health-iest heart in the world and die in a car accident. So, he's not being unsympathetic to what you're going through, but he's being himself. He's basically saying to you, isn't this *me?*"

"Yes." *(with a chuckle)*

"You know, I mean what can I tell you? He says, you know, if you're gonna go, you're gonna go. But, yes, there was a lot of blockage around his heart. Obviously a valve blew or something. 'Cause I feel like I have fat deposits of blockage around the heart. Yes, he might have had chest pains occasionally, a shortness of breath. He might have felt sluggish, but he's basically a young guy. You don't *think* that's what it is. You don't *think* you're on the verge of a massive coronary. You think you're just having a bad day. And I think this is why he and your father came in and said that things are happier now. That you have to start to get happy again. 'Cause one thing I will say about your husband, he'd never want you to kind of like bury yourself alive."

"I know."

"He'd want you to go on with your life. Well, I've got to give him credit—he's no B.S. artist. I mean, his feeling with his presence in the room, he's gonna come in and tell it like it is. And he says, I'm not going to come in and stroke you and give you a line of bull. I'm going to tell it like it is. Yes, I know what you're going through, and I know you miss me, he says. But I'm here. You talk out loud to me. You must believe I'm still around."

"All the time."

"And he states, 'I'm closer to you than you can imagine. But I don't want you to bury yourself alive. You have to go on with your life. The joy that you brought to me is joy that you can bring elsewhere—and to yourself, again.' Were you planning children?"

"No."

"Did he want children or something?"

"No."

"It's funny, 'cause he keeps bringing up children. He must work with children over there or something. He keeps talking about having children, so he must mean over there."

"I would say something if you wanted me to."

"Oh, no, no. But, ah, they're not his, but he does have children over there, he says. Maybe in a working sense, not in a paternal sense. You guys had an *interesting* relationship, yes?"

"Oh, yeah."

"Because he keeps saying that you had an interesting relationship. And—"

"Tell him, L! Sorry, I started to say—"

"Yeah, don't say anything. Don't worry. I'm not paying any attention. I'm too busy trying to listen. Was your relationship very platonic?"

"Mmm, platonic meaning—"

"Yeah, I mean you have like a brother-sister relationship, but you also have, you know, a *strong* demonstrative relationship."

"We were the best."

"'Cause that's the thing. This is why you have a very interesting relationship. I have to admit, it's *really* a true love relationship."

"Yes!"

"'Cause he keeps putting a big Valentine heart in front of you. He also extends to you red roses as a Valentine greeting. And he states that he will certainly be with you on Valentine's Day. This guy certainly would have remembered you on that day. And he says, I haven't forgotten—but you're not sleeping well, true?"

"True."

"You're a wreck. I'm not trying to be impolite, I'm being honest. 'You're a wreck,' he says. You just don't know whether you're coming or going. If God came to you tonight and told you that you were going to die, you couldn't die quick enough."

"That's a fact."

"And he says, but you've got to go on. He says, because, if you're gonna go, you're gonna go. He still lives by that. He says, if you're meant to be here, you would be here. You *have* to go on. He's like a New Yorker, he's straightforward, he's going to tell it like it is."

"He is straightforward."

"Name Larry mean anything at all?"

"Yeah, that's him!"

"Is that him? I thought he said Harry. I'm glad I listened! I was about ready to say is he saying Harry, and he said, 'No, I'm saying Larry. His actual name is Lawrence?"

"Yeah."

"Yeah. His actual birth name is Lawrence, I take it."

"True."

"But he's obviously known by Larry . . . or La."

"Mmm, I don't know La, but—"

"Well maybe not by you. Could be by somebody else. He prefers to be called Larry, it seems."

"Absolutely."

"Did he *fly?*"

"Yes!"

"'Cause I keep seeing him in an airplane."

"Yes!"

"I don't mean to sound funny, but it's like I was seeing a view of him flying over your head in an airplane."

"Cool."

"'Cause he says, you're my co-pilot."

"Yes!"

"Do you fly also?"

"Yes."

"Oh, O.K. I mean, like, do you fly? Like you're a pilot? Or you can—"

"I *was* his co-pilot."

"Oh, O.K.! Because he started joking that you're my co-pilot. I thought he meant it affectionately because of what he stated. So it means a lot more than I realized. 'Cause he says, you're my co-pilot and he's still with you. But do *you* fly also?"

"Yes."

"Yeah, 'cause he says, when you're flying he's your spiritual co-pilot. That he's with you also. Well, needless to say, this man is your guardian angel."

"Yes!"

"I'm not telling you anything you already don't know yourself. I'm *confirming* what you already know. 'Cause he says, he's *definitely* around you as a guardian angel. He must have had one *hell* of a heart attack, though, yes? I mean, he didn't suffer."

"I hope not."

"No. He says, he did not suffer. Believe me, he didn't know what hit him. He didn't have time to, he states. But it was that there was such blockage there that, *boom.*"

"That's what they say."

"It's like he blew. It's like a volcanic eruption. Like the pressure building, until finally *baboom.* Just don't feel that you let him down at the end. 'Cause he keeps saying, it's not your fault. You weren't there? 'Cause he's saying that—"

"I was . . . feet away."

" 'Cause 'you *couldn't* save me,' he says. He says, 'You're there, but you're not there.' "

(Nearly inaudible) "I wasn't awake."

" 'There's nothing you could have done about it. Don't feel that you failed me.' And he says, that's another reason he had a happy death, not only from going very quickly, but you're there. Obviously even if you're not aware of what's happening. Did he die in his sleep?"

"No."

"You were asleep?"

"I was asleep."

"Oh, O.K., 'cause he's talking about sleep, and I thought he was telling me that he died in his sleep. But, again, St. Joseph appears, which is a signal of a happy death. It's significant of a happy death. But again, as your husband states, he's closer to you than you can imagine. Yes, you need the physical presence—because you're in the physical body, there's nothing more compensating than the physical presence. He says, 'Yes, I know that you need that. However, the best I can do now is assure you that I'm near.' But again, as he states, too, he wants you to know that you *could not have* saved him. 'Cause you feel, if I were awake I could have gotten help. I could have saved him. If he was not meant to go, he would not have gone. He would have survived this and gone on with his life. The one thing about your husband, he *never* wanted to be a burden to himself or anybody else. So passing on like this is another reason he has a happy death. You been having a little trouble with your stomach area? If you do, it's basically nerves anyway. He knows you . . . you'll never be the same again, for a while. But he knows you just need the reassurance that he's near. And this is why he's glad that the Infinite Light affords him this grace to be discerned . . . so he can say to you, yes, I'm closer to you than you can imagine."

"If I ever get a chance to ask a question, can I?"

"O.K. Maybe you better do it now. Yeah, as long as most of the basic contents of the reading have come through already, I won't be judgmental."

"What I really want to know, Larry, is . . . when it's my turn—"

"Will he be there?"

"Will we be together *forever?*"

"He already told you—until we meet again."

"*Forever,* though. *Never* separated again."

"Umm, as he states, we've been together before *many* times. He says, what makes you think this is the only one or the only lifetime?"

"I don't ever want to be apart again."

"And he says, when you pass on, he'll be there waiting for you. This is what you have to look forward to in passing, and he says, and we'll be together. But he says, again he's not B.S.'ing you, he says, you do have to get through it. He says, it's easier said than done. 'I'm here, you're there. You're in the aftereffect of it. You're the survivor. You're in the more suffering part of it, because of the loss. But you have to get through it. You have to keep telling yourself that I am there with you, which I am.' That he has not separated from you. You thinking of moving?"

"No. No, uh-uh."

"He just wants to let you know it's all right, if you do decide to someday. Only because you might feel that you're leaving him behind."

"Did recently."

"Oh, you did already? Very recently? 'Cause he was talking about you moving and he said it was all right."

"Oh, I know what he means."

"O.K., as long as you understand. I thought he was giving me something for the future, so apparently he's giving me something for now. Umm, he knows that you've changed residences, but that it's all right. Because he wants—what you decide to do with your life is your decision and is your choice. He does want you to be happy and go on with your life. He did kind of live dangerously, yes. I don't mean in a bad sense. It's just that he was an adventurer. He wasn't afraid of a challenge, taking on an adventure or something like this. Obviously you and he did a lot of flying together."

"A lot."

"Because I keep seeing you getting around. Even if it's within your own state or whatever. Obviously you're getting around and getting around locally. His parents still living?"

"Yes."

"He keeps calling to them. If you think they could deal with this, he just wants to let them know he's all right. He doesn't care, as he says, whether or not they believe in this. 'Who cares. Someday they're going to pass on and find out I'm right, as usual, anyway.' *(chuckle)* So it doesn't matter."

"I'll tell them."

"As he says, he just wants them to know he's all right and at peace. They are bereaved parents. It has been a shock for them as much as for you. You just don't expect your son to just massively die of a heart attack. So he does call to his parents. Did he have siblings—brothers, sisters? Yeah, he keeps calling to his family."

"Yeah."

"So, obviously, whoever is left behind, he calls out. Obviously there's some grandparents there of his that have passed on, that are there with him also."

"Yes."

"But definitely as much as he was the utmost joy in your life, you were certainly, and still are, the utmost joy in his life. Are you kind of becoming reclusive?"

(No answer . . . but Roxie certainly was.)

"'Cause he does want you to go on with your life, but that has to be your choice. Hey look, you don't have to go out dancing until 4 A.M. You don't have to remarry if you don't want to—"

"NEVER!"

"But he does want you to be hap . . . Well, it's funny, he just said, 'Never say never.' He just wants you to know, he wants you to be happy. Whatever you decide to do—if up ahead you meet someone else, whatever, he wants you to be happy. Just have a life, but don't bury yourself alive. If you want to stay single the rest of your life, that's your privilege, that's your prerogative. But he says, just have a life. Because just remember, each day you live is one day less and it brings you closer to the finish line. And when it is finished, you'll pass on and you'll be there with him. But as he states, you still—he says, 'I've checked the records over here, you're not supposed to be here—not yet.'"

"Ah, soon?"

"Even though you would love to know that you're going next year. But he says, believe me, I'm the evidence of it. You don't have to go looking for it. When the time comes you *will* go."

"Were the words finish line his or yours?"

"Sorry?"

"When you said, finish line?"

"That was his. I'm just listening to what he says."

"That's appropriate."

"Yeah, 'cause the thing is, you have to realize, they can say things to me that I'll repeat back, that I won't think anything of. They'll know it means more to you than it does to me. 'Cause I'm just the instrument. I'm just going to tell you, oh, he's saying this. But, he does state that. He says that you have to go on with your life. That you will be with him again someday. In the meantime, he is with you spiritually. Which I feel you know already. I'm just confirming this."

"It's good to hear."

"Did he have trouble with his blood pressure?"

"No."

"It's funny. He didn't—"

"No."

"Because it *seems* that there was pressure buildup. Of course that could have been from this. But, to be honest with you, he basically seems to be pretty—"

"He had just had a physical."

"Yeah, he seemed to be in pretty healthy shape. That's the thing, he seems— if I met him, I would say, he seems fine to me. Well, as he says, you just never know. But there was definitely buildup in the heart valves and it must have been from deposits or something, because it's there. Did he have a *little lack* of communication with his family?"

"Maybe before I came along."

"O.K., because it's funny, there seems to be a *little* stress growing up. You know, in his family, maybe a little lack, and I'm doing it *very* remotely. I'm saying a little lack of communication. Things obviously became more harmonious later on. Which I think he's glad about in any case, that things did, thus become that way. You have a birthday coming up? By June?"

"Mmm, it's before June."

"Yeah, 'cause he said by June when you were hesitating. Well, you're obviously not going to be sitting in front of me, so he can't do it then, he has to do it now. 'Cause he is wishing you a happy birthday. So it's obviously at least by May. He says it's by June, so it's before June obviously. He does wish you a happy birthday. January is almost over, and he just wants to let you know he hasn't forgotten. And again, remember him on Valentine's Day, because—"

"I will."

"You'll certainly feel you're alone. And he says, he's sending his Valentine to you now. Also, what was I going to say? Oh, he's also wishing you a happy anniversary as well. That's later in the year, yes?"

"Yes."

"I feel I'm going beyond September."

"Yes."

"So, it's probably in the autumn, sometime. That there's wishing of a happy anniversary. 'Cause he says, it's much later in the year. I saw September. I was pushed. So, it would probably have to be November. Something like that, but—"

"Between September and November."

"Oh, October. O.K. He's surrounding the month, all right. 'Cause he pushed it ahead of September and then seemed to stop in November. So I figured I guess around there. But, in any case, he's wishing you a happy anniversary as well."

"Happy anniversary to you, too."

"That he will be near. And again, he wants, 'cause you're going to have your good days and your bad days, as you've already been having, so he wants you to think back on today, on those times when you're having a bad day. So this is your shot in the arm of the reassurance that he's near, that will keep you going. He says, 'cause again, he says, you've got to bring this to the finish line. *Got to!* You've *got to* bring this to the finish line. We're reunited again, everything comes full circle, and there's a fulfillment here. Even if you don't understand what it is right now, or care to understand what it is right now. He says, we have to fulfill and move ahead. You been having a little trouble with headaches?"

"Yes."

"Tension, under the circumstances. It's just emotional. He's telling me you're not in bad health, but you wouldn't care less if you were anyway, to be honest, as he jokes. But, he states that you're not in bad health, but you are out of harmony with yourself. Obviously from the tragedy. And this is why, again, I think your dad was saying and Larry was saying, things can be happier. Things should start to be happier. You have to kind of pick yourself up and move ahead. 'Cause you guys really had a *great* life together."

"Yeah."

"I mean, you go places. It's probably why he didn't want to be tied down with the traditional family role."

"Right."

"Because he enjoyed more the life. You had the friendship. You're traveling together. You're seeing places together, and you definitely had a very active life."

"Yeah."

"And a very fulfilling life. Where some people get up, go to work, come home, pay bills . . . Yeah, you guys did that too, but you had a *lot* more. I mean you had to pay your bills, but you still had a very adventure-oriented life. Did he like the mountains?"

"He liked everything."

"'Cause he keeps showing me him flying over the mountains—the scenery. He was a very *spiritual* person, in his own way."

"Yes."

"And he certainly liked the beauties of nature and such. Did you lose a pet also?"

"Yeah."

"Did you lose a dog?"

"Yeah." (*There had been many, but she knew I meant her little Rascal.*)

"'Cause he keeps talking about . . . Passed on?"

"Yeah."

"'Cause he keeps talking about the dog being there with him."

(*Sob*)

"Did it pass before him?"

"Yeah." (*Sob*)

"'Cause he claims that the dog barked him into the light. Ya know, welcomed him over *first*. Did you lose more than one pet?"

"Yeah."

"*That's* the children he's referring to. Now it makes sense. 'Cause he was busting my chops before, that I was looking at it *literally*, and then he said, the most recent pet that passed on, *dog*, that passed on before him, welcomed him into the light. Then again he said, the *children* are here with me, and he said, tell my wife there's more than one pet. So, apparently, this is what he's referring to, is that the *children* are there with him. It's all the pets that you and he shared, that were like your children. Which they certainly are. But the most recent dog, that obviously was really close to the two of you. You were both brokenhearted when the dog passed on, because you felt like you lost a child. He says that dog welcomed him into the light first. He jokes that he knew he was going to a good place. And the animal was there to welcome him over. You memorialized him, too, yes?"

"Yes."

"Yes, he keeps thanking you for the memorial. Was it something with an airplane?"

"Yes!"

"It's like his name is on a plaque, too."

"Yes."

"And then he talks about the airplane. The memorial through what he does best. Flying, or whatever."

"Do you want me to tell you?"

"No, as long as you understand. 'Cause this way he can give me more detail. Was it anything that involved a scholarship or something?"

"No."

"'Cause there's been finance exchanged for it, though, yes?"

"Yes." (*Donations went to both Father Phil's MIVA and to Motorsports Ministries.*)

"Yes, that's probably why I'm seeing finances exchanged. But other people are benefiting from it?"

"Yeah."

"That's probably why I'm thinking it's a scholarship. It's not a scholarship, but people are benefiting from the finance exchanged. Did you name an airplane?"

"No." (*She answered incorrectly. She named their plane "Flipper."*)

"He's talking about the name on the airplane. Well, whatever, it certainly has to do with an airplane, and he is thanking you for the memorial. Let me just go with that. 'Cause there seems to be a tremendous show-up at his wake and funeral."

"Yes."

"And it's obvious for the time he was here that many people thought very highly of him and liked him very much. Which indeed they did. And then, he also states, that he's glad for the support that was shown you. 'Cause everybody's pretty much shocked as much as you were about his loss."

(*Almost inaudible*) "Yeah."

"Did you fly here?"

"Yeah."

"On your own?"

"No."

"Oh, O.K. 'Cause he says he was flying with you. So apparently if you took Delta Airlines he was flying with you . . . or U.S. Air, or whoever. But he says he was certainly flying *with* you. Actually, too, he says you're *nervous* about flying—when it's not you?"

(Laugh) "Yeah."

"Yeah, he says, you're funny. You like to fly, but when you're in the driver's seat so to speak, you feel more confident, than when somebody else is."

"Right."

"But he's like, oh, don't be like that. You know that—"

"You were like that, too, Larry."

"You know, but he enjoys the flying. That he was with you spiritually on the plane, 'cause he knew you were coming. He *knew* this was his opportunity to reach out to you. He knew that . . . Since he passed on he did something where you'd find out about me. That you coincidentally heard about me or saw me on T.V. or something. This was his way of . . . even if you never were to get to see me, you would know he was somewhere else. He was near to you. You would at least have had that reassurance. He have a brother he was close with? Or brother-in-law, or something?"

"Mmm, maybe brother."

"Yeah, it's funny. It's like he's calling out to somebody like a brother. Unless it's a very good friend, that he looked upon as a brother."

"Yes."

"'Cause it could be that. 'Cause he's calling out to somebody like a brother. And when you're not *sure*, he's saying, well, it's actually a good friend and we're like brothers."

"Yeah."

"So apparently, there's a brother he was very, very close with—*a friend*, when I say brother I mean that, 'cause he looks upon him as a brother. I don't get a name, I get a feeling of him. So apparently Larry is calling out to him. 'Certainly tell him you have heard from me.' You taking a vacation?"

"Does this trip count?" *(She was going to spend some time with Larry's family in Pennsylvania before going home.)*

"Well, I think it's something more than this. I think it's up ahead, 'cause he talks about you having the opportunity for a vacation. 'Cause he says you're going

273

to need to get away by yourself, and you might up ahead. You know, even if it's local. You take a hike in the mountains or something. It's just that it's near. But, again, it's . . . You guys dated for a while, yes?"

"No."

"You *were* legally married?"

"Yes."

"Yeah, 'cause he says married. It's funny, though. I don't know if he's referring like to a past life, but it's like you *knew* each other before."

"It seemed like it."

"You know, 'cause obviously when you met in this life something clicked. Even if you dated for a short time and then married, it's like in the past you've been together *so long*. It was just obvious that you were going to get married. But it could be in like a past existence, or even over there before you both came to the earth or whichever. But, as *he says*, he's even doing his spiritual growth at a nominal speed over there, so that when the time comes—which will not seem long to him—but when the time comes, when you come there, we'll do it together, he says."

"Good! I keep asking him that."

"We'll do it together. That's probably why he's explaining this to you. So that you know, that he's assuring you that he'll *wait* for you more or less."

"I keep asking him."

"That he'll stay at a certain level. A level he'll know that you'll come too. So he can meet you. 'We can hook-up and work together.' 'Cause he *says*, there's no conception of *time* here. What seems, if you lived the next sixty years, we basically, you know, I'm looking at it as if it's like five minutes. It just isn't the same. And he says, 'It's not going to seem that the wait is long for me, even though it does seem long for you.'"

"Yeah, but what if I'm *old*, and he's still young?"

"Your body will be old, but not your *heart*. Remember, your physical body, which will remain here and go into the ground, will age, but *you* won't. I'm going to be forty-four this year, and I looked at myself in the mirror one morning, and it was like I still feel twenty-five, yet I see this forty-three-year-old man looking back at me. You know, so *(laugh)*. The thing is, it's just a state of mind. It's just a physical body, the costume we wear in this dimension. . . . But no matter *what*, he says, Larry will be there. He knows, no matter what, you're always going to miss him. That's not going to change. He's not going to B.S. you and try to tell you it is. It's not. You're always going to think back on him. You're going to think back on the happy times and memories. You were together—too short, in your opinion, and—"

"Yeah."

"But, as he says, better for that short time than never."

"Oh yeah!"

"But, as he states, you'll always miss him, but you have to go on and complete your mission in your life here. Because you're an individual soul on your individual mission, just as he was. And your lives did run parallel. It's just that one got their work done sooner, obviously, and moved on. But as he says, someday you'll get *your* work done and will move on."

"Tell me what I need to do."

"Exactly what you're doing. Just go on with your life. As he says, the stage is already set, just act out the role. Don't wish you were dead. Don't think you would rather kill yourself. Just go on with your life and fulfill. Because he says, you've *got* to get *here* by hitting the finish line. It will come when it's supposed to. So he certainly encourages you to move on. He wasn't a religious man, but he certainly is a *spiritual* man. And he asks that you continue to pray for him and just know that he's always *near* to you. You been having some *back* trouble?"

"Yeah."

"Yes, he's saying watch your back during your physical or athletic activity. A lot of it's *stress*, too. You're not sleeping well . . . you're just . . . you're a wreck. You're all out of sorts with yourself. He says, 'There are some days you feel like you're a complete *nut* and you've *lost* it.'"

"Yeah." *(laugh)*

"He says, 'Well, you are!' No, he's just joking. *(laugh)* He says, 'You are a nut. How could I possibly love somebody who's *not* a nut?'"

"Yeah." *(laugh)*

"Well, he was a nut, too!"

"Yeah."

"So he says, if the shoe fits, wear it, right? He was a nut, too, and so were you. Because the thing is, you were like two kids, like two teenagers who had a *blast!*"

"Yeah, that's exactly right."

"And he says, and that memory is there to sustain you until we meet again. I think with this, he's going to withdraw—from me, in any case—'cause he's going to start to fade down. They can only hold on to my brain for so long."

"I wish you wouldn't go, Larry."

"Well, he's not going from *you*. He's going from me. He's just going to cut me off to give my brain a rest, but he's not going anywhere from *you*, he says. He says, 'What have I been telling you the last hour.' He says, 'I'm telling you I'm not going anywhere.' He says, 'Just because I don't talk to this guy anymore, I'm going to cut off my communication with his brain, doesn't mean I'm going anywhere.'"

"Can you tell, George, before you cut him off, how I can know when you're around me and not think I'm just nuts?"

"Well, the thing is, as he states—and he's right—you just have to allow yourself to feel it. And just realize, that sometimes the most simple but yet profound messages will come when you least expect it. 'Just go on with your life and be happy,' he says. 'As much as you want to know I'm here and happy,' he says, 'I want to know you're there and happy also. And we *will* be together again.' That he assures you of. One thing about him, he's honest, straightforward and you can trust him."

"Absolutely."

"So, if he says that, you'll know that's a guarantee. He says, we'll be together again. He says, just hang in there, and he says, we'll be together again. 'Fulfill your purpose happily and come to the finish line and cross over to me.'"

"I love you, Larry."

"Well, with that, he signs off, sending his love to you. That he certainly loves you, too. 'And just try to hang in there and be happy again, until we meet again.' But he goes, along with your dad, your grandparents, different people in his family, his grandparents and such. He again calls to his own family. But he says, most importantly, you were certainly the specialty in his life and the novelty in his life, and you *still* are. And he says, definitely, 'Just know I'm *always* with you, as a husband and as a friend.' And with that he signs off, and the others do too, and . . . there they go."

Nine

COPING
WITH GRIEF

WE LIVE in a "get it done yesterday" type of society. Everything moves so fast and so much is expected of us *right now*. I am noticing more and more that the two most important words in our vocabulary when it comes to advertising any product are *fast* and *easy*. Whatever solutions we need in life, we seem to need them to be both fast *and* easy, otherwise they are not worth the trouble. That is, until you find yourself stopped cold by the loss of a loved one. Understanding how loss affects us and those around us and coming to grips with tragic circumstance is a long process. Healing takes time—sometimes a lifetime. Understanding and coping with loss become a sort of work-in-progress that will only be truly finished when we ourselves pass into the hereafter and begin to understand the reason we placed ourselves in that life lesson.

I do not consider myself a grief expert because I come from a different perspective in grief, mainly due to my ability to communicate with the souls in the hereafter and feel their hope and peacefulness. I have to rely on the messages that the souls send to all of us in an effort to help us understand the coping process. They are the *real* grief experts. Their messages have helped me immensely because they now understand this existence better than we do, and their advice and consolation are comforting and hopeful. That does not mean that I am spared the pain and suffering that people have to deal with when they have experienced loss. That part of what I do is cumulative and will, on occasion, also leave me emotionally drained and sometimes depressed after hearing about so much tragedy that people endure here. I also have had losses that have shaken my belief system—no human is immune. Loss hurts. I have learned, though, through the souls' unshakable conviction, to take the good with the bad and, through that, recognize that anyone who has been crushed by loss and survives is also a grief expert.

There is no recipe for coping with grief, and there is no "one size fits all" when it comes to making the pain go away long enough to understand the tragedy of losing someone we love. My ability is my way to help people with the coping process because, whereas the bereaved see their loved ones as gone, I see them as happy and joyful in the hereafter. People who are resentful of the fact that I did not grieve for my father's passing will never understand that while they remember him old and broken in his last days, I see him young, strong and happy. Were it not for the saving grace from the souls in the hereafter that spares me *some* of the pain of loss, I am sure the amount of tragedy I encounter on a regular basis would have driven me insane long ago. That does not mean that I do not miss my loved ones in the physical sense. Of course I do. Even if your faith helps you come to the realization that your loved ones continue to live, you still must deal with missing them in the physical and with the hole they leave in your existence.

Communicating with the hereafter has put me in a good position, however, to notice what is helpful and what is not when someone is bereaved, and I can say with certainty that nothing works for everyone all the time. Neither can anyone be told what is the correct amount of time or appropriate manner to grieve the loss of a loved one. It is more an emotional dance of "two steps forward and one step back" that only time and understanding will help heal. I also know that anger, self-pity and bitterness at the world are usually only a backlash at misfortune, but if allowed to fester, they become a poison that eventually destroys the vessel containing them. They prevent us from continuing to learn from our experiences of the earth—something the souls in the hereafter seem intent on our continuing. After a passing, most people will go back and forth in varying states of grief, from coping day by day to the feeling that their loss is a nightmare from which they cannot wake. Grief is as mental a process as it is a physical one. People need time to heal physically, emotionally and spiritually. They need to be given the latitude to heal at their own pace. It could take weeks, months or years to recover and come to terms with loss, but the souls in the hereafter implore us that we cannot allow ourselves to be beaten by loss.

While people learn from me about their loved ones in the discernment, I also learn from them in a very practical way about coming to terms with loss. I have noticed that most women grieve long and hard at the beginning and eventually come to a type of inner understanding, almost as if they can acknowledge that their loved one is firmly planted in their hearts. They also talk openly about their loss and share with others in a community fashion, which is very helpful. Most men, at the first hours and days of their loss, become stoic and provide the shoulder for everyone else to cry on. Then, as time drags on, the pain of loss gets squeezed into anger, overwork and sometimes alcoholism. Left unchecked, it becomes a dam of noncommunication and misfocused aggression that often leads to physical and emotional illness.

Crying is probably the most beneficial thing you can do in the beginning. The souls in the hereafter have told me that crying washes the soul clean. Talking is also good, and it is important to encourage friends and family to talk openly and frequently about the loved one passed on, if at least to remember the happiness and good times. So often people around us don't want to mention the names of loved ones passed on, but you should encourage them and yourself to say their names out loud. The souls in the hereafter love to hear themselves talked to and about because it helps solidify the understanding that they are still around and still around us. There is no shame in a man crying—it just shows that he is more of a man. So often during a discernment, the wife will become emotional and the husband will fight hard not to crack. Knowing it is senseless, the souls in the hereafter will keep driving at him in the discernment until the floodgates break, simply because they understand how important and valuable it is to release the pain and how very much it is needed to begin healing.

The time when families should be pulling together after the loss of a loved one is precisely the time when they fall apart. The souls in the hereafter can only explain to me that each person, in dealing with their own pain in their own way, pulls away because they are unable to handle someone else's pain as well as their own at that time. Also, because the loved one who passed on becomes the focus of everyone's attention, they seem to become more important than the other siblings or the spouse. Resentments, new and old, begin to creep into the grieving process, and, coupled with pain and anguish, become a recipe for broken relationships. Individuals as well as families as a whole seem to handle grief in differing ways. Some families seem to pull closer together, but others factionalize for a while. It is not uncommon for some spouses to become estranged or divorced. Souls in the hereafter describe it as "each to his own road," and though they sometimes advise and admonish from the hereafter, they also realize that there is not much they can do, because the work involved in our own spiritual growth must be done without their assistance. They do point out, though, that time truly does heal—probably the best advice they can offer.

When I have discerned loved ones in the hereafter for family members who have other siblings, it is interesting to note that very infrequently do the other siblings come to the discernment. Sometimes they just don't want to hear the information, and other times they feel they would rather handle the grief on their own. I try to encourage families to come together, since at the very least the discernment in itself is an interesting topic for discussion. Then, hopefully, the discussion could lead to some very candid discussion about feelings. When I am discerning for a family who has had a child pass, my eye always seems to wander to the surviving children, who listen intently but passively to the information coming from their brother or sister in the hereafter. It seems that they know instinctively that the information and emotion they absorb will have no outlet. So they sit, they listen, they wait for Mom or Dad to react, they watch. When it is over, they smile at me, and they go. All without a word. I think sometimes children who have lost a sibling feel that ultimately their grief will go unnoticed. Parents, caught in their own tragedy, turn inward, and relatives and friends assume children cannot fully understand the importance of having lost someone they have spent their whole life playing with, fighting with, talking with or just being with. If you take the time to understand the hiding mechanisms at work, you can see that they are hurting.

Having a sister or brother pass when you are young takes away a bit of your innocence and control. Children, until they become young adults, feel like they are immortal. The passing of young people is the cruelest reminder that nothing is forever. Most children are better able to understand that concept than you think. That is why the souls in the hereafter do the very thing we should do every day— talk directly to the children about it. In a discernment, the sibling passed on will speak directly to their brother or sister on earth in a friendly and direct way that seems to reach into their heart. Often, it might be only to remind them about better times or to tell them not to be afraid. In one discernment, a brother in the hereafter told his sister here that she now has his "official permission" to have the big bedroom, and he would do the best he could to help her pass the math final.

The messages are frequently that candid and sometimes very funny. It is their way of taking the edge off and showing that, although they are in the hereafter, nothing really changes. Whatever the message, we can learn a lot from the young souls in the hereafter and their concern for the happiness of the brothers and sisters they leave behind.

I cannot stress enough the importance of helping children to cope with their very special losses of parents, siblings or friends. Talk to your children as openly as the souls in the hereafter do about loss. So you cry. Your children cry, too, only they probably don't let you see it. They do have one consolation as children that we miss as adults—the ability to see their siblings in visitations that are vivid and extraordinary. Children can receive these visitations simply because no one has told them yet that it is "impossible." Asking children if they have had dreams about their siblings could open up a whole world of dialogue about loss that could be an inspiration for adults, too. All children are the same, here and in the hereafter. They want to be noticed. It is hard for them to live in the shadow of a deceased family member. They tend to lose their importance because they are still here. Most of the time children pretend they are not interested during a discernment (especially teenagers), but afterward they can usually tell others word for word what their siblings communicated from the hereafter and are proud of the fact that there is a bond so powerful that not even "death" can break it. What a great thing to know when you are young.

Loss of a child is probably the biggest reason why families fall apart, because it is an ax that swings in every direction—husband to wife, parents to surviving children, sibling to sibling. It has been estimated that 50 percent of couples who experience the loss of a child divorce within two years, and 70 percent of marriages dissolve within six years of the loss. These are very grim statistics, but not surprising to me. I have heard many times from a husband or wife that the only thing they see in their spouses face after loss is *death* and a constant reminder of how terribly life has changed. The pain of loss causes people to lash out in anger, and usually the only person with courage enough to stand in your path is a spouse. Blame and self-reproach invade the day-to-day relationship and start tearing at the family fabric. Soon, couples, unable to deal with the grief of those around them because they are dealing with their own personal grief, become cold and indifferent to the needs of the person they once cared for so deeply. Add to this the lack of closeness and intimacy, and the relationship quickly begins to dissolve.

Bonding together during the grief process is a job in itself, but a necessary one. The souls in the hereafter, already completely aware of the family strife, try to speak to family members in their own way and often have reminded their loved ones here to stay focused on the real reason for their anger and to try to work together to move forward on the road to healthy grieving. Relationships between parents and surviving children often become the victim of indifference or overprotection on both sides. My friend Connie was honest enough to tell me that she simply could not deal with her surviving daughter because her grief was too overwhelming. It was not until she saw an entry in her daughter's diary discussing her feelings of abandonment that she fully realized the need to reach out to her daughter, who struggled with her own grief. Another bereaved mom that I know in Michigan lost her son in 1993 and now struggles daily with the need to know where her surviving daughter is at every hour. Their children in the hereafter have told both these women to "mother, but not smother." Surviving children need to live as normal a life as possible after such a tragic loss, and not be punished for their mortality.

No one can speak as eloquently about coping with loss as the souls in the hereafter. They have an admirably fresh and direct way of helping their loved ones here understand that physical death is just a means to a magnificent end. They talk about their world and ours with such confidence that you cannot help but know that they are without a doubt happy and at peace. Their words about their world help us look differently at ours and the reason why we must continue on. There is nothing that I could ever say or do in a discernment that would have as great an impact as the hopeful and sensible information provided by those souls who help us pick up the pieces. I have seen their simple words have a life-changing effect on their loved ones. The souls know whence they come.

I HAVE BEEN BLESSED with knowing some very special people whose resolve and determination to fight grief "tooth and nail" help me to understand that the true direction of our spiritual road is borne out of tragedy. Connie Carey has an engaging style and an iron will that would intimidate a field marshal. Yet at the same time she also struggles to maintain her perspective in dealing with her own grief by helping other bereaved moms with her straight talk and generous heart. I asked Connie once if she ever could have imagined being such a positive influence for other grieving people. She told me, "I thought I was just going to be one of those soccer moms, watching those games and just being there as my children grew. Wow—have things changed." It is a perfect example of how things happen in our lifetime that thrust us into the people we need to be. We need to be in the position to understand and accept this change, because it is what we will need to fulfill our growth here. Understanding that life will be different after a loss is the first step forward, and whatever works is the correct way. "The year my daughter would have turned twenty-one, I had a cigarette and a can of beer at her grave," Connie told me. "I don't smoke or really even drink, but it helped me feel connected, and I celebrated for her adulthood." That is a very human way of coping, and a poignant way to celebrate the fact that, although they are separated, life for *both* continues. In a discernment Connie had, her daughter was able to speak to her, not as a bereaved mom but as a good friend, and offered some real wisdom about the coping process. This is Connie's story, in her own words:

"MICHELE WAS MY FIRST DAUGHTER and second child. She was a vivacious, easygoing and carefree young lady whom everyone loved. She treated everyone equally, and it did not matter what color, race or religion someone was, she felt that everyone had something very special about them that made them who they were. She was extremely close to her brother, who was twenty-one months older than she, and to her sister, who was two years younger. Since her brother was very quiet and a struggler, she stood up for him continuously. It was common knowledge that if anyone messed with Shawn then they would have to pay the consequences with Michele, which they often did. She and her sister Colleen had a very close relationship. They shared the same bedroom and spent many nights talking about their lives, teenage troubles and their plans for the future. There was always a lot of laughter in our home, and I was very reliant on Michele to keep things going within the family. She was always there when I needed her. She was involved in skiing, soccer, volleyball, dancing and skating, and she won several ribbons in gymnastics. A mom couldn't be prouder of her daughter. By the time she reached sixteen, she was modeling at several local malls and stores. She was 5'8" with long blond curly hair and blue eyes, and she was the idol of many young teenage boys at Wegman's Grocery store, where she managed a part-time job. As a family, everything was going our way.

"In the fall of 1993, Michele was so excited about entering her senior year at Westhill High School and already submitting applications to colleges. On September 19, a few of her friends from another school came to our home to pick her up to go hiking at 2 P.M. At 3:07 P.M., the careless driver, going seventy-two mph, hit a tree. Of the five young people in the car, Michele was injured the most critically. My daughter died four days later, September 23, 1993, of a cerebral hemorrhage.

"Our family felt that life was over. I was wrenched with the feeling that I was being punished somehow for not being a perfect mom, and my husband agonized over feeling that if he had been at home, he could have convinced her not to go. For several years I carried unbelievable anger over the driver of the car. He believes that the accident was not his fault, and it is very difficult to fight for a victim's rights in our legal system, which does all it can to protect the rights of the accused. All of my dreams for her future—graduation, prom, career, marriage, children—were smashed. I did not want to go on, and I found myself struggling with the anger that was seeping into every corner of my life. When my daughter Colleen would come home from school, I could not summon the will to talk to her, and she would just go to her room alone. My son was seldom around now, and at that point I just figured that it was for the best. I had nothing left to give them. I felt like a failure to my family, but there was nothing in me to help them with their pain and deal with my own also. We were all so hurt. My parents and siblings knew they could not help us so they chose not to be around to feel our pain. My faith disintegrated in the weeks and months following Michele's death, and the clergy struggled to understand why my grief was so intense. Hearing that your precious child is in a happy place is not enough for a bereaved mom to hold on to. My emotions were in turmoil.

"I knew that at some point I would either have to pull myself together or stop trying completely. I began to seek out anything that I could about death, passing and the Other Side. I began to feel driven by the need to know that Michele still existed. I read the books, attended the seminars and most important, learned to look within myself and to Michele for understanding. I was very fortunate to have Michele communicate through George Anderson that her life did not end on that day in September. I know now in my heart that Michele's life continues in a world close to ours, and I know she understands the hurt and undying grief that I struggle with every day and the anger, which I suppose will always be there but is lessening as I learn and cope.

"Part of my way of remembering Michele to the world and handling my own feelings of loss is through volunteering as an area sponsor for George when he comes to Syracuse, New York. It is my way of helping people who are going through the same hell that I went through. I have also learned a lot about myself and a lot about finding hope again after such pain. I feel Michele helping me with my work as I speak to other bereaved people, especially moms, and I feel stronger now knowing that she helps me every day in her special way. I know that in the physical sense I will not see Michele again until I cross over, but, due to my increased knowledge about their world, I know she is continuing her journey in a place where no one can harm her again. She has also made her presence very clear in the house from time to time, and she has blessed my daughter, Colleen, with well over one hundred dreams about her and her new life.

"I have had more than one discernment with George over the years where we as a family could listen to Michele's words and share together. When George returned to Syracuse in October 1997, I asked if it was possible to be there alone while Michele communicated. I felt I needed the opportunity for her to communicate with me "woman to woman" about things not only in her life but in my life as well. True to form, Michele did not waste a minute in helping me to understand and continue the path of my life here. The following is my discernment with George, one-on-one with my daughter, Michele."

THE DISCERNMENT

"Okay, there are three people who have come into the room, and I'll have to sort them out. Two women and a male—two *young* women. Now it is correct that you lost a daughter, right?"

"Yes."

"But you lost *two*?"

"No."

"Why do they talk about another daughter passed on? Does that make sense?" (*She is unsure how to answer.*)

"Did somebody else in the family lose a daughter? Somebody keeps insisting that there are two daughters passed on, or at least two young women."

"Oh, okay."

"Maybe I should have said that instead. Obviously, she's somebody's daughter, but two young women."

"Okay."

"One obviously is your daughter, but there's somebody else with her. Does that make sense?"

"Yes."

"There's somebody else claiming she's the daughter, she passes young, and I thought she could also be yours, but apparently not. But she is a relative, she states. That's right?"

"Yes."

"Okay, because she keeps insisting she's related. Now she keeps bringing up her parents. Is it correct that her parents are still here?"

"Yes."

"Oh, that's why she's saying she's the daughter. Okay, because she's busting my chops, insisting that she's telling me the right thing. Now this I don't understand—she keeps talking about cousin. Does that make sense?"

"Yes!"

"Okay, I don't know who she means *to*—your daughter—it could be anybody in the family, but she keeps talking about being the cousin. But she does speak about passing young, that's true?"

"Yes."

"She talks about hooking up with your daughter. Did she pass first?"

"Yes."

"Somebody is saying, 'Dad is here.' Is it correct that your dad has passed?"

"Yes."

"So that must be the male and the two young females who came into the room. I keep hearing somebody saying, 'Patty.' Does that make sense?"

"Yes."

"I feel somebody walking around saying, 'Patty, Patty.' I'm hearing *cousin* again. Is this the cousin I mentioned already?"

"Yes."

"That would be the young woman that was arguing with me. Now, she and your daughter are in the same age category?"

"Basically."

"They're in the same generation is probably the better way to put it. I guess anything is possible, but she gives me the feeling that she and your daughter have become very good pals over there. And they would be family, yes?"

"Yes."

"Now she keeps asking for her parents. If they can deal with this, she just wants to let them know that she is all right. She's calling out to them. Hmm—all right, without explaining, I keep seeing a big M in front of me. I know it must mean something, but did anyone ever sign their name with just an M or emphasis on the M?"

"Yes."

"I keep seeing it written in front of me, like somebody's signing their name, but emphasizing the M. Maybe being less formal with their name, but the emphasis is on the M. It's coming from your daughter, so it must have something to do with her. She would sign her name with the emphasis on M?"

"Yes."

"I see the word *code* in front of me, so apparently it's being done this way as a code, to give you evidence that it's her or something that is significant with her that I wouldn't know about. Also, your daughter thanks you for the memorial. Does that make sense?"

"Yes."

"Recently—within the last two years?"

"Yes."

"There's talk of a sister. You have another daughter?"

"Yes."

"Okay, because your daughter congratulates her. Is she hearing some kind of happy news?"

(*She is not sure.*) "Maybe."

"Is she employed?"

"Yes."

"Because it's something to do with employment. She seems to be hearing some sort of happy news that affects her personally, but I see career, so it is something to do with career. Your daughter brings up that you still suffer terribly in silence over her passing. It's a very inward grief, and she's not being unsympathetic, but she definitely gives me the feeling that you're not getting over this, period. Again, she's not being unsympathetic. I think your daughter just tells it like it is."

"Yeah."

"That's her personality anyway, but she says that this is something that you will not ever get over. She says, 'That's okay, just don't let your grief be your downfall.' That's what you have to dwell on. But she says, 'There is one positive thing. This has taken away all your fear. What's the worst that could happen to you now?' Plus—this is strange—but she says that this has also helped you to speak up."

"Um-hmm."

"It's made you less frightened and more determined. You may not really care to hear this, she says, but virtue has come out of this, that you may have noticed but are not really paying attention to. As she states, to every negative there is a positive, even if it's not the way we like it. Now, she speaks of anniversary. Are we around the time of her passing?"

"Yes."

"It passed though, yes?"

"Yes."

"Because she's telling me it's gone, so apparently it's passed. But she says that she's been very very close. You have dreamt about her recently, yes?"

"Yes."

"Yes, because she says she's visited recently, around the time of the passing. Because she knows that obviously it is a very difficult time for you to get through. So she says that she visited in dreams, and you had a vivid visitation. She gave me a good analogy—it's as if she lives in a foreign country, but different, because she's closer. She says, 'If I lived out of the country, how often would you see me?' She knows that lately you have been afraid of being left alone, and yet you are inclined to feel very alone."

"Um-hmm."

"There's nothing wrong with that. Hmm, she gives me the feeling of a brother. Either she has one or there is somebody that she was close to in that manner. Does she have a brother?"

"Yes."

"Okay. Now, why is she saying there are three? Counting her, you have three children?"

"Yes."

"Okay, I just wanted to make sure. She's calling to her brother also. There are also congratulations around him. And why is there a feeling of distance? Is he away?"

"No, he is married."

"Oh, maybe he is just on with his own life. Maybe that's why she's bringing up the feeling of your being alone, because there is distance between your children. Not that you are distant with them, but they are going on their own road."

"Right."

"There's talk of marriage. You are married, yes?"

"Yes."

"There's also talk of retirement. Is your husband getting near retirement?"

"Yes."

"Your daughter is showing me golden roses, and congratulates on retirement.

However, she speaks about her father retiring but still working, so apparently he doesn't fully go out to pasture. Again she shows me a big M, so it must mean something. It's funny, she says, 'M as in Michele,' so that is correct?"

"Yes."

"But why does she say M'shelly? Does that make sense?"

"It's Shelly." (*This was Michele's nickname.*)

"Oh, okay, because she said, Michele, and then it sounded like she said Sherry. That's interesting, because Shelly isn't a nickname for Michele. She's saying Michelle, M'shelly. She speaks of you working. You do work, yes?"

"Yes."

"Because she speaks of you working, and in your case she says it's more therapeutic than anything else. It's not a question of needing the extra money, but a question of keeping your sanity. But she says that you work with very good people."

"Yes."

"She compliments the fact that the people you work with, including those in authority, have been very sympathetic toward you. Plus, she states that in all essence it is not something they *had* to do. I mean, she's just calling a spade a spade. Since your daughter has passed on they have been very sympathetic and understanding. But as your daughter also states, they are parents also. This is something that has never been commented on, and she wants to thank them for being so good to you. Like if you're having a bad day, which as she jokes happens quite frequently, they are understanding. She says that you talk about her passing, but you do suffer in silence a great deal. I keep seeing a locked chest in front of me, which means that you lock it up. But this is the way you deal with it, and everybody has to deal with loss in a way they feel is best for them. Your daughter says that eventually you will see her again because you have no other place to come but there, and you know that one of these days you are going to finish here and show up there. It is as if she lived in New Zealand, and you knew that eventually you would save enough money to visit her there. You would be looking forward to it, knowing that you are going. But your life would still go on here in the meantime until you reached that point. She says that this is the way you have to look at it—that eventually you are going to come there, but your life has to go on here in the meantime, until you come to that day. I keep seeing you getting hit with a wave. Apparently you've had another wave of grief lately?"

"Um-hmm."

"Because I feel as though you're getting hit with it all over again. It just seems that this wave draws back now and again, but then it hits again. It's interesting, when that happens . . . you can actually feel her the closest."

"Yes."

"That's when you may dream about her. There's something that will happen to let you know she is near. There's also talk of a tree. Did you plant a tree in her memory or something?"

"Yes."

"Oh, okay, because she speaks about it—that could be one of the memorials she speaks about. I see a tree growing in front of me with her name on it or named after her. Your daughter also speaks of birthday. Do you know what she means?"

"Yes."

"I'm not going to interpret it. She spoke of birthday and just told me to tell you what I heard. But she does extend pink and white roses to you and says *birthday*. I don't know whether she means hers or yours."

"Mine."

"Okay, the fact that she extended pink and white roses to *you* would give me the impression that she means you, unless it is something she knows you will understand. So obviously then the birthday is yours. It's coming up?"

"Yes."

"There are three women who appear around you as nuns. One is St. Rita, who was a bereaved parent, and the other is St. Elizabeth Seton, also a bereaved parent. Those are the two who step forward. There are three, but I don't know who the third is. I haven't seen her yet, but I recognize the two as St. Rita and St. Elizabeth Seton. Your daughter says that you do pray for her, and she thanks you for it. You do it very personally."

"Um-hmm."

"Again, I'm getting the locked chest again. You do it between yourself and her. It's not like you go out and advertise it, so to speak. You may talk about it, but you keep a lot to yourself. Actually, there is talk of the rosary. Do you say the rosary for her?"

"Yes."

"But, to *yourself*—because that's what she shows."

"Um-hmm."

"That's what she shows me. And your daughter certainly is not super-religious—and neither are you—but you *are* spiritual and so is she. This is not organized religion—this is spirituality being spoken about. I saw Our Lady of

Lourdes appear around you and saw rosary beads appear, and your daughter says that you do say the rosary for her, but it's very personal between you and her. She's telling you to let you know that yes, she is receiving it and she knows that you are doing it on her behalf—just so that you know you are not wasting your time. When your daughter was on the earth, she was always in a hurry?"

"Yes."

"It's like she knew already that she wasn't going to be here very long. She must have understood on some level that as an individual she was fulfilling her purpose. And she tells me, as many of the souls have, that if you get your work here done sooner, you will find a way out. And she says that she passes 'accidentally,' is that true?"

"Yes."

"Because it was only the means by which she exited this dimension. She's telling me that the evidence of having fulfilled her purpose here was that she was always in a rush, trying to get everything done, everything accomplished. Like someone who is trying to settle things before their vacation. Plus, even just prior to her passing, she was doubly in a hurry. She might have seemed to be at a greater pace. As she states, this is something that you like hearing—finishing her work early and moving on—but she says that you are looking at it only from your point of view. You have to see it from her point of view, as an individual. Just as you have your life, she has hers, and she is being down to earth and very straightforward. She's explaining it honestly—just like when you fulfill your purpose here, you will go there. You may wish it was tomorrow, but it's not going to be. She says that when you do your life review, you will understand why this has all happened and why you had to go through it. And she says that the sense of triumph for yourself and the satisfaction of knowing you made it to the finish line will make it ten times more worthwhile than you can ever imagine. One thing I get from her—she is not a b.s. artist, so this is something you can trust her on—that someday, this will be fulfilled. Why is there talk about your husband's back? Your daughter just suddenly brought it up. She says, 'Oh, and tell daddy to watch his back.' But this is nothing new, true?"

"Right."

"Because that's the feeling she's giving me. I'm not telling you anything you don't already know. But obviously something you have to live with. Plus, in many ways since your daughter passed on, he suffers in silence. He may manifest his anxiety in a sensitive spot, which is the back. There's a pull in my back. Does he have lower back trouble?"

"Yes."

"He was injured there? (*She nods, yes.*) Because something hasn't healed right. Again, nothing you can do about it, and I'm not telling you something you don't already know. But there's a feeling that something did not heal right, apparently due to some sort of injury that he has to live with now. There's talk about you with a brother. Do you have a brother?"

"Yes."

"Is there a lack of communication between you and your brother?"

"Um-hmm."

"Oh, because your father just brought it up all of a sudden. But it's nothing new."

"Right."

"Your father says that you and your brother just can't seem to hit it off. And that's not an excuse—it's just a fact; there's nothing you can do about it. It's the way it happens to be, the way it is, and to be honest with you, it looks like it's always going to be like that. Ironically, though, I see that both of you are very much alike. I see horns locking, which is my symbol for your both being stubborn and being very much alike. You have tried to make it better, though. Yes?"

"Um-hmm."

"Because your father says that he knows in your heart you have tried, but it just seems to hit a dead end. I see symbolically somebody throwing in the towel, my symbol which says forget about it, there's nothing you can do. It's interesting— I see a lot of green around you. Could he be a little jealous of you?"

"Um-hmm."

"Because it stems from that. There's talk of him actually being jealous, and yet you might be tempted to ask him if he wanted to trade places. But he is actually a little pea-green with envy that things have gone better for you. Your father says that he's had kind of a difficult life, but a lot of the time he's inclined to make it that way. He can be his own worst enemy, and it's not a criticism but an observation. I see the figure of St. Theresa, the Little Flower, around you and she brings the grace of acceptance to you. She's more than likely the third nun that was around you. She's also the one that brings faith, strength and endurance. It's funny—you had devotion to her at one time?"

"Yes."

"Yeah, that's why. Out of the three nuns that were around you, she's standing out singularly, which would clue me that you obviously had great devotion to her at one time, and she still hangs around you as a guardian angel saint. Umm—you're a little pissed off at her?"

"Um-hmm."

"Yeah, because she just told me that. Not in those words. I just interpreted it that way. (She laughs.) But the feeling she gives me is like you are kind of mad at her. She knows that in certain respects you've given up on her, but she says that she's still hanging around you to let you know that she has not given up on you. But as St. Theresa explains, this is personal between you and her. If somebody has a purpose in their lives to fulfill, God himself cannot interfere with that person's soul growth. She says that you know what she is talking about. That's why your prayer wasn't answered the way you would have liked. St. Theresa just said that they hear all prayer, but sometimes they have to say no, because something else is working that they cannot change the plan of. But obviously you have prayed to her on your daughter's behalf, yes?"

"Yes."

"I am being told by St. Theresa that you have done that, and your daughter is confirming that your prayers have been received. The saint is saying, 'I may not have been able to answer the prayer the way you would have liked on the earth, but I have answered it in the next life.' You are still friendly with her, but you still have a bit of an ax to grind. Fortunately, St. Theresa is not taking it personally. (They laugh.) She understands where you are coming from, but she wants you to hear her side of the story so that you know why they cannot necessarily do what you'd like. She tells you, 'Would you honestly think that if it would be within my capacity to achieve this for you that I wouldn't have done it?' So perhaps return to your devotion of her personally. Out of the three nuns, she stands out the strongest around you because you have a link with her. You had devotion with her, but it's not for many years, yes?"

"Um-hmm."

"You felt abandoned, and she just wants to let you know that she has not abandoned you. Your daughter says that you haven't been sleeping well."

"That's true."

"Again, she's not—your daughter must have had kind of a wise-ass sense of humor, because she says, 'So what else is new?' It's not like you don't already know. Michele says to try to stop going over it in your mind again and again. It's like you constantly go over the episode, and you end up back in square one. And it leaves you doubly frustrated. I don't know why, but your daughter says, 'You could not have saved me.' And it's not your fault that she passed on. It's almost as if you think that you should have been there or could have done something. You didn't fail her, but you indirectly punish yourself by feeling responsible for her passing. She says this isn't true. She says, 'I could tell you this one thousand times, but if you don't believe it, there's nothing more I can do. I can't change the way you feel. You must do that.' She also says that it's not going to make the hurt or the pain go away, or the loss go away—that's *not* going away. But don't let it eat at you. She knows that you just wish you could die, period. *(She chuckles.)* And that's the bottom line. But she says that it's going to happen one of these days. It may not happen at the time that you'd like, but it will happen and it's inevitable that you will see her again. But until then you have to bide your time and fulfill your purpose here. As your daughter says, you're not going through this for no reason. When you have your bad days, she says to think of each day as one day less, and keep going. She knows that there are days that you just want to jump out a window, but you must keep going. You have to hit the finish line sooner or later. She's seeing into your future, and she says that there's more to your life up ahead. You as an individual have to fulfill it, as insignificant as it may seem. Not that you play favorites with your children, but for some reason, you and she 'clicked' the most?"

"Yes."

"She says that you were best buddies, and 'clicked' the best out of the three children. Not to begrudge the others, but it is a fact—you just seemed to be the best of friends as well as mother and daughter. That feeling just makes it harder losing her, because you and she, out of all your children, had the best relationship. She also says that there is nothing wrong in thinking that if it had been one of your other children, it would have hurt, but not as much. You and she were starting to get to know each other even better. There was a real link and rapport there. But she says that she is still your friend from the hereafter. The only difference would be that on the earth she also might have gotten married and moved somewhere else. But she says that eventually we will hook up again. According to your daughter, you love to argue, so—

(Laughing) "Yes."

"She says, 'Don't get into it—just tell her what I said—yeah, she loves to argue. Just say it and leave it alone, because you'll be here all night arguing with her.' As much as she'll come up with trying to make you feel better, you'll come back with something else cynical and you'll argue about it. She says it's not worth it. Michele jokes that when it comes to the bottom line she's right. That's her answer, and you'll find out someday that she knows what she's talking about. And because you and she were on the same wavelength, that's a scary thought, she jokes. Because, again, she knows that sometimes it bothers you. You think she didn't have a chance at life. She says that her life hasn't terminated, it's continued. Yes, *physically* it has terminated in this world, but she doesn't need her physical body anymore. You didn't love her body. You loved her. *She* is still alive. That's what lives in the nonphysical world of the hereafter. She says, 'You know I'm telling the truth because you've seen me in dreams, you've felt me around.' There have even been times when you've turned around and could have sworn you've seen her. You've had apparitional occurrences when you've least expected it, and you'd be driving, thinking of her, and a song comes on the radio that relates to her. You've had evidence that you can hold on to, and she says that sometimes you look too hard. Don't miss the forest for the trees. The most profound signs have come when you least expected it. You dread the holidays?"

"Yes."

"She says that the holidays are approaching, and you are already dreading them. Plus, she says, you get crabby. She says, 'Try not to be so much of a grouch this year.' She says that you have to try. You are *allowed* to try to be happy sometimes. It won't be like you are being irreverent or that you don't love her anymore—but try. It's funny, I'm being told that you'll move but you'll continue to work, even if you do it part time. It is best that you always keep your mind occupied. You are working more with bereaved parents?"

"Um-hmm."

"Because your daughter admires that. It gives you a chance to get some things off your chest. Sometimes—it's like that line from A *Streetcar Named Desire*— sometimes you need to depend on the kindness of strangers, and it proves to be a benefit. But you are doing it more independently?"

"Yes."

"It's more on your own, not like you're a part of a support group. More like something on your own that you are doing, where you get to share about her and people get to share about their loved ones. Plus I see you writing, so you may be writing up ahead for your own amusement or therapeutic release. Even after you move, it seems to follow you. Your daughter's passing and memory follow you but yet also keep you going. So again, she points out that there is a positive side to loss. Also, I hear the name Michael. Makes sense?"

"Yes."

"He just walked into the room. I don't know who he is, and he doesn't give me a clue, but as long as you understand, that's fine. He just wants to tell you that he's there with Michele. And Robert, too."

"Yes."

"That's around your husband's side. These are like—and I don't mean to be funny—'strays' that are showing up now to let you know that they are present. And Julie, too."

"Yes."

"That also seems to be around your husband, also."

"Yes."

"It sounds like somebody said Walter, too."

"Yes."

"He just walked into the room. He's present as well. These must have been people who passed on a while ago."

"Um-hmm."

"Michele has met people from generations ago and beyond that are there. But they also come to you, as insignificant as some of them may be to you, in a sense of comfort, trying to let you know that you are not alone. Sometimes you feel like you are suffering alone, but they want you to think back on this day when it happens again, and know that you are not alone. They certainly have been away from the earth for a long period of time, but they still can remember what it felt like to have the most difficult thing on the earth—feelings. Not that they don't have feelings in the hereafter, but they don't have feelings of hurt or loss. There are no negative feelings there—just warm and loving ones. It's only here that we have the conflicts of emotions. As Walter says, 'Sometimes it may feel like you are in the middle of a battleground.' Having these feelings is a tough battle. He appears in uniform, so I'm sure at one point or another he wore one, especially being of another generation."

"Yes."

"St. Theresa also adds, 'Yes, there are days here that feel like a never-ending struggle. And there is no resting place *ever*—not on the earth.' Even if you live to ninety, you won't find that resting place until you graduate to it in the hereafter. Even your daughter says that you have thought to yourself at times—you felt that after so many years you would reach a plateau or a resting place in your grief sooner or later. Someplace where it might be a little easier to cope and 'go with the flow.' Your daughter and St. Theresa say that until you reach the hereafter, there is no resting place here. When you feel you're having a bad day, acknowledge that some days will be better than others. It's okay to have your grief—just don't let it get the better of you. Why does your daughter keep bringing up pets? Was there the loss of some pets?"

"Hmm. Well, yes."

"Or did she love pets?"

"Yes."

"Okay, because she keeps talking about having all these pets there. So apparently she must have a number of them over there. Either they were from your family or ones she's adopted there. She keeps talking about having all these pets. She keeps showing me stuffed animals. Did she collect any?"

"Yes."

"Because I keep feeling—I wish you could be me for about five minutes—I felt I saw her appear in front of me, holding and surrounded by stuffed animals. She said, 'Just tell her what you see.' So there must have been a number of them in her room, like a collection. Again, this is something significant with her."

"Yes."

"In a lot of ways, her room is still as is."

"Um-hmm."

"She says that when she visits it, it still looks the same as when she was there in the flesh. Did somebody tell you to *not* keep it like that?"

"Yes."

"Well, she says that they should mind their own business. If that's what you want to do, leave it alone. Michele says that it's not hurting anybody. If you want to leave her room as is, do it. Because you even may have thought that if you moved, what would you do about her room? She says that if you feel like it helps you to set up what would have been her room in a new place, then do it. It almost feels like someone has told you to throw these things out or give them away. If that time comes and you feel you can do it, it's your business, but right now you're not ready for it. You just like things the way they are, and if this is what gets you through each day, then there is nothing wrong with it."

"Yes."

"Your daughter is not being mean to anyone in particular, but she says that sometimes people should mind their own business. Do it, and tell them that she told you to do so."

(*She laughs.*) "Okay."

"Tell them, 'Thank you for your advice, but I'll do as I please.' But again, she apparently works with animals in the hereafter, and shows me them herself. This is one of the things that confuses me—every time she appears, it looks like she is in a golden light. Was she fair?"

"Yes."

"Okay, then it is her I'm seeing. Because I can't tell when they appear whether I am seeing them in their spiritual self or as they appeared on the earth. She must have been blond and very fair. I'm seeing a blond-haired young woman."

"Yes."

"And it's interesting, because you're more of a brunette, and when she appeared in the light she looks very translucent—very blond and fair. Plus, you *bring* her stuffed animals? Is she buried with one or something?"

"Yes!"

"Oh, that's what she means. She kept telling me that I was overlooking something, and I didn't understand. She told me to look at the stuffed animals she was holding, and to mention about your *bringing* them to her. But she told me that she was buried with them, and it is another symbol of her giving evidence that it is her visiting you today in this manner. It's something that you certainly could relate to. Your daughter is telling me that she is going to let me go, but she certainly embraces you with love—now wait a minute, this puzzles me—she brings up the picture of St. Theresa. It looks like it was *put away* or something. Does that make sense?"

"Yeah."

"Then you understand?"

"Yes."

"Because she said for me to ask you about the picture of St. Theresa, and I did. As soon as she saw that you didn't respond, she told me to remind you about it being put away and then you would remember. She's telling me to ask you to take it out again and put it in her room. That's where it belongs. (*Connie told us later that in her grief and frustration at feeling her prayers to St. Theresa went unanswered, she took her picture of the saint and put it away in a drawer after Michele's passing.*) She's saying to put it near the candle. There's a candle in her room or something?"

"Yes."

"Because she's saying to put the picture next to the candle that's lit. You keep a candle lit in her room near Michele's picture. It's almost like I see her face again in a frame."

"Yes."

"She says to put St. Theresa's picture near the candle that you keep in her room. She says that sometimes you just sit in the room and visit, and this will give you the assurance that the prayers that you made to St. Theresa on her behalf have been heard in the hereafter. Michele jokes to 'bury the hatchet' with St. Theresa. They have to say no sometimes to our requests. This tragedy was something that your daughter had to fulfill, and she says that she cannot go against the natural law by sparing you this loss. Your daughter jokes again, 'St. Theresa is not the *bitch* that you thought,' for not responding to your prayers."

(Laughing) "Okay."

"But again she tells me to let go, and she's embracing you with love along with the others, and your daughter is calling out to her sister and brother and her father also, saying, 'Tell daddy you've heard from me.' She doesn't want you to think that she's not thinking of him too. But she says again to go back to praying to St. Theresa, and pray for the virtues she can send you—faith, strength and endurance—to help you keep going and continue fulfilling your purpose here. She says, 'One day you'll hit the finish line and thank me for listening to me for once in your life.' She must have had that *mess on your head* kind of relationship with you—like you would tease each other back and forth."

"Yes."

"Like a comedy act, but done with complete affection. But with that she signs off with the others, saying, 'Until we all meet again,' and there they go."

THERE IS NO WAY to know beforehand how people will deal with loss until they are thrown headfirst into that circumstance, and sometimes people surprise even themselves with their own behavior when it comes to coming to grips with tragedy. Like the old expression, death separates the "swimmers" from the "sinkers." Working with Dr. Risa Levenson Gold, a psychiatrist in Cold Spring Harbor, New York, has helped me to understand why loss can seriously affect some people physiologically and/or mentally and should be treated medically. Sadly, no amount of communication from the hereafter will help until the person can get to a point in their grief where they can reconcile their loss and put it into a proper perspective. There is a lot to be said for the correct frame of mind in listening to the communication from the hereafter. People who want to experience communication from loved ones in the hereafter must be in a position to understand and benefit from the communication. The communication will still happen, but the words would only be a bitter reminder that their loved ones are no longer on the earth. That is not the intent of the soul's communication. They do want to help, but loved ones here need to come to the understanding that they are communicating with souls in their new world not attempting to stop the clock and keep them alive on the earth through communication. People need to be in the proper frame of mind to hear and understand their messages and accept those messages as proof that their loved ones have made the transition from what we know as "death" to the magnificent world of the Infinite Light.

From my perspective during a discernment with a family, it is easy to tell where the rips in the family fabric are. Often the souls in the hereafter will concentrate on a specific member of the family, who they know has the most need for healing. They have the very unique ability to speak directly into the heart of that person in a way only that person will understand. If anything, the information helps to get the family talking again and focusing on their grief as a family. When I met with the Spencer family in North Carolina a few years back, they were puzzled that their son Josh, killed in a skiing accident, would spend more time communicating to his mother, from whom he was estranged, than his brother, with whom he had a very close relationship. Josh, having recognized his mother's pain at not having really had a relationship with her son, concentrated his messages to his mother, who desperately needed to be forgiven. This is something the family could never have known, but through the messages of their son, they began to understand completely where the need actually was. It also helped the family to deal with the loss as a unit. Sometimes, no matter what the advice or message from the hereafter, nothing they can do can help fix the rifts that develop. From the hereafter, all they can do is understand and console. Dianne Neville in Minneapolis lost her sixteen-year-old daughter Debbie in 1995. Hers was a sudden passing— her heart just stopped one day during ballet class. As with all who pass on into the hereafter at a young age, her passing was a crushing blow, especially to Dianne. Since the loss of her daughter, family life really suffered, having now also been estranged from her son. After meeting the son (who came separately to a discernment with his father, Dianne's ex-husband), Debbie helped make it clear to me that he was so frightened of losing his own child that it paralyzed the relationship with his mom. While Debbie did not make much mention of the family strife in his session, she did have many encouraging words during Dianne's session and promised to do what she could from her end to help bring harmony back to the relationship. She did concede however, that the road would be a long one, and perhaps not very fruitful until her son understands and accepts loss as something not to feared but understood. In the meantime, he will have to battle his fears in ways that will make sense only to him. It is probably one of the hardest lessons both mother and son will have to endure on the earth.

My only expertise in family grief issues comes from the family members in the hereafter who can, sometimes for the first time in their "life," speak openly and from the heart to their families on the earth. Sometimes their messages are quite astounding and help to pull families back together and encourage open dialogue, but they cannot work miracles. They try to make us understand, as they now do, that our experiences as a result of having lost a loved one in our lifetime helps fulfill our spiritual growth on this plane. That does not mean to say that families in turmoil due to loss should not do everything possible to find help—it is the very essence of what they mean in the hereafter about "finding our own road."

Shelley Tatelbaum is a Certified Grief Counselor, family grief expert and founder of the Center for Grief, Loss and Life Transition in Poughkepsie, New York. She is a dynamic and caring soul who also has had to struggle with her own gripping losses. Learning to come to terms with her own grief has helped propel her into a lifelong commitment to helping others understand loss. She offers meaningful advice here from her experienced perspective to help us understand that in order to overcome the pain of loss, we need to face it head-on:

"GEORGE'S INCREDIBLE GIFT and the hope and love he gives to people in grief is a blessing, but it is not a cure for grief. We still need to learn how to live meaningful lives without our loved ones. We still need the tools to help us cope with our losses during the holidays, the birthdays and the anniversaries. We still need to go through the grieving process and experience the pain that will ultimately lead us from the darkness into the Light. We never 'get over' our losses. We never want to forget our loved ones. We need, however, the courage to grieve and grow from our losses. Yes, we *can* grow and transform our suffering into the gifts that we did not ask for.

"Death forces us out of own ordinariness and zombielike sleepwalking through life. Depression and spiritual emptiness may settle in. Death creates a crisis of meaninglessness. Having faith during the period of grief can add hope, comfort, strength, inner resources and support to help us through the pain of sudden or even anticipated losses. Sorrow can have a profound influence on our soul. It can put our priorities into perspective, clarify our values and be the impetus for growth and finding a new meaning in life. It makes us stronger and motivates us to reach out to others and develop compassion. Grief is a process and not an event. We need to have patience with grief and we need to find a safe place for it. I still do not know how and why George has this ability, but I am sure about my feelings of how a belief in an afterlife affects grief and the grieving process. It makes us feel safe. It offers us hope. It allows us to move on in our grieving instead of becoming stuck in the *why* and *where*. It challenges our belief system at a time when death shakes many of our beliefs.

"How we live and not how we grieve is the most powerful testimony that we can give to our loved ones passed on. We do not have to show our devotion to our loved ones or stay connected to them by continued suffering. It is not a measure of how much we loved someone by how long and hard we grieve. George's messages from the souls of our loved ones consistently tell us to go on with our lives and to live life fully. Out of our wounds we can develop strength. Because we are wounded by the deaths in our lives, this strength allows us the opportunity to bring to ourselves and others compassion and appreciation for life and living."

THERAPY OR GRIEF RESOLUTION, either in group or individual form, is sometimes necessary to resolve conflict and always beneficial, at least in identifying problems and offering new perspectives. No matter how hard we take a loss, the hereafter has told me that the door to acceptance and reconciliation is never closed, and help is there when you need it both professionally and from our loved ones in the hereafter. You also have the best of help—your loved one—in your corner.

Ten

ANIMALS — HERE
AND HEREAFTER

FORGET WHAT YOU HAVE HEARD in Sunday school or Catholic school, animals *do* go to "heaven" or the hereafter. I know that this has been a hotly debated subject, but judging by the pets that come through during the discernments, I can tell you quite certainly that they are there.

Animals provide a very important role in the hereafter. As I stated previously in the chapter about suicide, animals in the hereafter bridge the gap between anxiety and peace for people who have just crossed over. Those who pass into the hereafter who have been fearful or distrustful of people will be visited by animals first, because animals are nonjudgmental and eager to please. These souls who may have had trouble relating to people on the earth immediately take to the animals, which provide companionship and a sense of well-being. I was very glad to hear that an upstate New York hospital for the criminally insane has picked up on this idea. They instituted a program whereby patients, as part of their rehabilitation, care for a whole host of animals in a zoolike setting. They have found that a remarkable bond develops between the patients and animals. The animals don't see the patients as "different" or dangerous, and the patients have someone to love and care for, maybe for the first time in their lives. It is great to see this type of spiritual therapy put to good use on the earth. This system works very much the same in the hereafter, and for the same reasons. Although this is one of the main purposes of animals in the hereafter, many of the souls who come through to me speak glowingly about the animals that first greeted them upon their passing and who eventually remain to live with them permanently.

In some discernments, people in the hereafter have told me that the family pet was there to help them cross from this world to the next. This never surprises me, since most people trust their pets more than people. Naturally, they would be more inclined to follow the family pet to the Light than a distant relative whom they might not know. Dianne Arcangel, a pioneer in the field of deathbed apparitional experiences of the terminally ill, has told me that she has documented many cases where animals make their presence known in apparitional form to someone in order to ease their transition into the hereafter. Even people who have never owned pets, especially in circumstances where they have taken their own lives, will tell me that they were inclined to follow a puppy or kitten into the Light because animals are nonjudgmental and love unconditionally.

There are many circumstances where animals work for our benefit as we prepare for the hereafter. I used to think that an animal's passing just days before a child's passing was a rare occurrence, but as I talk to more and more parents who were animal lovers, it seems that this is not as rare as I thought. Martha Weir suffered the passing of their German shepherd, Maggie, quite suddenly and unexpectedly. It was two days before her fourteen-year-old son James was struck and killed by a car while riding his bicycle. During the discernment James told me that Maggie, sensing the impending passing, chose to go first in order to provide a familiar face to cross him into the hereafter.

There are many people who come to the discernments with the hopes of hearing from their pets as well as their loved ones. Elaine Stillwell, founder of the Long Island Chapter of Compassionate friends and a very special friend of mine, had come to me in 1989 after her two children passed in an auto accident. Since then, we have kept in touch and recently got together for another discernment. During the discernment, her children, Peggy and Denis, talked about their dog, Max, and the fact that they were making space for him in the hereafter. Although they understood that the loss of Max would be hard for Elaine and her husband, Joe, her children thanked her in advance for this gift to them, and promised they would take good care of him as they had on the earth.

I am not sure why some people have a problem with the idea that pets survive in the hereafter. It makes perfect sense to me that the pets I loved so much will be there right along with those friends and relatives that have touched my life. I was told during one discernment that anything that we love, that is loved by us, will be waiting for us in the hereafter. The pets we love, here and hereafter, are just as much our family (sometimes even more so, because they don't cause as much trouble) as our family members. On the other hand, I have had someone come for a discernment and listen wistfully as Mom or Dad is discerned, but who completely fall apart as soon as the family pet comes through! If you own a pet, I do not have to explain to you how important they are to our well-being. A few of my friends have actually had the apparitional experience of seeing my first cat, Boo-boo, in my house. I feel her presence around me many times, especially at times when I am upset or under strain. Animals, both here and hereafter, have the unique ability to sense our need to be comforted, doing so willingly and without expectation.

It is interesting to note that one parable, exempted from the modern Bible, centered around Jesus and the animals. In the parable, Jesus explains to a group of villagers tormenting a cat, "Whatever is done to the least of my father's creations is done unto him." I was reminded of this parable when a woman in Los Angeles came to me for a discernment primarily to make contact with the pets she loved that passed on. While most people might consider this bizarre, as an animal lover I could completely understand her need to know that they were at peace in the hereafter. What surprised me in this discernment was the appearance of Jesus who stated simply, "Whatever is done to the least of the animals of the earth, so do you do unto your Father in Heaven." I hope this helps people to remember that pets are one of the Infinite Light's greatest gifts to us on the earth. They show us pure and absolute love, the kind that awaits us in the hereafter.

I have conceded that the souls in the hereafter are much smarter than I am in knowing best how to appeal to their families, but I have found that pets in the hereafter also have the ability to get around my thought processes in an effort to appeal to their loved ones here. My cynicism tells me that all people love their pets and of course they still feel attached to us, but sometimes the pet will actually try to fool me into thinking they are human so that I will have to listen to their messages and the information they tell me more carefully. I sometimes don't know that a soul is a pet until they tell me. This is their insurance that I won't just discount their communication by saying, "The pet says hello," and leave it at that. Some people come only for communication with their beloved pet, and the communication is filled with the same emotion as those of the human kind. When they need to get their messages across, they will utilize whatever means necessary to make their point.

Geri Hashimoto is a woman after my own heart in that she is a "cat person." You have to be a "cat person" to understand how strong that bond can be, and Geri's discernment proves how human our pets can actually be. Geri tells the story in her own words:

"WHEN I REACHED GEORGE after trying for about four years, it was almost immediately following the loss of my 'daughter'—my twelve-year-old cat, Annie. While most people would relate the death of a cat as "just a cat," her loss was devastating to me as I had raised her from one-day old. Our bonding from that day on was not only unusual but far transcended a pet/owner relationship. I've had my share of cats in this lifetime and one cat now that is almost equal to Annie in closeness, but nothing compares to my Annie. I felt as though I wanted to go with Annie when she died as my loss was so great. Even now I cannot explain the grief and loss I feel. I wanted to write about my experience so that others can understand that animals do indeed have the ability to 'talk' to us if the need is there.

"When my father came through at the start of the discernment, I thought I was going to faint. I felt a chill up my neck and then I became lightheaded, as my father and I never had a good relationship. Perhaps it was fear or maybe shock. My father always hated my cats because I treated them as if they were more important than he was. They were. He particularly hated Annie, and when she was diagnosed with squamous cell carcinoma in her neck just six months after my father's death, nothing could convince me that he wasn't taking her to pay me back out of meanness. On the earth, he would have done that if he could have. There were several people I hoped to hear from, but the only thing I *really* needed to know was if Annie was all right in the hereafter. I didn't care who came through as long as I could know just that one thing—that she was safe and that my father hadn't harmed her.

"When I walked into the group discernment that evening, I almost felt hopeless seeing all those people who, certainly, must be more in need than me. All I wanted to know was about a *cat* and that couldn't be very important when these people lost *people*. But before long Annie had come through to George as my 'daughter' passed on, perhaps because my need was so great. Whatever the reason, it just further opens my eyes that animals also go to the hereafter and share love and bonds with the people they were on this earth with. How comforting it is to know she will be there when I arrive in the hereafter.

THE DISCERNMENT (part of the group
discernment that pertains to Geri)

"Let's see who we go to now. Umm, this could be a guy or a gal. I hear the name 'Geri.' Does anyone take it?"

"It's my name."

"Okay, that's fine. Someone just said, 'Call to Geri. Tell Geri Dad is here.' So apparently it is your Dad and that is why he is calling to you by name. Now your father speaks of Mom. Is your mom passed?"

"Yes."

"Okay. Your father says your mom is here, too. He spoke of it that way, so apparently your mother is present. Your father speaks about the loss of a child. Does that make sense?"

"Yes."

"To you?"

"Yes."

"Okay, because he keeps saying the child is here also. Loss of a child. I didn't know who he meant. And in this case, it's you. Wait a minute. He speaks of it twice. Did you lose more than one? You haven't miscarried, have you? Was there another loss of a child in the family?"

"Uh, I don't know."

"I don't know. Somebody keeps telling me to hold my ground. Your father is bringing it up, and I'm going to hold my ground though."

"I might know what it is." (*Geri had lost a male cat, her "son" Kat, in addition to Annie.*)

"Okay, because he's not killing me about it—no joke—but he is stating . . . I just realized what I said! (*Everyone is laughing.*) Yes, definitely you have lost a child and then he said it again. But he doesn't push the issue on that obviously as much as your loss. Your father also speaks of a brother. Did he lose a brother or brother-in-law?"

"He has a brother on the earth." (*She had forgotten about his brother-in-law, John.*)

"Ahhh, wait a minute. He's bringing up the loss of a child again—one of each sex."

"Yes." (*Now Geri is sure he means both cats.*)

"Does that make sense?"

"Yes, it does to me."

"That's why. Okay. He could have been calling to his brother. Let me leave it in that he is calling to a brother. When you said that he said, 'Oh, bring up the two children again, one of each sex.' Now he speaks of a son. So apparently it is correct that there is a loss in the family of each sex. Now he speaks of son. Did you lose a son? You obviously lost a daughter. Somebody must have lost the son."

"Well, yes, I understand." (*Geri was not sure how she could answer when she knew he had zeroed in on the loss of Annie, a cat that was like her daughter.*)

"He's saying one of each sex. Your daughter is present, so it must be your daughter coming through and this other. He feels like a cousin so I don't know if this other soul would have been a cousin to your daughter or something."

"Okay."

"Or *somebody* must have had a son, and it probably would have been like a cousin to your daughter. It's a minor point so who cares. Your daughter is present. Your father says when you sort it out you will recognize the loss twice. Two children. So, I don't know—but your daughter is present. She is coming through with your parents. Wait a minute. Your daughter speaks of another grandfather. I don't know if she means a grandfather to you or your father-in-law who has passed."

"My father-in-law has passed."

"Has passed on? Is that correct?"

"Yes."

"Because your daughter . . . your father-in-law must be with her also. She's speaking about another grandfather with her."

"Not my grandfather."

"No, no, *she* said *her* grandfather, that's what I'm saying. Hmmm, I don't even know where to begin. It sounds like . . . does the name Lee or Leah mean anything?"

"Lee. My father's name is Lee."

"Oh, 'cause I keep hearing the name around you. So that must be your dad confirming he is present. Obviously your daughter passes young, no doubt. There is also the essence of tragedy. Is that true?"

"Ummm . . ."

"Because the way she states it—(*to the souls*) Do you mean you had health troubles or are you trying to lead me somewhere else? (*To Geri*) But she does pass from a health related condition?"

"Yes."

"That's what she states. As much as there is a struggle, she kinda knows she's gonna pass on. That's what she says. So, I take it she must have had something serious enough."

"Yes."

"Now, this could be symbolic, so listen to my wording. She gives me the feeling that she passes on from something serious enough like a cancer."

"It is cancer."

"That's what I'm assuming, but I want to make sure she's not trying to lead me into another area. So it's in the cancer family—this illness—because she says she passes from something serious like a cancer."

"Yes."

"Affecting the blood? Well—"

"I don't know."

"Okay. Also pressure to the head, too. Maybe it starts in the blood and lodges in the head. Who knows. Because she says affecting the blood and pressure to the head."

"It was the neck."

"So she had, like, some sort of tumorlike thing or whatever because it seems it's in me and then all of a sudden it shoots up me and goes into the head region. She keeps telling me she is speaking fine. Did this affect her voice?"

"Yes."

"'I'm talking fine,' she says. 'That's why I'm talking so much.'"

"Yes, I understand that."

"Obviously some sort of tumor that causes trouble with hearing, too."

"Yes."

"There must have been pressure around her ears."

"Yes, yes."

"It feels like it's behind my ear."

"Yes."

"And then all of a sudden you're here. I feel like something was blocking my hearing in the right ear. And she said that she's hearing fine. I'll be honest with you. I feel like I had a lump or something back here. (*He points to the back of his neck.*) Yeah, because I have to admit it's a serious illness like a cancer, but it's a weird cancer."

"Yes."

"That's probably why she was telling me it's like a cancer, because it is, but it's not one you hear about frequently. She keeps telling me, 'Would you think you'd get it here?' And I'm thinking, 'No.' That's funny, because it starts with a little lump or something. It's something like a bump back there."

"Yes."

"She keeps calling out to Daddy and family. (*Geri referred to her husband as Annie's "daddy."*) And also blesses you for being so good to her prior to her passing. Again I'm seeing the movie, *Terms of Endearment*. If you watch it you can relate to it personally. Yes, but she says she was operated on, so I take it that she was?"

"Yes."

"But, obviously it didn't help. But, as she states, she respects the fact that you did everything possible to make her well."

"Yes." (*The doctors couldn't remove it. It was on her vocal cords and was noncurable.*)

"I don't mean to, you know, create trouble, but it's almost like you feel you were led down the primrose path—as if the treatment would help, but it doesn't help. (*Geri laughed. She had chosen holistic treatment, which kept the cat comfortable until they moved from Las Vegas to Florida.*) I see St. Jude appearing behind you as a symbol that as you were going through it everything seems to have turned out to be hopeless. Your hope was high because it seemed for a while there things were working, and then they plummeted again."

"Yes."

"And I see your hands tied in front of you, which is a symbol that your hands are tied. It comes to the point where you just don't know what to do. She also says she drifts into a sleep. Is that true?"

"Yes."

"Because she says she passes in like a coma or sleeplike state."

"Yes." (*Geri had to put her to sleep to stop the suffering in the end.*)

"Again, I see St. Joseph appear as a symbol of a happy death. So she passes peacefully into the hereafter and also emphasizes that she wasn't frightened. You might have been more afraid that she would be scared over there and wouldn't know what happened. She says that she wasn't frightened and that she's welcomed into the hereafter. But she keeps emphasizing about you being with her so apparently you were with her to the end."

"Yes."

"She kinda jokes that you wouldn't even go to the bathroom because you were afraid she'd pass on while you were out of the room."

"That's right."

"She said that you stayed every second. She jokes. She says, 'I know you—you're a perfectionist. If you had been out of the room when I passed on, you would have held it against yourself forever that you weren't there when I passed.'"

"Yes."

"And so she said that of course that wouldn't have been the case, but she says, 'Try to tell my mother that.' Also, thanks for the memorial."

"Yes." *(Weeks later Geri did a whole wall of pictures of her and two poems in calligraphy about how much she missed her.)*

"So obviously good things are being done in her name. Hmmm, I don't mean to be funny but your daughter must have had a good sense of humor because she kinda joked at you and said, 'In my mother's case it's a little bit like, "Call me when the shuttle lands,"' because since she passed on you don't even know you are alive anymore."

"That's right."

"But as your daughter states, you have to try to come back to yourself again because she is all right and at peace as much as you'd rather have her here, as long as you know she's all right it will make it a little bit easier. And she is all right and at peace. She says 'I'm here with my grandparents.' She talks about your dad again, so I assume your father passes before her?"

"Yes."

"Because she claims that Lee welcomes her into the light."

"Really!"

"So he must have been one of the first people to welcome her over. Your father also feels he could have been closer to you, is that true?"

"Oh yes."

"He says that's why he welcomed your daughter over, he says, because he owes you big."

"That's true."

"And he states—I don't want to sound Catholic here, but it was part of his redemption to welcome your daughter into the light to—"

"Yes."

"Kind of make up."

"Yes, I understand that."

"As your father says, to make up for the fact that he was kind of a SOB, and we all know what that means."

"Yes, he was." (*Everybody laughs.*)

"Well, thank heavens he's not anymore. As your father says, 'call a spade a spade.'"

"That was his exact terms. He used to say that all the time to me."

"But this is why he welcomed her into the Light. It was his job to try to make up for his review that he was an SOB. So as he states, your loss is his gain because he and your daughter have become very close over there."

"Really!"

"Your father states that on the earth he just did not know how to show or express love. It was as foreign to him as craters on the moon are to me."

"That's right."

"But he says that through your daughter he's gotten quite an education in that. Plus, he saw from the hereafter what you were going through and what an ordeal it was. He says he and your mother have settled out their differences."

"Oh my God, that's really something."

"Apparently he's quite a changed man over there."

"Oh my God, he must be!"

"Because he also apologizes for the abuse."

"Yes."

"So he must have been abusive both physically and emotionally."

"Yes."

"Because he says emotional scars never really healed. And again then, he says your head was always being messed on growing up. Then when your daughter passed on, in the back of your mind it's like you're thinking, 'I must have done something wrong that this happened.'"

"Yes."

"And that just isn't true. So, as your daughter states, you have to let that go. And she can tell you to, but *you* have to do it. Why does your daughter say the 'younger'? Is she your youngest?"

"Yes she was."

"Youngest child?"

"She was the youngest."

"Sorry, sorry, sorry. She says to me, 'I just said the younger!'—(*to the souls*) Okay, okay—calm down, Hercules. She claims coming in dreams."

"She came in one dream."

"Yes, but that's coming in dreams. And again, maybe there's ones that you don't recall. Hmmm, she talks about you moving. Were you thinking of it?"

"Oh, God, again?" *(Geri had moved three times in three years.)*

"Well, I want to let you know that it's all right. And it could be again that you might feel you are leaving her behind or whatever. You have to go on with your life. As she states there is no choice in the matter. Your father speaks about temper. Was he inclined to have one?"

"I don't know if he's talking about his or mine."

"Because he's talking about temper and I'm kinda blaming the poor guy, figuring he wasn't the nicest—"

"Well."

"So maybe it's yours. You gotta get it from somewhere. Maybe you got it from him. Believe it or not your father extends you white roses as a spiritual blessing and a peace offering."

"Really."

"He says he hopes you forgive. And, your mother seems closer though, yes?"

"To me?"

"Yes."

"Yes, she was."

"Definitely she was the heart and soul of the home and she must have put up with a lot of bull."

"Yes, she did."

"And your mother says, 'I'm here,' and she sends her love to you, but it's obvious who has the need as the parent to do the talking."

"Right."

"And whoever has the need is going to come through for that reason. So as your mother says, 'Don't think I'm not talking to you,' or whatever. She says that your father needs it. So she ways, 'For once I'm shutting up and letting him do it.'"

"Yes."

"But as they say, your daughter is safe here with them. Your daughter also speaks about a pet. Did you lose one?"

"Yes."

"Prior to her?"

"Yes." *(That was Kat.)*

"She talks about the pet welcoming her into the Light. But obviously the one that goes before her is there also. Because it's the family's pet. And again, losing the animal, you kinda felt like you lost your last link with her. So he says the animal is here with her, which is something you have wondered about, so I think she just wants to state that. But she asks that you continue to pray for her and just that she is all right and she's back to her old self. The physical body was ill but the spiritual body was not. And don't torment yourself over this tragedy because your father admits he made you feel like a valueless person. So you're thinking somehow you've deserved this, and it's not true. So your daughter says you have to clear your mind from that type of thinking because you obviously still have a purpose here. Hmmm. As your daughter states, she must have been very spiritual in her own way and kind of smarter than her years, because she states if you've gotten through this much bull in your life you'll get through this one also, not because it's bull but because you've been through enough struggle in your life and you will get through this one also. Your daughter says that you'll have to show up here eventually and it's just a question of getting to the finish line. Each day is one day less. But fulfill and move on. But again, you'll always miss her, but as long as you know she's all right and at peace, you're going to be able to go on a little bit, and she is. As she says, go home and have a good night's rest. But, as she states, clear your mind from a lot of the bull of the past that was instilled in your mind from your father, or you can do a number on yourself. And if you don't clear that—you know, it can't be achieved in a day. We're talking years of indoctrination, but start to break it away. You still have to chip away at it, she says, to make it break. At least if she tells you, you can believe that she's telling the truth. So again, all right, she sends her love to you and to her dad. And her family. And just know that she's all right and at peace until we meet again. And they all step aside."

BECAUSE ANIMALS ARE SO PRIZED by the Infinite Light for their ability to love and forgive both here and hereafter, the souls there have also told me that cruelty toward animals is a much greater offense to the Infinite Light than even cruelty toward another human being. Why? Because animals, at the hands of humans, are unable to defend themselves properly and must suffer the pain inflicted upon them in silence. What makes it worse for animals is that once beaten or abused, the animal will still have a disposition of love and trust, only to have the abuse happen again until trust is eventually beaten out of them. I know this firsthand, because my cat, Winks, had been abused when I found her in the animal shelter. I was told that she was brought back many times by families who had hoped to give her a loving home, only to find that she hissed and bit. When I brought her home, she purred and rubbed her face into my hand, and not twenty seconds later, bit me and ran under the bed. In the ten years she has been with me, her behavior has not changed much. Mine did.

Take care of your pets—for their sake and for your life review's sake. They are the closest thing to God that we will ever find on the earth.

Eleven

LEARNING FROM THIS LIFETIME ON THE ROAD OF GRIEF

THE ROAD AHEAD

At no time in my professional career as a medium have I ever seen such a hunger for the spiritual as in the last few years. It seems to be growing at about the precise time our culture is falling apart. Maybe it is because of that fact. I think that we are beginning to strip away that arrogance that kept us tied to the premise, "You only go around once. *Grab* what you can." People used to be afraid of an afterlife mostly because they were afraid of accountability from this lifetime. Now I think that people are actually hoping that the next life will make up for the disappointments and tragedies in this one. It *will*. The souls there waste no time in telling us exactly that.

So what does lie on the road ahead? I suppose it all depends on who you ask. The souls tell me during the course of discernments that life here *is* becoming more spiritual, and more people are sitting up and noticing the patient signs from the Infinite Light that are often right under our noses. These signs can be as tiny as a butterfly in December or as large as a stranger on line at a supermarket who, by asking what's wrong, keeps you from ending your life over grief (these things have actually happened). In the discernments, as in life in general, we are surrounded by those who have a vested interest in our spiritual road—the souls and the Infinite Light—and they continually help us to walk the straight path. This is part of their *own* spiritual development in the hereafter. They have also promised great things for those still on the earth. They tell me that we are unbelievably close to a cure for cancer, and that the cure for AIDS is right under our noses. They caution us, however, that while some will rejoice in the lives saved, others will be bitter that it did not come soon enough to save their loved ones. At this, again, the souls there promise that there is a reason for everything in the universe, and we will understand when it is time.

Closing this book for me is as hard as closing the discernments that I do for grieving people. I know that while families are hearing from their loved ones, the connection with them takes away the pain of their physical loss. Unfortunately, that feeling is temporary, and afterward families are back to the reality of living and grieving and waiting for the day they will see their loved ones again. The souls have a lot of advice to us here on the earth and usually waste no time in telling their families that, no matter how badly tragedy has thrown them, they must continue on the road they are on in order to benefit from their experiences when they also cross to the Other Side. They know for a fact that we will be reunited, and while they don't feel the pain of separation that we feel, they recognize it within us and try to help. Helping does not mean spoon feeding or carrying us, but doing what they can from their unique vantage point to walk with us where we need to be. Very often the souls in the hereafter will tell their families that they are around as a type of "guardian angel," but joke not to make that job too difficult for them by getting so caught up in our grief that we cannot continue. They are always willing to help in small ways but remind us that the road is *ours* to walk until it leads to them. They show themselves as shining examples of what peace we can count on when it is our time to leave the earth, and they hope we learn by that example.

THE SEEDS OF HOPE

The souls in the hereafter are better teachers than we think, and they often take no credit for having planted the seeds of hope in our heart. It just seems to happen that as we need to understand, the answers fall before us. That is the work of those souls who care for us and walk peacefully and silently with us for the rest of our lives.

Colleen Carey, daughter of Connie Carey, whom I mentioned earlier in this book, lost her sister at a time when so many things are moving too fast for a young person ill equipped to handle such tragic loss. Just as her sister had done in life, she helped Colleen to understand and accept the change from her vantage point in the hereafter. Colleen sent me this poignant reminder of how powerful hope can be and how much it is needed:

"WHEN MY SISTER MICHELE first died I had little or no hope whatsoever. How could I after losing the one person who understood me—my sister—my best friend? But as time progressed and I searched for my own way to deal with my loss, I began having vivid dreams in which Michele showed me her world so I could deal with mine. In the past five years, I have had many visitations from her, but one stands out in particular: In my dream, Michele was holding my hand while we walked through wide, remote grassy fields. After walking for what seemed like hours, we came upon a beautiful crystal-clear stream. I remember not wanting to get my feet wet but she led me through. Finally we came upon a gold winding staircase, and we walked up the stairs. When we got to the top of the staircase, there was a magnificent glass window with a breathtaking waterfall on the opposite side. Michele slipped through the glass and began wading in the water and letting the waterfall cascade over her hair and shoulders. I didn't want her to leave me, and I tried to follow. I couldn't slip through the glass and it frustrated me. When I looked up at Michele, she said, 'You can't come over here. This is my world.' I believe in my heart that Michele showed me heaven, and that is where my hope began to grow."

IN THEIR OWN WAY, the souls show us glimpses of the grace and peace of their world, even if they aren't as profound as Colleen's. It may be as simple as a moment of laughter when we feel we can't go on, or a sense of peace when despair threatens to consume us. But they do need us to believe that there is a place in their world for us if we can only continue our life in hope until we meet again. I used to tell people that there is no cure for grief, but I was corrected by the souls in the hereafter. The cure for grief is finishing life here and seeing our loved ones again. At that instant, all pain and grief will disappear. It is a moment that the souls there look forward to as much as we do. That wonderful moment will come for each of us, but in due time. We are still left with the pain of loss that will temper the rest of our existence here, but it is a necessary part of learning. The only thing that seems to help is time and understanding. We must understand that tragedy is not punishment, and we must understand that we are a very small part of a very big universe. I have been told by the souls that the hereafter is a dimension parallel to ours, and, in some rare instances, we are able to peek beyond the veil that separates the dimensions, if only for a few seconds. Usually these brief signs from the hereafter are our loved ones' way of helping us to understand that they are closer than we could even imagine, and that better things await us. In the meantime, they ask that we consider them to be what they truly are—alive and living in another place.

As I stated at the beginning of this book, what I do for people is really only "second best." Nothing will replace the physical loss of a loved one, but second best is knowing that nothing is gone forever. Sometimes just knowing that the hereafter is a place that can be recognized by us because our loved ones are there can be the difference between hope and desperation. Discernments do end, but life continues with or without our permission. Our loved ones try to teach us in their own way that we can either fall down over the weight of our grief or we can learn to carry it and go on as we continue our journey. The choice is ours.

Working with the souls in the hereafter and their loved ones here has changed my life. There is so much I owe to the souls in the hereafter and their encouragement. I also owe a great deal to their grieving loved ones for teaching me how strong the bonds of love are that they can bridge years and dimensions and still remain as vibrant as ever. So much can be taken for granted on the earth, and opportunities abound to advance our own soul growth every day of our lives. This is what the souls try to teach us and also why we are still here. I try never to forget the words these souls speak during the discernments. Through these brave families who come to me to listen to the words of comfort from their loved ones, I learn a little more about human nature and the capacity in us all to accomplish great things.

Each of us on the earth has work to do. That is why we are still here. We should be grieving for ourselves that so much is left to learn. There are so many lessons that need to be experienced before we can walk through that portal to a world where no tears live. Instead, we grieve for the very people who have finished their work and dropped the heavy burden that is life on the earth. They have been rewarded for their lives, whether long and tortured or short and confusing. In a way, their communication is the biggest pep-talk in the universe. It is the soul's way of helping us to understand that if we could only hang on to the finish line, wherever it may be, there is such reward that awaits us in a world of such beauty it cannot be understood on this plane. They know, and they try to help us know to make our burden lighter.

People still ask me about Lilac Lady. Since my childhood, to my knowledge, she has not visited me again. But I still think in many ways that she is still around. I think she represents the hope of great things to come when my life here is done. The souls in the hereafter have the capacity to do great things for us, but they can't change our lives, mine included. Just like the children's story of Humpty Dumpty, all the souls in the hereafter could not change the things that I must go through as part of my own soul growth on the earth. But inasmuch as I don't get any answers to some questions, I am shown the possibilities in my life where I can follow their example and I can, in turn, help others to understand that the souls are always there—even if they don't always make it known. I know at the time of my own passing that Lilac Lady will return like an old friend, among the other people and animals I have shared the earth with. I hope they will be pleased with what I tried to accomplish here.

The road to the Eternal Light is a long and crooked one, filled with obstacles but peppered with places to rest and contemplate. As with any road, some of it is smooth and clear, and it has side roads that take us out of our way. In the end, however, all these roads lead to a destination. On the road of our spiritual lives here on earth lies the flicker of all things great in our universe—the Eternal Light that makes all things possible and becomes greater with each step. You are not alone, and your loved one has never left you. Life makes us weary, but we walk. Loss makes us fall down, yet still we walk. The Infinite Light shows us every day the promise of things to come, and so we *must* walk. Walk on toward that Light in peace, love and most of all—hope.